AROHAN

Samarpan is a Hindu monk, teacher and writer of several books, articles and memoirs. He has delivered popular talks at various educational institutions, and his orations on scriptures are available online both as videos and transcriptions. He teaches ancient and modern scriptures at the deemed university of the organization to which he belongs.

Also by the Author

SPIRITUAL FICTION

Tiya: A Parrot's Journey Home

Param

Junglezen Sheru

Kratu

PHILOSOPHY

Carving a Sky

RELIGION AND SPIRITUALITY

Living Hinduism

The World of Religions

The Hindu Way

Veda Vihangam – The Essential Veda

YOUTUBE

https://www.youtube.com/c/Samarpanananda

ARCHIVE.ORG

https://archive.org/details/@swami_samarpanananda

AROHAN
Ascent with Gita

SAMARPAN

PAN

This edition first published in India 2024 by Pan
an imprint of Pan Macmillan Publishing India Private Limited,
707 Kailash Building
26 K. G. Marg, New Delhi 110001
www.panmacmillan.co.in

Pan Macmillan, The Smithson, 6 Briset Street, Farringdon, London EC1M 5 NR
Associated companies throughout the world
www.panmacmillan.com

ISBN 978-93-6113-092-2

Copyright © Samarpan 2024

The moral rights of the author have been asserted.

All rights reserved. No part of this publication may be reproduced, stored in or introduced into a retrieval system, or transmitted, in any form, or by any means (electronic, mechanical, photocopying, recording or otherwise) without the prior written permission of the publisher. Any person who does any unauthorized act in relation to this publication may be liable to criminal prosecution and civil claims for damages.

1 3 5 7 9 8 6 4 2

This book is sold subject to the condition that it shall not, by way of trade or otherwise, be lent, re-sold, hired out, or otherwise circulated without the publisher's prior consent in any form of binding or cover other than that in which it is published and without a similar condition including this condition being imposed on the subsequent purchaser.

Typeset by Manmohan Kumar
Printed and bound in India by Thomson Press India Ltd.

A humble offering to
Lord Sri Krishna
whose divine message
has been the light for humanity
for thousands of years

CONTENTS

Prelude: Before the Beginning   xv

Gita: Word of *Bhagavan*   1
    Importance of Gita   1
    Bhagavan, a spiritual reality   3
    God, the teacher   5

I: The Sorrow   12
    Parikrama at Omkareswar   12
    Gita begins   20
    Background of Gita   23
    The moral dilemma   26
    Arjuna's emotional turmoil   28
    Confronting the consequences of war   30

II A: Know the Real   32
    Stay awake in your strength   34
    Is God for real?   36
    Importance of a mentor   37

Your smile reveals your strength ... 40
Don't make an issue out of a non-issue ... 41
You don't live only once ... 42
Real never perishes ... 44
What is death like? ... 48
The significance of a philosophy of life ... 50
Is it a problem or a situation? ... 53

II B: Commitment to Work ... 55
Dignity in life, death and duty ... 55
Stay balanced at all times ... 59
Commitment to work is Karma yoga ... 60
Work effortlessly with no baggage ... 63
Perfection in work is yoga ... 65

II C: Way of the Perfect ... 66
Who is perfect? ... 67
Freedom from senses versus freedom of senses ... 70
The peril of indulging the senses ... 71
Genesis of anger and the ruin caused by it ... 72
The way to peace ... 74
Awake in wisdom ... 75
And fulfilment! ... 76

III: Karma Yoga ... 78
Perform action as *yajna* ... 79
Strive for mutual interest ... 83
Be a role model ... 84

Don't be preachy ... 86
Change is a slow process ... 87
The robbers in life ... 88
No track changes, please ... 90

IV: Knowledge Liberates ... **93**
Why spiritual knowledge is the highest ... 94
Knowledge is eternal ... 97
Why God incarnates ... 98
How to approach God ... 100
Think divine to be divine ... 101
Importance of spiritual knowledge ... 103
Who can have spiritual knowledge? ... 103

V: Giving Up All ... **107**
Who is truly a monk? ... 108
How a monk works ... 111
God does not take your good or bad ... 112
The results of spiritual wisdom ... 114
Achieve here and now ... 115
Pain takes you forward ... 116

VI: Meditation ... **118**
Who is meditation for? ... 120
You alone are your friend and enemy ... 122
Essential habits to be a yogi ... 124
What is concentration like? ... 126
How not to be destroyed ... 128

How to concentrate 129
Rebirth of the failed 130

VII: Knowledge and Beyond 135
It is difficult to be spiritual 136
Creation 138
God runs through everything 142
Who loves God? 143
Can one worship other gods? 146
It is difficult to know God 146

VIII: The Way to Brahman 149
Supreme spirit, soul, karma 152
The last thought before death 154
Freedom from rebirth 156
The glory of yoga 159

IX: The Royal Knowledge 161
Creation cannot be explained 161
Is God the Creator? 164
God: the divine father, mother and sustainer 166
God shoulders the burden 167
Rituals to worship God 170
Spirituality in one sentence 174

X: God Everywhere 177
God alone is virtues and shortcomings 179
Buddhi yoga: how God blesses a devotee 183

God has become all	184
God in gambling!	187
God is in every glory	187

XI: God's Cosmic Form — 189

What are spiritual visions?	189
Should you search for the perfect Guru?	192
Presence of all in one	194
The cosmic form of God	195
Arjuna's prayer to the Lord	197
The real nature of Sri Krishna	198
The ultimate prayer	200

XII: Bhakti, the Divine Love — 204

Who are the best devotees of God?	205
Struggles in the worship of the formless	207
God saves His devotees	208
Struggle, struggle, struggle!	210
Virtues to have in life	212

XIII: Matter and Consciousness — 216

The world of matter	220
Who can be spiritual?	222
The nature of consciousness	223
Why spirituality?	226
How to be spiritual?	227
Beyond illusions	228
Is God responsible for our mess?	229

XIV: The Dynamics of Life — 231
- Choosing the right company — 231
- The three qualities within us — 234
- How we get ensnared — 236
- Are you evolving? — 238
- The way to freedom — 240

XV: The Way to God — 242
- *Samsara*, the world — 243
- The way out of samsara — 246
- Creation and rebirth — 247
- God and His glory — 250
- Lord – beyond all — 251

XVI: The Divine and the Unholy Qualities — 254
- The source of ethics — 254
- The Divine qualities — 256
- Honesty, integrity, values, virtues — 257
- Are you unholy? — 259
- What leads you to hell? — 263

XVII: Three Attitudes — 265
- You are what your *shraddha* is — 267
- Know a person by their food habits — 268
- Three types of worshippers — 270
- Types of self-control — 271
- *Dana*: making gifts — 273
- Cultivating noble qualities — 274

XVIII: Freedom	**277**
The dynamics of action	279
Three kinds of understanding	282
Three kinds of acts	283
How good a worker are you?	285
Three types of *buddhi*	286
The holding power	287
Is your happiness of the right kind?	288
How work becomes worship	289
The result of leading an ideal life	291
God rules all from within	293
The essence of Gita	295
Drawing the net	296
Gita Rolls On	**298**
Select Bibliography	300
Thank you!	301

PRELUDE
Before the Beginning

Each soul is potentially divine. The goal is to manifest this divinity by controlling nature, external and internal. Do this either by work, or worship, or psychic control, or philosophy – by one, or more, or all of these – and be free. This is the whole of religion.

– Swami Vivekananda

My conscious journey into understanding the dynamics of life underwent a trajectory change when I was in my early twenties. An unusual situation arose at our centre that demanded an urgent and unconventional solution – I, a novice monk, had to break into the house of a bank manager to get the keys of the bank locker right away. The manager, whose responsibility it was to open the locker to deliver the question papers for the Board examination scheduled for that day, had absented from duty.

Upon reaching the manager's flat, I found the door locked. Looking for clues, I jumped up to the ventilator and saw that the keys were on the table with a note, implying that he wanted them to be taken by whatever means.

I contacted the administrative authorities, took some policemen with me, and at the suggestion of the neighbours, tried entering from the backdoor, which had been left unlocked.

The gentleman, who was leading the way, entered the living room, screamed, held his hand tightly on his mouth and ran back.

I was next in line. When I entered the room, I saw a sight which I have never forgotten. How do you react when you enter someone's house whom you knew well and who was more than successful in life, and are welcomed not by him but by his body hanging from the ceiling with a rope round his neck?

I felt numb.

I also felt compelled to question the dynamics of life – what made the chain run and what made it snap.

My journey through life continued, bringing in its wake more unnatural deaths, break-ups and breakdowns, lows and despondency, and other such impediments. But that scene has continued to occupy the most space among my bad memories.

Over the years, I have found that there are numerous books that teach us how to manage one's life, and masters from every age have illuminated the way to blessedness. However, in a changing world that spews new minds, new situations and new problems continually, it is impossible to have one fit-all solution for everything.

A closer look at life shows that the problems and demands of humanity have remained unchanged over ages; they only get clothed differently. We all seek comfort, security, material pleasures, inner happiness, long life of our dear ones, good health, wonderful family, supportive friends and likewise. And so, the solutions to life's problems also have been the same, only packaged differently.

Of all the books that explore life as a complete whole in the Hindu spiritual tradition, Gita is the most respected and popular work, primarily because it teaches the philosophy of life at all levels and shows that if you do not fight your war now, your demons will soon catch up with you and cause much more harm. It also guides the way to self-seclusion and realizing one's true self to those who have no inner or external war to fight.

Gita is like the mirror of life. If you shut your eyes to it, you will see nothing, and if you gaze deep into it, then your true nature will come tumbling out to give you a reality check. So, with its help, one can understand what they are and what they need to do with life. It can also help sense the way out of the morass in which they might be to attain anything – beatitude, wealth, fame, peace, liberation – just anything!

People often ask whether Gita is relevant in the present times. The answer is a big YES. It is just as relevant today and will continue to be so in the future, as it was when it was first delivered millennia ago. Until a person becomes spiritually illumined and realizes their true divine nature, they will remain bound by the polarities of success and failure, making them aggressive and depressive by turn.

Feeling imprisoned, they may yearn for the strength to break free from the bonds, which Gita provides through its life-saving message of freedom and oneness: the two essential pillars of strength.

Looking back, I believe that the unfortunate bank manager, mentioned earlier, would not have taken the extreme step if he had understood life better with the help of Gita.

This work, *Arohan: Ascent with Gita,* approaches the sacred scripture in a manner that a common person can understand and relate with. Presented as a discussion between a young man and a monk, the purpose of this work is to bring before the readers the realities of life on a larger canvas, avoiding the polemics and philosophical wrangling often found in scholarly commentary.

This work does not translate or explain all the verses, since the purpose is to arouse an interest in the minds of those who find it challenging to navigate the philosophical complexities of Gita. The selection of the verses is mostly random to show that Gita is like a bowl of nectar – drink from anywhere and you will be blessed. Indeed, *Arohan* may well prepare you for a deeper dive into the sublime waters of this eternal divine song.

The work is also my tribute to Gita, which is the first scripture I studied seriously, and to my great teachers who took special care of me while explaining its depth in detail. I also profusely thank Gita Press, whose publications have been the guiding light in my spiritual journey. Even this work owes greatly to Gita Press.

I also offer my most sincere pranams to Swami Nikhilananda ji of the Ramakrishna Mission whose translations of Gita and the Upanishads have been the main frame of my understanding of scriptures. Help has also been taken from the work of Swami Swarupananda's translation of Gita, which was overseen by Swami Vivekananda himself.

The English translation of the verses in this work is not literal but free-flowing, to align with its theme. Except for some verses from *The Song Celestial* by the great poet Sir Edwin Arnold, the entire work is from my memory.

To make the reading of Sanskrit verses easier, words have at times been separated from their conjunction form.

GITA
Word of Bhagavan

In Whom is the Universe, Who is in the Universe, Who is the Universe; in Whom is the Soul, Who is in the Soul, Who is the Soul of Man; knowing Him – and therefore the Universe – as our Self, alone extinguishes all fear, brings an end to misery and leads to Infinite Freedom.

— Swami Vivekananda

Importance of Gita

This chapter may appear difficult and technical to some readers, and it may even require more than one reading. Those not interested in it may skip it, but to understand the ideas that abound in Gita, it is advisable to grasp the essentials of this chapter.

Gita belongs to the tradition of living scriptures, meaning that it has inspired people for thousands of years. Composed in mere seven hundred verses in eighteen chapters, it is spiritually deep, philosophically broad and intensely practical. Each of its chapters is named as yoga, implying that one can improve their life, and become increasingly aware of their indwelling Divinity, by following any of the chapters, in part or whole.

Gita is considered sacred for the Hindus, many of whom memorize it in childhood, while others recite it daily, contemplate upon it, and strive to realize the spiritual truths that it contains. It is also customary for a Hindu to recite it when they begin their journey beyond the physical universe.

Highlighting the importance of Gita, Sri Ramakrishna had said that a monk may give up everything, but he must keep a copy of Gita with him. Swami Vivekananda, during his wandering days in India in the 1880s–90s, always kept a copy with him.

It is not known for sure how old Gita is, but it is a sacrosanct belief that it was delivered in the battlefield of Kurukshetra by a tranquil Sri Krishna to his friend-disciple Arjuna, who, overwhelmed with sorrow, horror and confusion at the thought of killing his own kith and kin in the impending war, laid down his arms and refused to fight, citing many 'compelling' reasons for his decision. It was the kind of conflict where his duty demanded that he go ahead with the war, while his emotions and sense of virtue dictated the opposite.

What Sri Krishna then spoke to him by way of teaching came to be known as Gita, which alleviated Arjuna from his confusion and mental mess – something that we always face in the world. In the process, Sri Krishna also revealed to him the spiritual reality behind existence.

Bhagavan, a spiritual reality

What is this spiritual reality that Gita discusses?

The idea that 'I' exists separately from the distinct 'world' is universal among all beings. This sense of duality, drives all beings to live 'individual' lives in the world, and to leave the likes of their own for the future.

Of all living beings, it has been the privilege of human beings to ponder over the meaning of 'I' and to wonder if there is an underlying unity in the vastness before them.

'Yes', say the spiritual masters.

'But how?' comes the next question. That is when the quest for spirituality begins. It is then that the noble minds start probing into the deeper layers of existence. (Here, 'noble' is used in its original meaning, implying 'rare, inclined towards purity', without any reference to hereditary or titular status in society.)

The first step in that direction is when one realizes that the conscious reality of a person is known as 'self', and of the universe is 'God' or 'Universal Self'. To realize this truth, one has to get down to silencing the mind through purity and meditation. Those who strive to do this consciously and sincerely are known as yogis or spiritual persons, very few of whom succeed fully. These blessed ones can be from any age, race, continent or gender.

In the depths of meditation, they realize that the world, created by the senses and mind, has consciousness as its substratum, the way the ocean is to its waves. This consciousness is real, infinite and forever, and is not bound by anything of this world, nor does it have any characteristics of matter whatsoever, like creation-destruction, good-bad, etc. The only thing that can be said about it is that 'It is'. This universal and eternal substratum is known variously as God, Atman, Brahman, etc. No name, form, quality or action can describe it, since It is Infinite; not merely big or huge, but that which can neither be defined nor be comprehended by anything that is finite.

The existence or non-existence of this infinite consciousness, Brahman, can neither be experienced by the mind, nor can be proved through reasoning. The mind and senses, by their very constitution are finite and hence they deal only with the limited. Thus, no science, poetry or art can ever capture the essence or majesty of the Divine. As Sri Ramakrishna put it beautifully, 'one cannot put three litres of milk in a one-litre jar'.

God, being the reality of all, creates, sustains and dissolves the universe. Why and how this is done, cannot be answered, since there was nothing at the point of creation other than God, the pure consciousness. The sages say that the act of creation is achieved by His divine power, called variously as Prakriti, Shakti or Maya. These three names, and many other such names for the power of God, are often used interchangeably, although they may have subtle differences in connotation.

We have used the word 'Bhagavan' for God in the title of this section in consonance with the term used for God in Gita. The term 'Bhagavan' literally means God, the entity who always has the divine qualities of knowledge, strength, vigour, etc.

The power of God has been described by the sages of yore to be *trigunatmika*, meaning, it is composed of three *gunas* (qualities): *sattva, rajas* and *tamas* (approximate translation could be stability, kinesis and inertness). These qualities, like a heap of marble, stay in perfect balance when there is no creation. Human language is incapable of defining this timeless and attribute-free state. But they become active and try to overpower each other once the balance is disturbed. This state of disturbed balance is known as creation, which is a product and derivative of the three gunas only. It is then that the cosmic mind, worlds, beings and the individual mind is created. And yes, it now becomes the domain of language!

God, being the master of His power, is beyond the gunas. Whenever there is creation, He appears as various deities with form and qualities, who are worshipped by devotees, and who fulfil their desires in various ways. When there is no creation, there being no subject or object, God remains what He truly is – indescribable. Due to this He is often referred to as being formless and beyond qualities.

God, the teacher

Once creation is set in process, beings of infinite varieties populate the universe and lead their lives according to their inherent tendencies across indefinite cycles of birth and death. The only way to break this vicious rut is to gain the higher knowledge of spirituality, which cannot be attained through ordinary means. So, God Himself gives this knowledge to contemplative minds or to His chosen ones.

However, spiritual truths, although profound, tend to become mere dry information for their upholders and practitioners as time passes, like a palace that turns into a heap of bricks and stones due to neglect. It is then that an incarnation, known as *avatara*, comes and sets dharma, the spiritual path, right once again by presenting the eternal spiritual truths afresh, and ridding the garden of Creation of various weeds and pests that have sprung up in the meanwhile.

Even though God is beyond everything that makes this universe, He can, by His own power, appear as an avatara in the universe. Whenever He chooses to incarnate, His birth and deeds are not impelled by natural forces like Karma. He thus remains desireless, ever free, all-powerful, ever-present, all-knowing and merciful all the time. In the Hindu spiritual tradition, the Divine is never perceived to act out of vengeance, akin to a gardener plucking out unwanted growths without any animus.

It is through the words of the avatara that the scriptures get validated once again, spirituality gets infused among noble minds, and the evolutionary process gets an upward push, away from the stagnation in which they had been stuck for a long time through their never-ending cycle of ignorance – desire – action – birth – death. Spirituality breaks this cycle by cutting at the root of ignorance. To be spiritual means to *know* that you are one with God – desireless. There can be no duty for you, no bondage, neither birth nor death. You are free, eternally free; master of all; beyond pleasure and pain – bondage was never anything beyond your own imagination, a product of your mind.

The Divine Lord of all once incarnated as Sri Krishna and was born to Devaki and Vasudeva. During the Mahabharata war, he became the charioteer of his friend-disciple Arjuna, who got immersed in guilt and sorrow at the sight of his near and dear ones ready to kill each other. He presented this as a conflict situation between his duty as soldier and his obligation of non-violence towards his own kin, and refused to take part in the war.

Sri Krishna then reminded Arjuna of his duty, known as *svadharma*, that has to be performed by all without any emotional involvement, which can be accomplished through complete surrender to God, or by being dispassionate in one's attitude towards life and the world. Once a person becomes dispassionately committed towards duty, they become fit for spiritual practices that ultimately elevate them to the realization of oneness with God.

The fact is that the situation of Arjuna was not at all a conflict situation, *dharma sankat*, which arises when two choices are equally right, as we find in the many instances in the life of Sri Rama. In this particular case, it was more a case of mental mess created by emotions – the eternal enemy of intelligence. The decision to fight the war was unanimous, and both the armies had assembled there by their own choice and by way of *Kshatriya dharma* – the duty that demanded an able-bodied Kshatriya take part in a war when invited or challenged. So, how could there be a case of conflict for anyone?

In fact, there is no mention in Vyasa's Mahabharata of any other warrior going through that kind of despondency as Arjuna had. More importantly, towards the end of Gita, we find Arjuna himself expressing his gratitude to Sri Krishna for dispelling his initial delusions, which then allowed him to become conscious of his duty once again.

What Sri Krishna told Arjuna was later composed as Gita by the great sage Vyasa, who incorporated it in his monumental work, Mahabharata, in the section named *Bhishma Parva*.

All this may be true or may be a story to set the stage for conveying Gita's spiritual message. The fact, however, remains that the world is scorched by pain caused by the materialistic outlook born of ignorance, and resulting in greed, emotional imbalance, transgression of duty, failure to honour one's own word, selfishness, cruelty, jealousy, hatred and other such feelings, which continue to cause immense sorrow all over. This is where the importance of Gita comes in. It shows how the reality behind the universe is not what it appears to be; the Divine alone is real while everything else is transitory. The goal of life should be to know this truth; to strive through legitimate means to excel in worldly affairs; and also strive to realize one's unity with God.

Identification with matter will cause suffering, while being with the spirit of God will liberate – this is what Gita says.

Indian spiritual traditions talk of dimensions of existence as the physical, the subtle, the causal and the infinite. The physical universe is characterized by action; the subtle universe is of deities and other divine beings where enjoyment is in abundance; the causal universe is where one can be face to face with God who appears as with some form; and the ultimate one, the infinite, is the state of pure consciousness, known as Brahman. It cannot be known by the mind since the mind has to be completely stilled for that state to be revealed. A person can only become one with It and regain freedom forever from all cycles of existence; at this point, the individuality created by the mind-ego complex merges into the Divine permanently, like ice melting into the ocean.

Gita accepts these states of existence and presents all of them on a single canvas, with a particular focus on the physical, causal and the infinite. The realm of the subtle universe, inhabited by the gods and other such beings, does not find importance here. Philosophically, Gita aligns more with the Upanishads than the main body of the Vedas.

It is also important to note here that Gita presents a complete picture of existence, and hence to claim that Gita talks only about this aspect or that, as insinuated by many commentators and writers, is a great injustice to this majestic work. Gita is as infinite in its outlook as God is. To try to put limits on it is a futile exercise.

Lord Krishna, in his message to humankind through Gita, says that there is no difference between the Personal God, that is, God with form, and formless Reality; every path leads only to Him; and every act of worship done to whomsoever, reaches Him only, since Consciousness, God, incarnation – are one and the same. The goal for all is to let go of their identification with the petty 'I' and be what they truly are – YOU, the Divine.

It is then that one realizes that all struggle in life, extending aeons in the past, and all actions performed were ultimately aimed at letting go of our limited 'I'-ness so that the higher 'I' of the Lord may take over and play through us.

A work of sublime greatness invites many adaptations and interpretations. Gita is no exception. For thousands of years, it has been explained and commented upon by innumerable saints, philosophers, thinkers and scholars to elucidate its content, to make it relatable for the prevalent age and times. Every one of these was no doubt valid for its time. Of these, the commentary by Adi Shankaracharya is considered to be the most rational and comprehensive, although this too is not accepted by all, since different minds are at different levels of evolution and hence require different interpretations of the work.

Swami Vivekananda wanted scriptures, including Gita, to be interpreted in light of the life and teachings of Sri Ramakrishna, who showed through his spiritual experiences how spiritual truths are universal, ever-present and must be realized to make one's life blessed. To use an analogy, spirituality is not to be used like a fashionable garment that is only worn on special occasions; rather, it should be used as a daily wear garment.

So, it is in the fitness of things that Gita be presented to today's dynamic generation, that they too may identify the relevance of these timeless and ancient spiritual truths to the challenges of the digital age. It is with this idea that this book has been written.

We hope that this work, which is a presentation of the words of Bhagavan, will serve as a handbook for understanding Gita, the Hindu religion, spirituality and how to handle one's problems in life.

I

THE SORROW

Parikrama at Omkareswar

Omkareshwar. A small temple town with the famous *jyotirlinga* of Lord Shiva, where the great Shankaracharya (c. 8th AD), whose words are the ultimate in explaining Hindu scriptures including Gita, met his guru Govindapada and received *sannyasa* from him. It is quite near the financially rich and industrially vibrant city of Indore, where I had come to plant money to grow a tree of money in the form of industrial plants.

Unfortunately for me, there were some unsavoury developments, so I visited the temple town to soothe my frayed nerves. Our newfound opulence in the hands of the untrained has led to unexpected fragility, a reality that we rarely admit but which can be easily felt in the proliferation of 'pop Gurus'. The saying 'as the Guru, so the *chela*' used to be popular, but now it is, 'as the chela, so the Guru'. I personally never went to any of those *tamashas*, even though I was hit seriously.

There was a large crowd at Omkareswar, comprised of both devotees and religious tourism. Years ago, my parents used to come here on pilgrimage, but nowadays life has become all about making money and spending it, mostly to show that you have arrived.

With my thoughts racing to catch each other, I sat on the bank of Narmada amidst pebbles and rocks, observing the temple in the dying light of the day. Until a few years ago, one could find a *Shivalinga* all around the place, but now, due to the all-consuming project of making life comfortable, only stones remain. Earlier it was God as stone, and now stones have become the new God for the builders who know how to make money by placing the right stones in the right place.

I glanced around. A monk sat at a distance lost in his own thoughts, looking at the flowing waters.

To the world, said I, and threw a pebble into the river.

To power and pelf! Another pebble.

If there were fish in the river – though I am not sure if there were any left after the dam construction some years ago – they would have wondered at the rain of stones. Rain! A marvellous occurrence. Water, which is supposed to be under the ground, starts falling from above, and we marvel at the phenomenon.

Would the fish, living amidst the pebbles of the rivers, think likewise? I thought and threw another one into the river.

To life, I muttered ferociously. This time the resonating splash from the water was loud, which probably rocked the contemplative mind of the nearby monk. He looked at me, got up, walked some paces and sat by my side.

Angry? said he.

These monks! They tend to untap their wisdom, conjured up through sense, nonsense and common sense, at the first opportunity. To my credit, I had made fair donations to various religious organizations at the prodding of my family members and so knew some of them. Money for words! Nice exchange.

Not at all, Swamiji.

There was no need for me to tell him that right then, I was in the mood to murder someone for the chaos that surrounded me.

Private person, aren't you?

What did he mean by that? We are all private persons. Only the emotionally hollow parade their stories in public. No, I wasn't hollow.

To be polite, which is the business of all businessmen, I asked about him. He had come to deliver talks on 'Ethics in Business Management' at a management institute whose graduates I often employed. Going by their behaviour, I was not sure if they would be interested in the subject on which he had come to speak.

Oxymoron, isn't it? Business and ethics do not go hand in hand. Most businesses are a zero-sum game, with the policy of 'your money, my pocket', so scruple is not our strength, you know, said I.

He looked at me with a deep, piercing look, unlocking some of my deeper knots. I felt uncomfortable.

Much later, I chanced to read an incident when John D. Rockefeller, the filthy rich man of America, had met Swami Vivekananda. The great Swami had measured his hidden weaknesses at a mere glance and narrated them to him, rattling the tycoon. After a few days he made a large donation to some charity, and challenged Swamiji with, 'Now you can thank me.' And Swamiji had famously replied, 'It is for you to thank me.'

I don't think that the monk sitting by my side had gauged me that much. He said, Ethics and spirituality are everywhere, *bhai*. There is no act of life or thought of the mind that is not permeated by spirituality. The problem lies in your perception, and that is why you suffer.

It was a bit confusing. If I were to be so confused in my business, my bank balance would have shrunk by some zeroes, causing mayhem in the stock market.

There is more to life than making money and surrounding oneself with minds and gadgets to stay intoxicated, said he.

He was surely perceptive. Judging someone is not very difficult, you know. Not only the clothes, but the way a person speaks, sits, looks and gestures speaks volumes about them. You don't have to be a yogi or a shrink with a questionnaire to know about a person. We, in our business, too, measure people by a mere look. However, he appeared deeper than us.

We continued to conversate as the bloom of the evening darkened the flowing water. Like the increasing darkness all around, my confidence about myself and my success ebbed, as his words flowed.

Have you overcome your fears? Are you immune to sorrow? Do you have the strength to be happy with nothing to give you company? Have you mastered rejection? Do you stay steady even amidst your failures? Have you overcome the urge to be the winner at all times? Don't you ever feel loneliness at a party?

I wanted to ask him if he was a master of his life but out of politeness, I kept quiet. Nevertheless, these were powerful blows. I did not even know that so many problems could assail a person. He, however, had saved the choicest for the last.

How well can you bear the loss of your loved ones, and how good will you be when you have to face rejection from the love of your life?

Stop! I kind of screamed. Some raw pain had been stepped upon.

Well, we don't teach you how to make money, but we do save you from becoming human monsters, or human animals – confined to foraging, fighting and mating. Do you even realize how you people are dismantling the society that has been built brick-by-brick for thousands of years by our sagely ancestors? From sages to savages – what a journey!

What do you mean? How am I responsible for the chaos that you are hinting at?

Not you directly but your ilk, the money monsters, for whom the body is the only temple and beauty the only deity.

I could not take that lying down. With due respect to you, Swamiji, when so much of blood has been shed in the name of religion, why should anyone give a fig about it?

To be honest, said he, I don't understand how anyone can shed blood in the name of God who is the creator and sustainer of all. It beats rationality to see how any religion can permit such a thing. If you look back at history, do you find Hindus fighting in the name of religion or shedding blood of others? No, never. A true religion makes a person surrender to his divine nature, which is gentleness and inner peace. If these two are lacking from a religion, then there is something seriously wrong with it.

However, do please remember that there are two reasons for this bloodbath – political ambitions camouflaged under the mask of religion, and fanaticism born of ignorance. That way, non-religious violence has been worse: Changez Khan's army killed more than four crore people; the Communists under Lenin, Stalin and Mao, the arch enemies of religion, are responsible for the death of more than ten crore people only in the twentieth century. You can check the stats on internet.

And, if you want to ban religion for the mayhem caused by the vicious, you have to ban Science, too, since it is much more directly connected with the devastating atomic explosion on Hiroshima and Nagasaki! Bhai, violence is in the nature of humans. If you do not control it through religious values of peace, then the thunder of guns and the blaze of swords is bound to annihilate lives.

God! Swamiji could indeed silence his opponents.

Even then, do you think that we should believe in God instead of taking care of the present?

To know about God and spirituality, said he, one has to silence their mind through purity and meditation. Those who strive towards that are known as spiritual persons. Silence your mind and you will know the truth.

Just one small question, Swamiji: why are there different ideas about God, and why do most religions not accept the idea of incarnation? I was finally awake to the talk.

The knowledge of God depends on how He chooses to reveal Himself to a person, which again depends on the purity of one's mind and the longing for Him. He may appear to someone as formless and to others with, say, thousand arms – He may appear in any form that He chooses. After all, He is infinite, and He is the Lord and master of all. No one can claim exclusive knowledge about God. The crucial line is 'a defined God is no God'.

I really loved the statement, 'a defined God is no God'. Over the years, after I first heard it, I have used it many times to silence overactive zealots.

I persisted, If God is for real, then why is there so much disparity, and why so much suffering? If God is just, then why do bad people not get punished while good people suffer so much?

The idea that God is just comes from religions with a tribal mindset that demand quick justice, said he. Even the definition of good and bad in those religions comes from their books, which are heavily loaded in the favour of the believers. The whole concept looks more like mob justice. And why should God have a bias towards good people?

Contrary to all this, in the Hindu religion, there is no absolute good or bad, nor is our God a despotic one – favouring some and wrathful towards others. Moreover, it is a misconception that bad people do not suffer. In fact, they suffer much. Only we do not notice that. And sometimes, their good Karma protects them in this life. After all, we, the Hindus, do not go by the childish theory of one birth to explain universe and creation.

Speaking spiritually, do not transpose your own ideas and understanding on God, since He is beyond mind and beyond any law of cause and effect.

And so, the conversation continued further. Towards the end, he said that the way I was throwing pebbles into the river showed some kind of deep agitation, and so he had come to talk to me. Impressive, I thought.

He then invited me to join him for a morning walk the next day at the Parikrama known as the *Mandhata Parikrama*, the circumambulating path around the Mandhata mountain on which devotees walk. It is about eight kilometres long around the island formed by the rivers Narmada and Kaveri. The island is imagined to look like ॐ, Om, and is dotted with ancient temples and monasteries.

He then added, we, the poor, have to move according to the timings of trains and buses. But you being rich, must be the master of your own time. So, manage your time and join me.

Swamiji was persuasive. Willing or not, I joined him the next day on the parikrama.

Gita begins

The next morning, I crossed the footbridge on the Narmada and reached the point where the Swamiji had asked me to meet him. He was waiting. We wished each other and started our walk.

Before we could exchange anything meaningful, I was startled to see a Sanskrit verse and its Hindi translation inscribed on a stone slab erected on the side of the road of the parikrama path. It was the famous first verse of Gita, which I knew partly:

धर्मक्षेत्रे कुरुक्षेत्रे समवेता युयुत्सवः | मामकाः पाण्डवाश्चैव किमकुर्वत सञ्जय

Dhritarashtra asked: *Sanjay, what did my children and those of Pandu do when they assembled in the sacred land of Kurukshetra for the war?*

Here, too, O Lord! I exclaimed. I had read somewhere that God is the biggest land grabber in India.

Why? What is your problem if Lord is present here, too? You can go anywhere, convert religious places into money mines, and you think God has no right to be here? And why? You think a person is bereft of God? Wherever there is anything, God is there.

One interesting thing about these monks is that they are always arsenal ready. Give them half a chance, and the firing begins. He was probably right, so I kept mum.

He asked if I knew what Gita is.

Of course, Swamiji. We, in India grow up with these stories, and I also know a lot about it from other sources.

Like?

Gita is all about war, war and war. Get up and fight! Tell me, Swamiji, why preach about war and bloodshed in an already blood-baying world? To be fair, it also has some noble words, though they became outdated long ago. But India, the worshipper of the past, continues to chant it, and the gullible listen to the sermons by the *babajis* on its verses, even though whatever these verses have to convey are removed from the present-day reality.

Really! exclaimed he, with amusement in abundance.

What's more, it puts women and the deprived in a bad light while praising the caste system. It talks about detached work. Now tell me, whosoever has heard of such a preposterous thing like detached work! The little success that I have today is because I worked passionately all my life. Passion, Swamiji, passion. Passion drives the world!

The climb, my words and emotions made me pant.

Swamiji looked mighty amused, as if he would burst out laughing any minute. It was pretty insulting. With that look he broke out in a soft, melodious chant of the first few verses, and then asked me if I had ever felt chaos in life.

Of course, I said.

How bad was it?

Bad, I said.

Was it anything like this? Saying so, he read out, *My limbs fail me, my mouth is parched, I tremble all over ... I am not able to stand upright, and my mind is in a whirl.*

The emotion conveyed by Swamiji was too powerful to miss. He said, you have not even faced such life devastating emotions, how can you then understand how life-saving Gita can be? Let me tell you that Gita has solutions to all human problems. You only have to look for them in the right place. It is set in the battlefield to show that howsoever bad your plight in life, you can always lift yourself up by its words.

He was not even looking at me now. Talking to himself, as it were, he walked, stopped, sat, spoke, looked at the horizon, and stressed on the importance of Gita in everyone's life. I tried to stay with his thoughts, but I realized how difficult it was to be in sync with the thoughts of a mind that is teaching greater things.

Walking with him and listening to his animated words, I felt an urge to spend a few days with him, listening to his explanation of how Gita is related to life. Probably the time had come for me to learn something new.

In the beginning itself I realized that I needed to record all that he was saying, so I started recording his words without letting him know. It was probably unethical but at that time, I wanted to save him from being self-conscious. How wrong I was in assessing him that way! I am sure he would never have remained totally conscious of his words.

What I learnt from him every day, I noted down on my tab at night before I went to sleep. It has been years since that riverside conversation took place. Finally, at the ceaseless prodding of my friends, I have organized it to present before you what I understood of the life-saving message of Gita, as learnt from Swamiji at Omkareswar.

He did not explain every verse to me. Initially, when I pointed out the missed verses to him, he said, I am not giving you a new commentary on Gita. To learn it traditionally, you should find a suitable translation of Shankaracharya's commentary. Personally, I do not trust anyone else.

Background of Gita

We proceeded – Swamiji with his words, and I with my thoughts – looking at the beauty of Narmada and letting a few words slip inside my consciousness.

I was thinking about how looking at something from a height is such a wonderful experience – you take the whole thing in one single panoramic shot – when my musing was interrupted by Swamiji's. Do you know how it all started?

Startled, I asked what he meant and then realized that he wanted to know if I knew the background of Gita. I did, but I remained silent.

A long time ago, said Swamiji, maybe 5,000 years ago according to some, there was a famous kingdom, Hastinapur, near present-day Meerut, whose king was the blind Dhritarashtra. He had one hundred sons, who came to be known as the Kauravas. The eldest of them was Duryodhana, who was the crown prince and the de facto king.

The cousins of the Kauravas were the five Pandavas, and the chief warrior among them was Arjuna. Due to various reasons, the Kauravas and the Pandavas were constantly at odds. A large sequence of unfortunate events (my grandmother had narrated the Mahabharata to me in childhood, so I had an idea what these events were) finally led to a terrible war, in which a huge number of soldiers, warriors and kings assembled at Kurukshetra to show their solidarity and valour in the battlefield. Soon, both parties had huge armies of elephants, chariots, horses and warriors.

Lord Krishna was friendly with both the Kauravas and Pandavas, and so he had tried to stop the war through negotiations but failed. Now in the war, he was the charioteer of Arjuna who was his friend-disciple, while his own army was with the Kauravas. Imagine this! Sri Krishna's own soldiers, on his payroll, trying to kill him in the war simply because they were on the opposing side. This is what is known as *dharma yuddha* – the righteous war. In it, you may choose any side, but once the choice is made, you have to be true to your side even if that means killing your own. It is more like a game in which the highest stake is life itself.

When the battle bugle was sounded, Arjuna wanted to have a look at the chief warriors arrayed on both sides. The sight disturbed him hugely. Teachers, disciples, elders, relatives and other close ones ready to kill each other. He became inconsolable with grief at the possible loss of life. Grief-stricken and confused, he refused to take part in the war.

What Arjuna was experiencing was actually self-delusion, since he and all other warriors had come prepared for the war, knowing well their duty and its consequences. What happened with Arjuna is not a one-off incident. Such cases of delusion are often described with high-sounding terms in the present times, like 'conflict situation'. But these are only human failings, which require the right guidance,

THE SORROW 25

as Arjuna sought from Sri Krishna, who then delivered his message, which was later composed in 700 verses by the great sage Vyasa, who incorporated it in his monumental work, the Mahabharata, in the section named Bhishma Parva. And thus flowed Gita – suckling the spiritually thirsty, religion-hungry and emotionally drained.

Many debate whether the Mahabharata actually occurred, and if there was really a Lord Krishna who delivered it on the battlefield. We may never get a 'scientifically' proven answer to these questions. But it is undeniable that our world is right now in the throes of conflict, between nations, between communities, linguistic groups, religious groups, business conglomerates, neighbourhoods, families – you name it. This conflict is almost entirely driven by fear and greed. That is exactly where Gita comes in, like it did a long time ago, and reveals that the reality behind the universe is much more than what we take it for and thus, we suffer.

And what is that? I asked.

Let us wait for that. The whole of Gita is only about that.

Coming back to the story, King Dhritarashtra, sitting in Hastinapur, wanted to know how the war was going, so Vyasa, the great sage that he was, gave Sanjay, the counsellor-charioteer of the king, yogic power to see and hear all that was happening during the war without ever getting harmed. Sanjay was taking part in the war on the side of the Kauravas.

As per the Mahabharata, on the tenth day of the war, Bhishma, the grandsire of both the Pandavas and Kauravas, was mortally wounded in the war. Heartbroken, Sanjay came to inform the king of the major blow, who became devastated at the news. He then wanted to know in detail all that had happened. That is how began the narration which is now known as Gita.

In the opening verses of Gita, Sanjay narrated the war situation as it had been. Duryodhana, the son of the King, was his usual confident self before the war, and he described the chief warriors, their strength, weapons, flags and trumpets, and made a comparative description of both armies to Drona, his war teacher and also one of his chief warriors.

It was then that Arjuna requested that Sri Krishna take his chariot to the middle of the battleground so that he could survey the chiefs of both the sides. What he saw then was shocking even to the battle-hardened heart of Arjuna. Facing each other were the great warriors of the land ready to kill and get killed. What's more, nearly every warrior had his relatives facing him in the deadly battle. And for what? So that either Duryodhana or Yudhisthira could rule!

The moral dilemma

Arjuna's shock at the sight of the warriors was immense. The future wailing of the widows, cries of the orphans, destruction of human resources, and the blood-soaked earth moved his heart to extreme depression and despondency. That is when he verbalized his emotions as:

सीदन्ति मम गात्राणि मुखं च परिशुष्यति, वेपथुश्च शरीरे मे रोमहर्षश्च जायते |
गाण्डीवं स्रंसते हस्तात्त्वक्चैव परिदह्यते, न च शक्नोम्यवस्थातुं भ्रमतीव च मे मनः |

(Seeing these kinsmen gathered here to fight), *my limbs fail me, my mouth is parched, I tremble all over, my hair stands on end. My bow, Gandiva, slips from my hand and my skin burns. I am not able to stand upright, my mind is in a whirl. (I.29–30)*

Look at the poetry, said Swamiji. What depth, what portrayal! If a person experiences any of these physical sensations, then know that they need help right away. Have a support system, as Arjuna had, or go to a doctor as is the usual practice; but don't just let the negativity born of turmoil overpower you.

I remembered the famous poem, 'Home they Brought her Warrior Dead'. Indeed, it was her support system that saved the widowed young lady.

Swamiji continued. The next verses show the anguish of Arjuna.

न काङ्क्षे विजयं कृष्ण न च राज्यं सुखानि च, किं नो राज्येन गोविन्द किं भोगैर्जीवितेन वा |
येषामर्थे काङ्क्षितं नो राज्यं भोगाः सुखानि च, त इमेऽवस्थिता युद्धे प्राणांस्त्यक्त्वा धनानि च |
आचार्याः पितरः पुत्रास्तथैव च पितामहाः, मातुलाः श्वशुराः पौत्राः श्यालाः सम्बन्धिनस्तथा |
एतान्न हन्तुमिच्छामि घ्नतोऽपि मधुसूदन, अपि त्रैलोक्यराज्यस्य हेतोः किं नु महीकृते |

O Krishna! I desire neither victory, empire, nor pleasure. Of what avail is dominion to us and of what avail are pleasures and even life, if these, for whose sake victory is desired, stand here in battle, giving up their life and wealth. See how teachers, uncles, sons, grandfathers, maternal uncles, fathers-in-law, grandsons, brothers-in-law and other kinsmen stand here in this war. Even though these were to kill me, I would never wish to kill them, not even for the sake of dominion over the three worlds, what to say then of this earth! (I.32–35)

Arjuna then gave high-sounding reasons from religion for not fighting, even though he had come prepared for the war knowing all this.

Arjuna's emotional turmoil

यद्यप्येते न पश्यन्ति लोभोपहतचेतसः, कुलक्षयकृतं दोषं मित्रद्रोहे च पातकम् |
कथं न ज्ञेयमस्माभिः पापादस्मान्निवर्तितुम् | कुलक्षयकृतं दोषं प्रपश्यद्भिर्जनार्दन |

O Krishna, even though the mind of the Kauravas is overpowered by greed, and hence they see no evil in the annihilation of families, nor do they seem to see sin in hostility towards friends, but why should we, who clearly see the crime involved in it, take part in this war? (I.38–39)

कुलक्षये प्रणश्यन्ति कुलधर्माः सनातनाः,| धर्मे नष्टे कुलं कृत्स्नमधर्मोऽभिभवत्युत |
अधर्माभिभवात्कृष्ण प्रदुष्यन्ति कुलस्त्रियः | स्त्रीषु दुष्टासु वार्ष्णेय जायते वर्णसङ्करः |

On the decay of a family, the traditional religious rites of that family die out, resulting in loss of dharma for family, which makes the women of the family go wrong. This causes intermingling of varnas (occupational categories) which ruins the way of life of people. (I.40-41)

सङ्करो नरकायैव कुलघ्नानां कुलस्य च, पतन्ति पितरो ह्येषां लुप्तपिण्डोदकक्रियाः |
दोषैरेतैः कुलघ्नानां वर्णसङ्करकारकैः, उत्साद्यन्ते जातिधर्माः कुलधर्माश्च शाश्वताः |
उत्सन्नकुलधर्माणां मनुष्याणां जनार्दन, नरके नियतं वासो भवतीत्यनुशुश्रुम |

Admixture of Varnas leads the family to the hell and is the destroyer of the family. Deprived of the right offerings, their ancestors fall from the heaven. Such a mixture also results in the destruction of traditional religious values of the families and the clan. We have heard, O Krishna, that hell is inevitable for those whose families' religious practices have been destroyed. (I.42–44)

Every religion has two aspects – spirituality and religious practices. Hinduism is the religion of freedom, and so it allows a person to follow the family and local practices as a way of life, without letting go of the supreme spiritual truth. Here Arjuna is talking about the loss of *kula dharma* – family traditions, and *jati dharma* – the community duties. These two have been the mainstay of Hindu religious and social practices till recently. The preservation of these dharmas depended a lot on the female members of the family, and hence the worry.

One important feature of kula dharma and jati dharma was offering of *pinda* in the form of rice balls and water to dead ancestors according to the traditions. The war being a major cause of destruction, these traditions were sure to suffer.

Interestingly, Lord Krishna never gave a direct answer to this issue in Gita. This is because these traditions are dynamic and hence bound to change. It may also be argued that Krishna had come to restore dharma, which had been distorted notwithstanding the prevalence of these social institutions, and thus he was not averse to their demolition either. Also, who better than the Lord Himself can appreciate the transitory nature of all human institutions!

The verses starting thirty-six show how Arjuna presented the conflict situation. In his defence it must be said that he was not entirely wrong. Some scriptures recommend killing of an *atatayi*, while many others assert that no killing should be done. *Ahimsa*, non-killing, is a higher dharma than even killing in self-defence.

Confronting the consequences of war

अहो बत महत्पापं कर्तुं व्यवसिता वयम्, यद्राज्यसुखलोभेन हन्तुं स्वजनमुद्यताः |
यदि मामप्रतीकारमशस्त्रं शस्त्रपाणयः, धार्तराष्ट्रा रणे हन्युस्तन्मे क्षेमतरं भवेत् |

By being ready to slay our own, out of greed for empire, we are getting involved in a great sin. Believe me, if the sons of Dhritarashtra, armed with weapons were to slay me, unresisting and unarmed in this battle, that would be acceptable to me.

एवमुक्त्वार्जुनः सङ्ख्ये रथोपस्थ उपाविशत्,विसृज्य सशरं चापं शोकसंविग्नमानसः |

Sanjaya said:

Speaking thus in the battlefield, Arjuna put away his bow and arrows, and sank into the seat of his chariot, with his mind distressed with grief.

Thus is described why and how Arjuna refused to fight. The reason he gave was the degeneration of the social order that would be the result of such a great holocaust; with so many people of the warrior caste dead, inter-clan marriages would be inevitable, which would ultimately pollute the religious rites and ceremonies. According to him, the very religious order of the universe was in the danger of getting disturbed. So, he then put down his famous bow, Gandiva, and collapsed in the back of the chariot – a living portrait of melancholy and despondency.

Swamiji concluded with, You know, people are always in some kind of despondency, and hence in need of a saving message. Lord Krishna gave that saving message to the world through Arjuna, who was in a desperate situation sunk deep in the mire of grief.

Was I relieved to be back at home at the end of the day.

II A

KNOW THE REAL

It was our second day of walking together.

We talked of the small things of life, interrupted with occasional greetings of 'Narmade Hara' by the pilgrims to the Swamiji, as a mark of respect to the great tradition of spirituality represented by the sannyasins. It was heartening to see that there were still people who respected others, a quality which was becoming scarce in the mall of consumerism.

India is different from other countries in many aspects, one of which is the way people are greeted in a particular town. In the Himalayas it is 'Hari Om!', in Vrindavan 'Radhe, Radhe!', in Varanasi 'Om Namah Shivay', in Ayodhya and many other places it is 'Jai Ram ji ki', and likewise. Here, at Omkareswar, it was in the name of the sacred Narmada. As for me, I was open to all kinds of gods, greetings, philosophies – starting from atheism, agnosticism, nihilism to Vedanta – meaning, I was into none. I knew passion and goals; the rest were secondary details.

Swamiji responded to every such greeting with enthusiasm, even though they were all unknown to each other. Ah, India! We may soon be burying this culture of bonding with unfamiliar individuals within the embrace of inclusiveness.

We walked some distance in silence when he asked me if I knew the most powerful statement in Gita. I had no idea, so I kept mum.

When Arjun had exhaled his lamentations, said Swamiji, Sri Krishna expressed his surprise at the sliding down of the powerful. He then exhorted Arjuna to burn down his apparent weakness and be what he truly was – a mine of strength.

People often ask, 'Of what use is Gita in modern times?' My answer is always the same, it erases the clouds and cobwebs of your mind and restores you to what you already are. If you have the strength, it will come out firing on all cylinders, and if you feel you do not have anything within you, it will show you how to regain it, since all strength is within you.

Hawa gyan! I muttered under my breath. All strength within oneself, indeed!

You said something, he asked.

Nothing, I said.

When he persisted, I explained the expression 'hawa gyan', which is roughly equivalent to a tale told by an idiot, full of sound and fury, signifying nothing.

I appreciate your understanding, he said, and laughed loudly as if I had just told him a joke. As for hawa gyan, when you go and tell isolated communities that men have landed on the moon, they too will laugh at your back, saying hawa gyan. Einstein's theories were considered hawa gyan by most scientists, and when the great Einstein was told that an atomic bomb can be made from his equation, he treated that as hawa gyan. Whatever cannot be grasped by a mind, it promptly labels it as hawa gyan.

He continued in the same breath, You know what, the way you make fun of us, the monks, we too make fun of you people, your obsessions, cravings and above all, the sheer *nautanki* in matters of spirituality.

I do not take that as a compliment, sir! I said.

Wah! You can make fun out of your ignorance, and I cannot laugh even if I know the truth! What kind of rationality do you educated have?

Swamiji continued. We are weak because we feel weak and want to feel weak. In the story of the Mahabharata, Arjuna was a great warrior, but you just saw how pathetic he appeared. This is the fate of all of us. We all have strength within us, as you will learn when we come to that part of Gita, but we behave like cowards out of our ignorance. That is when a teacher or the words of a master in the form of scriptures is needed to uplift a person. It is exactly this kind of life-saving words that Lord Sri Krishna taught all of humanity through Arjuna.

Stay awake in your strength

कुतस्त्वा कश्मलमिदं विषमे समुपस्थितम्, अनार्यजुष्टमस्वर्ग्यमकीर्तिकरमर्जुन |
क्लैब्यं मा स्म गमः पार्थ नैतत्त्वयि उपपद्यते, क्षुद्रं हृदयदौर्बल्यं त्यक्त्वोत्तिष्ठ परन्तप |

From where has this dejection come to you? It is un-Arya like, disgraceful and detrimental to the attainment of heaven. Be not unmanly; it does not behove you. Cast off this weakness and get up. (II.2–3)

What power, what strength! said Swamiji animatedly. This is what I need, you need, India needs and so does the world need. Wake up, o lion! Hallucinate not that you are a lamb. Let sparks of strength fly out from every pore of your body and every syllable that comes out of your lips. Let flames erupt wherever you stand, let people feel the flow of your volcanic energy wherever you go. And that won't be to scorch them, but to assure all that you are there for them. Let your presence be like that of a lion in front of its cubs – training them up to be the king of their empire. Make all those who come in your perimeter, a mine of strength.

God! Swamiji was fired up. What passion! But was it passion or conviction? I decided not to grade him, unlike modern institutes where the learners grade their teachers!

Swamiji continued, If I had the power, I would have these verses written at the entrance of every institution and would want everyone to have this idea etched in their hearts. Do you know why people suffer? Simply because they forget that dignity and majesty are their inborn qualities. Instead, they behave like rats in a dark kitchen, stealing the crumbs and scampering in fright at the slightest sound. Why do you crave for love? Why are you an attention seeker? Why are you moving around with a glorified begging bowl? It is all because you insist on inhaling weakness, the way Arjuna was doing in the battlefield.

Begging bowl! It is the monks who went to the rich with their bowls, and here we were being criticized. Anyway.

Arya means cultured, he added to his earlier comments. And the desire to have a better afterlife, which can be attained through noble deeds, is a common belief of the religious. By reminding him of his present and the future, Lord Sri Krishna exhorted Arjuna to get back to his dignified self instead of wading into cowardice. This message is not only for Arjuna but for all of us, for the whole world.

Is God for real?

I interjected between his breaths, You mentioned Sri Krishna as God? Why should it be so? Why believe in God? What is the proof of that? Do you yourself believe in God? Moreover, different religions have various Gods, why pick one out of them? And how can one believe in the idea of incarnation of God, which is a recurring theme in Gita?

Too many questions! We will be handling all that as we proceed, said he, and then dropped a bomb; No one can believe in God till they have known Him face to face and talked directly. Every believer is a fake.

I loved his statement 'Every believer is a fake', and since then I have used it on many occasions to demolish the unguarded.

To be sure what he was telling, I asked, What about you, Swamiji? Do you believe in God?

You won't believe whatever my answer would be. If I say yes, you will think me to be puff-head, and if I say no, you will think me to be humble. Your questions should always be based on what you already know, and what you need to know to increase that base. The rest is all hawa talk!

Was he being vindictive? I was not sure.

He continued, I believe in the words of masters. And why not! These masters were unselfish, learned, wise and established in the deepest of meditation. You can believe in the words of Marx, Freud, Einstein and Darwin, so why can't we believe in the words of the spiritual masters? And what are scriptures? These are the records of the words of the enlightened masters. So, there is nothing wrong in believing their words, and working to realize them in your own life. If you fail to get the expected results, you can then claim to have proved them wrong; till then you have no right to criticise them.

Importance of a mentor

कार्पण्यदोषोपहतस्वभावः पृच्छामि त्वां धर्मसम्मूढचेताः,
यच्छ्रेयः स्यात् निश्चितं ब्रूहि तन्मे शिष्यस्तेऽहं शाधि मां त्वां प्रपन्नम् |

Overpowered by confusion and emotions, I pray to you, as a disciple who has taken refuge in you, to tell me what to do. (II.7)

Do you know what our big problem in life is?

The number of times Swamiji asked this question during our talk made me wonder if we indeed have so many 'big problems'. If so, we must be creatures of marvel to stay afloat in this problem-ocean.

Everyone should have a mentor in life, he said. Mentor not in the sense that you people use help to achieve targets at work, but in the sense of a teacher and counsellor whom one trusts in all aspects of life, who deals with you, not just with your problems. It is natural for a person to feel squeezed and crunched in life, which can prove to be life-threatening, or at least life-altering. It is then that these mentors pull you out of the morass. You know, long ago, one of my elders had told me this, and I am glad that I always stuck to great counsel from able mentors in my life.

It is nice to know that you too have feet of clay, Swamiji!

He did not pay attention to my comment, and instead continued.

A devastated Arjuna wrecked by the havoc caused by his mental storm, extended his arms towards the Lord, as if entreating him to take him out of the emotional whirlpool. You will find this idea of surrender to the teacher repeated in every scripture. Even Gita talks about it multiple times. You may not need a mentor to make money, but a mentor is important if you want to keep your life running smoothly, and also to grow in spiritual life.

Swamiji went silent for a minute, probably revisiting some old pain of his. How I would have loved to know what he was thinking just then!

Breaking the silence, he asked me if I had ever been to a professional counsellor.

No, Swamiji. But I know some regulars.

Do you know why they fail to get much help from the counsellors? That is because the job of those holding your hand is to walk the last mile with the help-seekers, to make sure that they get out of the mess. That is rarely done by the counsellors.

You may not know, Swamiji, but counselling is one of the lucrative jobs today. I wanted to take out my anger on some of those I knew.

Of course, that must be. People do not like to invest in human relations anymore. You love to enjoy the best of the world by having nuclear families in a bubble society, without investing in relations. Who will help you when you stumble? Mark my words, emotional breakdowns are going to be a major disease in the near future. With no mooring, trusting no one, opening up to no one, people are going to be worse than fragile. Change yourself, bhai, before it is too late.

What to say!

How can you know if you are truly strong? asked Swamiji, and then he himself answered. Nothing can touch the strong, so they continue to smile even when there might be emotional shambles all around.

Crazy people, too, behave that way.

How true! The difference is that the crazy cannot inspire anyone, but the strong can do that by a mere look, touch or a word.

If you have to explain what God is to a child, how will you?

As you know, even kids understand what love is, so I will tell them that God is love. He stays in everyone's heart, and He makes people love each other. Where there is no love, know that there is no God. However, to a scientist I will say that God is knowledge. And both these explanations perfectly fit God!

Your smile reveals your strength

तमुवाच हृषीकेशः प्रहसन्निव भारत, सेनयोरुभयोर्मध्ये विषीदन्तमिदं वचः |

Sri Krishna then smilingly addressed a sorrowful Arjuna, standing in the midst of two armies. (II.10)

Sri Krishna, ah! The paragon of strength and confidence, born of knowledge. It is unfortunate that the great Lord's name is often only associated with love and Vrindavan, whereas he should always be remembered for his undiluted smile even amidst the worst crisis. It was with his smile that he won hearts, and also handled all the problems that came to greet him.

This is one thing every leader should adopt in life – smile in a crisis situation and resolve it in a snap. That can happen only if your strength is born of a complete knowledge of the situation. Most leaders are not like this, so they mask their weakness either with arrogance or with a fake smile that screams of incompetence. The magic touch of a leader lies in his being tranquil and compassionate. The screaming types can demand, but they cannot command. Authority may come to the unworthy, too, but moral authority comes only to a true leader.

Was I competent? I was a leader looking after the welfare of a large work force. I was caring and kind, but I am not sure if I had the qualities that Swamiji was enumerating.

Don't make an issue out of a non-issue

The teachings of Lord Krishna in Gita begin from this verse on. Our great teacher Shankaracharya began his commentary from this verse.

अशोच्यानन्वशोचस्त्वं प्रज्ञावादांश्च भाषसे, गतासूनगतासूंश्च नानुशोचन्ति पण्डिताः |

You mourn for them who should not be mourned for, and yet you speak words of wisdom. Know that the wise grieve neither for the living nor for the dead. (II.11)

Since you don't have complete knowledge of things, you often make an issue out of a non-issue. I am sure you must have read many stories where someone was screaming because something had not been done, only to be told that the work had been completed long ago. The foolish ones! Just look around, and you will find people everywhere swamped by this issue of the non-issue.

Swamiji then narrated an incident from the life of a great American instrumentalist, Albert Spalding, who once shouted at his agent in Europe – where he was performing – as to why there were no ads in papers that morning. After he had ranted enough, the agent smilingly told that it was because all the tickets for the show had sold out long ago! Spalding reminisced how stupid he felt at that!

Swamiji continued with his explanation. And why shouldn't you feel devastated if someone dear to you is about to die, or is gone forever? How is that not an issue? That is because we are not mere bodies but Atman, the conscious entity behind all existence.

न त्वेवाहं जातु नासं न त्वं नेमे जनाधिपाः, न चैव न भविष्यामः सर्वे वयमतः परम् |

Never was there a time when I did not exist, nor you, nor all these kings; nor in the future shall any of us cease to be. (II.12)

We identify ourselves with the body, but in reality, we are Atman. Pure consciousness – eternal, pure, conscious, free. As Atman we never cease to exist, but as bodies we keep changing.

You, just like everyone else, said Swamiji, may get startled at the abruptness of this teaching, but this is a common tradition in India – to begin a great work by narrating the ultimate truth. They do not always lead you gently from one step to another, rather they offer you the ultimate truth and if you continue to be interested, they lead you upward gently.

Swamiji, all that you are saying sounds good in words. But who cares if we are Atman or not? We are certain of this life now. Isn't it fair that we enjoy it to the full? Isn't it better to be the master of the well we know, rather than to hanker after the ocean we can't even imagine? You may not be aware, but most of us now believe in the truth that 'you live only once' – YOLO. So, enjoy as much as you can while you are alive, is the new belief current with people.

You don't live only once

I must say two important things here, he said. The first is that death does not end your existence, as we will see as we proceed. The second is that there is nothing wrong with enjoying the world. In fact, out of the four goals of life as classified in the Hindu religion, the first two are *artha* and *kama* – acquiring wealth and enjoying life. But for real enjoyment, you have to be a master and not a slave. And that is what Gita teaches, 'Be the master of the world'.

However, when you are scampering around due to your fears and worry that you may not be alive tomorrow, can you behave like the master of the universe? Can a person in hurry enjoy life, or even food? To enjoy means to feel every moment of the act. When you are in a hurry, how can you enjoy?

Our ancestors had realized the truth and practised the fact that 'You are eternal'. They were the masters of the universe since they were in no hurry and in no fear that it will all end with their death. Leave YOLO for the dim-witted, it takes you nowhere due to the fear of death stalking you. Your only temple then is the body, momentary pleasure is your worship, and infinite number of worries is the *prasad* that you get.

There was a pause, and then he asked me if I had ever read any book on the power of positive thinking and its ilk?

These books are for the mediocre, Swamiji. Those who can, they do, those who can't, they teach and the lowest of intellects keep learning all their life.

Swamiji laughed loudly at that, saying, Harshness does not behove you. Do you know how people feel pepped up after reading those books, and how some people get inspired to die and kill in anticipation of a quick entry to the heaven by reading their sacred books! So, just imagine the strength that will flow through you when you realize that death is a mere chimera, a change of state, a phase for you, since you are beyond birth and death! Can you imagine the flow of power that will then be for people across all spheres of society? Can you think of the immense dignity and flow of power that will come to mankind if they realize that they are one with God?

So, what is death? It is a mere gateway to a different state of being, just like childhood and youth are.

देहिनोऽस्मिन्यथा देहे कौमारं यौवनं जरा, तथा देहान्तरप्राप्तिर्धीरस्तत्र न मुह्यति |

The way one passes from childhood to youth to old age, just like that, one passes into another body at the time of death. So, the wise are not deluded by death. (II.13)

We will be returning to this fact again and again as we proceed. For the present, just know that rebirth and phases of life, including death, are not theories but facts of existence.

Real never perishes

But Swamiji, nearly the whole of the world has not heard of the idea that 'I am infinite', and rarely does anyone believe in it. Even the Buddhists, whose philosophy originated in our land, do not believe in this, and see how they are raking in popularity in the West? And have you noticed how the meditation techniques based on their philosophy of this and that, and popularized by different organizations, are becoming popular in India? Also, see the dancing and singing types, who have spread all over the world. Even they don't accept the idea of 'I am Brahman'. What would you say to that?

Bhai, why do you relate popularity with correctness? If popularity were to be the yardstick, then film stars would be the greatest scientists and saints!

I had not thought on those lines. My USP – speciality – was to make money, so my philosophical musings had been sketchy, based on what I had learnt in my childhood, and now from media posts and conversations at parties.

I told you earlier and will tell again, the fact that Atman is not a philosophical idea but a truth that can be realized by anyone if only they will go for it and practise the required *sadhana*.

How can Atman be the ultimate truth? The answer to it is quite simple: Vedanta, of which Gita is one of the texts, uses a very simple argument to demolish all opposing philosophies as explained in this verse.

He then read out from the stone carving in front of us.

'नासतो विद्यते भावो नाभावो विद्यते सतः, उभयोरपि दृष्टोऽन्तस्त्वनयोस्तत्त्वदर्शिभिः |

The unreal never comes into existence, and the real never ceases to be. The wise know this difference and behave accordingly. (II.16)

Philosophically, this is one of the most profound statements in Gita, and it acts like a *Brahmastra* that can burn down any mental agony that you might be having in your life. How? It says that if a thing is real, it will never become non-existent, and if it is not real then it never existed!

This is the simple truth of existence – the real never goes away, and the unreal never comes into existence. The body is unreal, since it goes away, but you are real, and so you will never go away. The idea of nirvana lies in this – the creation of body and mind will cease once you know what is real. And what would be that? YOU. Not the *shunya* of the Buddhists.

So, if you have a sense of losing something, know that it was not real. You should not feel upset at its loss since it was just a chimera. When I was a child I was once travelling by a bus during summer. I clearly saw water on the road ahead and eagerly waited to see it being splashed by the wheels of the bus. But that water never came, and instead, it always stayed away in the distance! I was disappointed. I still see 'water' on the road when I travel, but now it amuses me, instead of upsetting me. So, cry not over what never existed!

He then asked me if I was ever scared of ghosts as a kid. I humorously replied that I still get a creepy sensation when alone on a dark night.

Imagine, he said, the mere idea of a ghost terrifies you, which is not even a reality for you! Then what unfathomable strength can well up inside you when you realize that the 'Real never perishes, and you are that!'

Hmm. What else could I say to all these new thoughts raining upon me? The word 'raining' reminded me of the stones that I had been showering on the river two days ago, and how it had resulted in a different kind of rain! Life is so crazy!

Once you realize your true nature to be Atman, your idea of yourself and others will undergo a tectonic transformation, and you will then always remain full of joy, positivity and inclusiveness.

These ideas are repeated in the next verses, which I think do not require explanation.

अविनाशि तु तद्विद्धि येन सर्वमिदं ततम्, विनाशम् अव्ययस्यास्य न कश्चित् कर्तुमर्हति |
अन्तवन्त इमे देहा नित्यस्योक्ताः शरीरिणः, अनाशिनो अप्रमेयस्य तस्मात् युध्यस्व भारत
य एनं वेत्ति हन्तारं यश्चैनं मन्यते हतम्, उभौ तौ न विजानीतो नायं हन्ति न हन्यते |

Real is that by which everything in the universe is pervaded. No one has the power to destroy it – the Immutable.

Only the material body is perishable; the soul is ever indestructible, immeasurable, and eternal. So, get up and fight!

He who thinks the Self to be the slayer, or as slain, does not know the reality. Atman neither slays any, nor can it ever be slain. (II.17–19)

न जायते म्रियते वा कदाचित् नायं भूत्वा भविता वा न भूयः,
अजो नित्यः शाश्वतोऽयं पुराणो, न हन्यते हन्यमाने शरीरे |
वेदाविनाशिनं नित्यं य एनम् अजमव्ययम्, कथं स पुरुषः पार्थ कं घातयति हन्ति कम् |

The Self is neither born, nor does it ever die; nor having once existed, does it ever cease to be. It is without birth; eternal, immortal and ageless. It is not destroyed when the body is destroyed.

How can one who knows the Self to be imperishable, eternal, unborn and immutable kill anyone or cause anyone to kill? (II.20–21)

This idea of Atman being beyond all actions, what to say of slaying or getting slayed, comes repeatedly in the Upanishads and Gita, as also in the words of the spiritual masters.

Fine, Swamiji! But what about people like me who neither believe in these nor act accordingly?

The world is the great playground where we are enjoying our bit, he said. Once tired of the play, we would want to be what we are. Till then the play will go on. So, worry not! Enjoy if you feel like enjoying, but do not force yourself into enjoyment, nor into spirituality. That is why we, the Hindus, never proselytized, knowing well that the seekers will reach the teacher.

What is death like?

One interesting thing that I have observed these days, said Swamiji, is how Indians are sliding into desperation to have a long life. For thousands of years, we learned to laugh at death, but death is having the last laugh at India in the present times. It has succeeded in putting fear into the hearts of the descendants of the bravehearts who knew very well that childhood, adulthood, old age and death are all apparent changes playing on the changeless YOU.

The desire to hold onto life madly, known as *abhinivesha* in Sanskrit, is the characteristic of the lowly, not of the culturally elevated. You may feel sad that you lost a great companion in the departed, but you should really feel happy for the one who is gone, since they are moving on to their destiny. Why grieve for that which is natural?

वासांसि जीर्णानि यथा विहाय नवानि गृह्णाति नरोऽपराणि,
तथा शरीराणि विहाय जीर्णानि अन्यानि संयाति नवानि देही ||

The way one discards old clothes and puts on new ones, in the same way the jivatman discards the old body for the new. (II.22)

I wanted to know if a person could return from death, since Atman was real. I also knew of a story about Nachiketa, in which the young sagely boy had returned from death.

He said, Death means the disintegration of the molecules that made the body. So, it is not possible for a person to return from death, unless he did not die in the first place. Death also means that the Karma of *jiva* with that body is over, so the reversal is not possible. Bhai, life is a journey, which cannot be made by looking into the rear-view mirror. So, one should not pay much value to death, the return of a person, or even about contacting the dead. These are all signs of weakness.

नैनं छिन्दन्ति शस्त्राणि नैनं दहति पावकः, न चैनं क्लेदयन्ति आपो न शोषयति मारुतः |
अच्छेद्योऽयम् अदाह्योऽयम् अक्लेद्योऽशोष्य एव च,
नित्यः सर्वगतः स्थाणुरचलोऽयं सनातनः |

This Self cannot be cut, nor burnt, nor made wet, nor dried. It is unbreakable and incombustible, and it can neither be dampened nor dried. It is everlasting, in all places, unalterable, immutable and primordial. (II.23–24)

Accept death as a natural process of change of the body and focus on the reality behind life, which is far more important, he said. Atman being infinite and subtler than the subtle, nothing can act upon it – neither sword, bullet, water, fire – simply nothing, for how can the unreal act on the real?

The significance of a philosophy of life

Let me tell you the greatest problem of all those who feel low, depressed, hollow, sad, listless, etc., said the Swami. It is all because they do not have a philosophy of life, and instead stick to the philosophy of convenience, like 'Live one day at a time', 'The present is the only reality', 'Who has seen tomorrow?', 'Enjoy life before it is gone'. There is only one expression to explain the thoughts of such people – fools guiding the foolish. Do these people have a worldview? Do they have any philosophy of life? Aren't they trying to drag us back to the level of animals who live exactly by these principles of 'eat, mate, fight and flight?' Millions of years of evolutionary struggle are going to waste because of these whatevers!

You can change your life for the better and achieve stability in life simply by having a philosophy of life. So, the Lord laid before Arjuna the three philosophies of life.

अव्यक्तोऽयम् अचिन्त्योऽयम् अविकार्योऽयम् उच्यते,
तस्मादेवं विदित्वैनं नानुशोचितुम् अर्हसि |
अथ चैनं नित्यजातं नित्यं वा मन्यसे मृतम्, तथापि त्वं महाबाहो नैवं शोचितुमर्हसि |
जातस्य हि ध्रुवो मृत्युः ध्रुवं जन्म मृतस्य च, तस्मात् अपरिहार्येऽर्थे न त्वं शोचितुमर्हसि |
अव्यक्तादीनि भूतानि व्यक्त मध्यानि भारत, अव्यक्त निधनान्येव तत्र का परिदेवना |

Atman is not within the ken of the sense or the mind, nor is it knowable by any instrument since it is unchangeable. Know Atman to be thus and grieve not. (II.25)

If you believe yourself to be the self that goes through rebirths endlessly, even then you should not grieve since death and rebirth are inevitable. (II.26–27)

If you believe yourself to be a product of matter, then know that all beings are unborn before coming into existence, and vanish forever after death. So, why grieve for something that comes only in between for a while? (II.28)

There are only three possible realities about us, as beautifully explained in these verses.
1. You are the infinite Atman, which was, is, and will continue to be. The goal, in that case, is to know your true self and be free of all delusions that try to pass in the name of life. This being so, you should not grieve over death.
2. Some schools of Hindu philosophy believe that the soul goes to various spheres after death, enjoys, and after the exhaustion of the Karma, it returns to the earth. The cycle goes on eternally.

Sri Krishna tells Arjuna that if this is his outlook, he should not feel upset, since those who die will be born again. You may feel upset if the death was due to bad or violent acts that go against dignity, but death itself should not devastate you, and instead you should strive to have a fulfilling life of self-expression and dignity to improve your Karma. If you do not do that, you will then be back in a new body to face the garbage that you leave behind.

3. The popular belief is that we cease to exist after death, YOLO. In that case, existence is a chance combination of matter, as the materialists believe. If so, why should one crib for the few years that they are here in a body? Why should death trouble them? Or pain? Or excitement? If

it is all meaningless, purposeless, in that case why even bother to enjoy life?

Instead, as will be explained later, if you try to earn respect till you are conscious of your existence, you will have a dignified and peaceful life. How to do that will also be explained later.

The importance of having a clear outlook towards life is best illustrated by the story of the Brahmin Dandi Swami and Alexander the Great. When Alexander's general wanted to take Dandi forcibly to meet him, the Swami refused and said, 'Even if you take away my head to your king, who is not a son of God but a murderer, you cannot take away my soul, which will depart to my God and leave this body like we throw an old garment.' This is the kind of conviction you get once you are established in a philosophy of life.

Just to remind you, all these three outlooks are actually perceived by people with various levels of spiritual understanding and realization, of which those who believe that death is the end of everything rank the most primitive.

Whatever your outlook, you have to strive to be the best physically, socially, mentally, morally, spiritually. To do so is known as dharma. This is one important teaching of Gita, and of the Hindu dharma. Every Hindu scripture teaches the essence of dharma and how to be established in that. Period.

Although Gita tells us of these three outlooks towards life, it was meant to jolt Arjuna out of his stupor. The truth, according to sanatan dharma, is very simple – 'Atman alone exists, and you are that.' Gita merely explains it, narrates its implications, and shows the way to realize this truth. If you live by this truth, you will become the master of this world and if you realize it, you will be the master of all, forever.

I asked him the popular question, If rebirths are to fulfil our desires from previous lives, then why are animals, birds and snakes also believed to have rebirth?

Rebirth, according to scriptures, is caused by the acts we perform and the spiritual knowledge that we acquire. It means that lower organisms and animals are stuck in the rut of dying and being born again and again and yet again in the same species. Whenever God incarnates in some form, He gives an evolutionary push to the whole of creation. It is then that there is an evolution of consciousness for all. It is then that the lower ones advance a bit and are born in a new species. That is how creation continues indefinitely.

Is it a problem or a situation?

One important statement in these verses (II.27) is *tasmāt aparihārye arthe na tvaṃ śocitum arhasi* – lament not over the inevitable. A problem can be sorted out, while a situation has to be accepted. If your tap is leaking, you need to repair it, but if you have an incurable disease, it is a situation with which you have to live. Very often we confuse a situation with a problem, and so keep running here and there to find a solution. If I have to use glasses, it is a situation with which I must live. There is no reason for me to crib then.

Bhai, I have overcome many problems in my life by realizing their true nature as situations. This one half-verse can change your life forever.

We both were tired after such a heavy discussion and so we wanted to end it. It was also getting late for Swamiji, so we ended the discussion at that.

Swamiji concluded with, There are three distinct sections in this second lesson. The first section lays down the philosophy of life with a special focus on our real nature as Advaita. The second section talks about the way to attain this reality through physical and mental activity, whose sole aim is to make the mind pure. The third section is about how a sage who has known himself to be Atman, behaves. Can we discuss the other two sections tomorrow?

Of course, said I.

It was in the dead of night that I completed my note on our discussion, without understanding much of it. The sound of the flowing Narmada seemed to be egging me on, saying 'Hold on!'

II B

COMMITMENT TO WORK

When we met the next morning, Swamiji began with an outline of Karma yoga, which essentially means dignity in work, life and death.

Dignity in life, death and duty

I told you about the three possible outlooks towards life. None of these permit cowardice, or dereliction of duty. Dignity! Dignity! Dignity! If there is one word that I would like to teach people all over the world, it is 'Dignity'. Be dignified in your life, work, rest, recreation, enjoyment, duty, defeat and death. A soldier may have to kill his enemies, but there must be dignity in it. Undignified acts are the luxury of the barbarians – the human animals. The Aryan will always be dignified in acts and will respect others – even their enemies.

As a child, I was hugely inspired by the story of King Puru and Alexander. When the invader asked the defeated king how he expected to be treated, King Puru proudly replied, 'The way a king treats a king.' Just see how dignified the king was even in his defeat! This has been the Indian tradition and culture.

Whatever your act, even if that be begging, borrowing, asking for favour, demanding your rights, anything – you must remain dignified. And this is what Sri Krishna told Arjuna – 'Be dignified.'

स्वधर्মমपि चावेक्ष्य न विकम्पितुमर्हसि,
धर्म्याद्धि युद्धाच्छ्रेयोऽन्यत्क्षत्रियस्य न विद्यते |
यदृच्छया चोपपन्नं स्वर्गद्वारमपावृतम्, सुखिनः क्षत्रियाः पार्थ लभन्ते युद्धमीदृशम् |
अथ चेत्त्वमिमं धर्म्यं संग्रामं न करिष्यसि, ततः स्वधर्मं कीर्तिं च हित्वा पापमवाप्स्यसि |
अकीर्तिं चापि भूतानि कथयिष्यन्ति तेऽव्ययाम्,
सम्भावितस्य चाकीर्तिः मरणात् अतिरिच्यते |

Considering your duty as a warrior, you should not be shaken. Indeed, for a warrior there is no better engagement than fighting a righteous war. Lucky are those to whom such opportunity comes unsought, which is like the gateway to the heaven to a Kshatriya warrior.

If you run away from your duty of fighting, O Arjuna, then you will lose your dharma and also your honour, which is an abominable act to commit. People will forever speak ill of you. For a person of respect, infamy is worse than death. (II.31–34)

I commented, Even then, Swamiji, it is difficult to digest how it can be the right thing to kill one's own in whatever war and with whatever justification.

This is because you do not know the whole story of the Mahabharata. These people had fought earlier too, and it was a common practice for the warrior class to impress their superiority on all. It is something like a boxing championship or Sumo fighting, only that in a righteous war, it is a group fight with life at stake. So, do not blame Gita for this. Also, the whole point of this life lesson is that when it comes to the upholding of your dharma, nothing else takes precedence, be it family ties, friendships, or alliances. Why? Because these attachments are all transient, whereas dharma is eternal.

Coming back to our discussion, if you make a mistake in life, then own up to it, face the consequences and maintain your dignity all the while. People will forgive your mistakes, but they will never forget your brittleness in the face of a crisis. You will be the laughing-stock even after your death if you prove to be a shirker.

I interjected, What is this dharma that you are talking about? Isn't there enough killing going on in the name of religion?

Religion is not dharma, said Swamiji. Dharma is that which is your core nature, as burning power is of fire, and wetness is of water. The essential nature of human beings is divine, so our only dharma is to strive to be that. However, to be able to do so, the society entrusts certain responsibilities to various groups, as say, the military protects the borders and the police look after internal security. The duty of the Kshatriya class in earlier times was to protect the society from the evil forces, even if that demanded killing in a war. So, it was the duty of Arjuna to take part in the war, which had become inevitable.

A similar call of duty is demanded when a police officer has to arrest or shoot at their own son if he goes rogue. You might have watched some movies and read books that depict such conflict with elan.

Yes, I had. I also realized how I had clapped and shed tears while watching a father shoot at his son who had gone wrong. But, we being what we are, we support some acts and then criticize the very same at some other time.

Swamiji continued, You had talked about Gita being all about war, which it is not. The duty of a Kshatriya is to fight for the cause of dharma, so Sri Krishna told Arjuna:

भयाद्रणादुपरतं मंस्यन्ते त्वां महारथाः, येषां च त्वं बहुमतो भूत्वा यास्यसि लाघवम् |
अवाच्यवादांश्च बहून्वदिष्यन्ति तवाहिताः, निन्दन्तस्तव सामर्थ्यं ततो दुःखतरं नु किम् |
हतो वा प्राप्स्यसि स्वर्गं जित्वा वा भोक्ष्यसे महीम्,
तस्मादुत्तिष्ठ कौन्तेय युद्धाय कृतनिश्चयः |

The great warriors who hold you in high esteem will think that you fled from the battlefield out of fear, and thus you will lose their respect for you. Your enemies will defame and humiliate you with unkind words, disparaging your might. What could be more painful than that for you?

Performing your duty, you will go to heaven if you die, and if you gain victory, you will enjoy the kingdom on earth. Therefore arise, Arjuna, and do battle with determination. (II.35–37)

The beauty of the Lord's words lies in their simplicity and practicability. He cuts through all ifs and buts to say, 'Perform your duty or perish in infamy.' Period.

Stay balanced at all times

सुखदुःखे समे कृत्वा लाभालाभौ जयाजयौ, ततो युद्धाय युज्यस्व नैवं पापमवाप्स्यसि |

Take part in the war as matter of duty, treating happiness and distress, loss and gain, victory and defeat alike. This way you will never incur sin. (II.38)

This is how every duty should be performed – do not get emotionally attached to it. This is also the gist of Karma yoga which will be elaborated now, and also in the third chapter.

What does it mean to stay balanced? Imagine a gentleman going for a walk daily with his dog. The dog knows the path that the master takes, so he runs forward and looks back to see if his master is coming. At times, the master may change his path, which will make the dog crestfallen, retrace its path to catch up with the master, and as per his habit, he will start running forward again.

This is what happens in our life, too. Our expectations run ahead on the familiar path but we have to retrace our steps when ground reality proves to be different. Gita teaches you that the sense of failure and disappointment is born of expectation. Meaning, expectation ran ahead but had to come back to the reality of the world. So, instead of swaying with your success and failure, stay balanced. This demands strength, which is born of practice and discipline.

Commitment to work is Karma yoga

You must have heard of Karma yoga, said Swamiji. Many have even tried to paint Gita as a book of Karma yoga, which is simply unacceptable. What Gita says is that if you want to attain the highest in this world, or a better afterlife, or desire to go beyond the cycle of birth and death, you need to perform Karma yoga.

I am not an admirer of Karma yoga. I believe in working with passion.

That is the reason why Gita teaches and I am explaining that to you. Why learn a subject if you already know it!

That was a good one, I thought.

There is a difference between ordinary work (known as Karma), and working for a higher purpose, which is Karma yoga. We all work – breathing, eating, sleeping, praying, meditation, worship, thinking. All of these produce visible external results and internal mental impressions. These impressions – physical, verbal or mental – goad a person towards future action of 'avoid or seek'.

For example, if you put your finger in fire, the pain caused by it will make you stay careful in the future. Similarly, you will wish for experiences that you liked and loved to repeat. More actions will produce more impressions, and thus there will be a never-ending cycle of desires-acts-results-desires.

Karma yoga cuts through this vicious cycle by training a person not to hanker after the results. Whatever a Karma yogi does, he does with a complete sense of commitment towards the action without caring for its outcome, since they know that they did their best, and the result is not in their hands. Think of a sprinter in a competition. If they keep looking forward and backward as to how well they are performing, will their performance be appreciable? No, not at all.

Thus, Karma yoga teaches you to be committed to work, and not to the result. As for results, your own past acts, or someone else's acts may make others more successful, but the inner enrichment that you acquire cannot be taken away from you. It propounds unattached action, but certainly does not advocate purposeless action. All action is directed towards intended ends. The distinction is between intention (*sankalpa*) and desire (kama). Intention is born of dharma, while desire is rooted in *triguna* (more on this later). By all means, intend to achieve your business or professional goals, and then set about acting on them with all the might at your disposal, while remaining clear that the result is not yours to command. This, when practiced diligently, will leave you free from both dejection and elation.

As you continue practicing Karma yoga, favourable results will start coming your way, but probably you would have outgrown the need for that.

People today take MBA degrees from prestigious institutes of India and abroad. But I have rarely seen people with degrees to have commitment towards work; they are committed only to results! *Arre* bhai, stay committed to your work, and then results will come sooner or later. But no, they plant a sapling today and want the fruits tomorrow! The same is true of family, relations, friendship – everything. These young ones only want results without any commitment towards the acts.

He then raised his voice and said, The ordinary ones crave for results, while the great workers care only for the acts. Karma yoga is the key, bhai. Practise it and you will see how great you become in life.

Out of curiosity, I asked, is it possible for us to fully practise it?

Karma yoga in the sense that you should be completely detached with results can be practised only by the incarnations of God, or by the greatest of sages. Lord Buddha was a Karma yogi, so were Lord Jesus, Swami Vivekananda, and such greats. But we, the ordinary mortals, can only struggle, fail, get up and keep moving towards perfection. As you walk the talk, the progressive sense of freedom, joy and peace that begins to pervade your being, even in times of failure and setbacks, will amaze you, as will the growth in proficiency and productivity in your field of work. You will reach a point where you will surrender even the goal of achieving that perfection to the Divine, being content to enjoy the journey.

My head was reeling. I was into business and action, but I had never thought that the wheels within wheels ran so deep!

One great advantage of Karma yoga, he said, is that even if you practise very little of it, or intermittently, the change in your outlook accumulates, like a bank balance, in your character, till it starts showing with time. It also takes you out of the mess of the world, whose only characteristics are fear, misery and expectations. Death won't kill you, but these will.

नेहाभिक्रमनाशोऽस्ति प्रत्यवायो न विद्यते, स्वल्पमप्यस्य धर्मस्य त्रायते महतो भयात्

For a Karma yogi, there is no loss or adverse result in case he fails, and even a little effort made to perform Karma yoga saves one from great danger. (II.40)

We usually associate religious duties with virtue and sin, meaning that if you do not perform your religious acts, you will accrue sin. There is no such thing in Karma yoga – what you have remains, even if you do not add to it. Simple.

He then read out from the slab the most famous saying on Karma yoga from Gita.

Work effortlessly with no baggage

कर्मण्येवाधिकारस्ते मा फलेषु कदाचन, मा कर्मफलहेतुर्भूर्मा ते सङ्गोऽस्त्वकर्मणि ॥

You have the freedom to act, but you do not have the authority over the results of your acts. Also, never be bonded to outcomes [which creates new impulses to act], nor be ever lazy. (II.47)

The message from the verse is:
a. Never be idle. Not even for a moment;
b. Work as if your whole life depends on it. Finish your job at hand in the best possible way. May you proudly claim that others can be your equal in doing that, but no one can be better;
c. The result of what you do depends on many extraneous factors on which you have no control. For example, a farmer's healthy crop may get ruined because of bad

weather. So, do not let your mind race ahead towards results. Accept with dignity what comes to you;

d. If you wish to be spiritual, which very few do, then do not keep creating new entanglements for yourself. Remember that our bad habits do not drown us, but entanglement does.

He then smiled and asked if he had been clear.

Loud and clear, I replied. Only that I am not in a position to accept what you say.

This is the age-old problem of prejudiced thinking. People do not like to adopt new ideas. That is why most of our learning terminates by the time we exit teenhood.

He continued: The word 'unselfish' is a technical term, meaning 'not obsessed with the results'. There are many ways to stay detached from the results of your acts. For instance, you can use your willpower, treat your work as an offering to God, or perform your acts as sacred yajna. Just choose what suits your mentality and become a yogi. The next lessons will show some of these methods.

To keep it clear in your mind, always remember how a mother cares for her newborn without expecting anything from her. Ultimately, Karma yoga is when the act itself is the result!

Perfection in work is yoga

बुद्धियुक्तो जहातीह उभे सुकृतदुष्कृते, तस्माद्योगाय युज्यस्व योगः कर्मसु कौशलम् ||

A karma yogi can get rid of both good and bad in this life itself. Therefore, strive for Yoga, which is the art of doing work perfectly. (II.50)

The beauty of Karma yoga! You don't have to die and go to heaven to reap the fruits of Karma yoga. The results will be here itself in the form of mental tranquillity, which is an essential condition for the practice of meditation, the last step to spiritual attainments. Elsewhere, Gita says, *samatvam yoga ucyate* – yoga means to stay balanced all the time.

So, learn the art of yoga, bhai. Be a yogi. Be established in the art of work by staying detached from the results, knowing that it is not in your hands. Be not obsessed with it. This will make you great.

Karma yoga is about doing, and not about wishing. So, yoke yourself to this great yoga, and become blessed here and now.

II C

WAY OF THE PERFECT

The discussion on Karma yoga had been heavy for me and my way of life, so I decided to take a break and sit down for a while. I was also not used to so much of walking, that too up and down as we were on the parikrama path. Once we resumed walking, Swamiji started explaining the last part of the second chapter that deals with the way of the perfect.

Swamiji began with, I love your expression 'hawa gyan', which Gita would appear to be if it did not give practical ways to attain perfection and the way of those who have attained that state. Discussing the qualities of the greats is not meant to be a paean of their glory, but because those who wish to attain perfection need to emulate those qualities. I read somewhere, to be an astronaut, you have to think and behave like an astronaut. Just like that, to be a great person, you have to think and behave like the greats.

Who is perfect?

Arjuna wished to know how a person, established in perfection, behaves.

स्थितप्रज्ञस्य का भाषा समाधिस्थस्य केशव,
स्थितधीः किं प्रभाषेत किमासीत व्रजेत किम् |

How does one sthitaprajna – *who knows Atman – behave? How do they talk, sit and walk? (II.54)*

The interesting thing about this question is that Sri Krishna himself was such a *jnani*. If you read some of the original works like Mahabharata or Bhagavatam, you will realize that whatever the Lord said in the next verses by way of qualities, he himself had all of those. Such a person is known as sthitaprajna, one whose intellect has become steady and fixed.

To the question, the Lord replied:

प्रजहाति यदा कामान्सर्वान्पार्थ मनोगतान्, आत्मन्येवात्मना तुष्टः स्थितप्रज्ञस्तदोच्यते |

A person who completely casts away all the desires and stays satisfied in his own Self by the Self, are said to be sthitaprajna, men of steady wisdom (II.55)

The desires that roam free in our minds are the forces that make us sway like a reed in a tempest. There is simply no way that a person full of desires can ever attain tranquillity of the mind, and consequently a steady wisdom.

Those who clean their minds through Karma yoga and then through meditation realize that they are neither the body nor the mind, but Atman; their desires get completely wiped out, since they are fulfilled in every sense. Only such people are perfect, and worthy of real respect.

I asked if Swamiji knew of some such person.

Bhai, knowledge of anything is subjective, so there is no way to know if a person has reached that state. That is one of the reasons why we have so many Gurus claiming to be *atmajnani*. As for your direct question, yes, I have seen some monks who had the qualities of sthitaprajna as described below.

दुःखेष्वनुद्विग्नमनाः सुखेषु विगतस्पृहः, वीतरागभयक्रोधः स्थितधीर्मुनिरुच्यते |
यः सर्वत्रानभिस्नेहस्तत्तत्प्राप्य शुभाशुभम्, नाभिनन्दति न द्वेष्टि तस्य प्रज्ञा प्रतिष्ठिता |

One who remains undisturbed amidst misery, who does not crave for the favourable, and who is free from attachment, fear and anger, is spiritually illumined.

One who remains unperturbed under all conditions; who is neither delighted at getting the favourable nor feels dejected at the unfavourable, is man of spiritual wisdom. (II.56–57)

As you can guess rightly, these qualities come naturally to the spiritual greats, but need to be cultivated by those aspiring for inner growth. Think of Don Bradman, the legendary cricketer, to whom the game came naturally. Compared to him, a budding cricketer has to do sadhana to achieve a semblance of success. This is true of all fields of activities like writing, acting or anything else.

The bottom line is, have an ideal; follow in their footsteps to attain success. There is no other way. Do not try to carve out your own path like geniuses who are born to show the path to the world. They are the mould in which we have to cast ourselves, and not everyone can be a mould. Period.

I loved the way Swamiji emphasized on 'Period' after saying something strong.

Even then, Swamiji, is it possible for anyone to go beyond the emotions like anger? In my young days, I used to read *Amar Chitra Katha*, in which there were many stories of sages who got angry and cursed others. What would you say to that?

Have you heard of the 'dry bite' of a snake? In such cases, a snake bites but does not inject venom. If a sage is truly established in the knowledge of Atman, he may get angry at something but that will be only for show – a dry bite. Their emotions are like a burnt rope that holds shape but cannot bind.

Oh! My mind was getting dusty with the debris from a lifetime of preconceived notions crashing to ruins.

He continued. An implication of *tat tat prapya shubhashubham* as narrated here is to treat situations as they come, and never to carry your past baggage in your conversation and action in the present. It is in our temperament to bring up the past or keep the past in consideration while handling the present. Naturally so. But if you wish to be great, you should treat every situation without any past prejudice. Be cheated a hundred times, let people laugh at you, let them call you naive, but you stick to your value of staying free of prejudice. Let your past inform you, but don't let it imprison you.

It is difficult, said I.

I have known people in administration who treated their subordinates without any past baggage of acts. So please do not say that this cannot be done. The difficulty is directly proportional to your attachment to your own judgment, and is inversely proportional to your commitment to fulfilling your dharma.

Freedom from senses versus freedom of senses

यदा संहरते चायं कूर्मोऽङ्गानीव सर्वशः, इन्द्रियाणीन्द्रियार्थेभ्यस्तस्य प्रज्ञा प्रतिष्ठिता |
विषया विनिवर्तन्ते निराहारस्य देहिनः, रसवर्जं रसोऽप्यस्य परं दृष्ट्वा निवर्तते |

One who can withdraw the senses from their objects just as a tortoise withdraws its limbs into its shell, is established in wisdom.

Others may succeed in restraining the senses from latching on to the objects, but the taste for the sense objects remains. However, this lurking taste too ceases for those who are spiritually enlightened. (II.58–59)

Do you know what your problem is?

Oh no! Not again. I asked, Do you really think that we have so many problems?

Of course you do. Unless you know who you truly are, you will always have problems, and some of those will get prominence according to the situation. And forget about setting out for perfection, you don't even know what that state is like, he said.

The highest state is when you become free from the snare of your senses. What is this modern generation trying to attain with ideas of YOLO and all? They want freedom of the senses, while India has always stood for 'freedom from the senses'.

This difference, although it looks innocuous, is profound; it makes one worldly and another godly. But who is going to listen to us? People who go to God or Gurus to find ways to make more money, can you really expect them to care for these niceties?

He continued with fervour, This drawing away from the senses must not be forced, as happens with a diseased person. Rather it is the evolved state where you outgrow the joy of the limited because you have experienced joy of the higher. The kind of books, toys, games, comics, shows and music that you liked in your young age, you do not enjoy anymore, except for the occasional nostalgic visit down memory lane. Your progress towards higher ideals is exactly like that – you outgrow and become immune to the attraction of the sense pleasures.

The peril of indulging the senses

यततो ह्यपि कौन्तेय पुरुषस्य विपश्चितः, इन्द्रियाणि प्रमाथीनि हरन्ति प्रसभं मनः |
तानि सर्वाणि संयम्य युक्त आसीत मत्परः,
वशे हि यस्येन्द्रियाणि तस्य प्रज्ञा प्रतिष्ठिता |

The senses, if given licence, violently hijack the mind of even a wise person striving after perfection. So, a sthitaprajna, having controlled the senses stays absorbed in the Transcendent. In a word, a sthitaprajna has their senses under complete control. (II. 60–61)

One of my favourite stories from the Indian traditions is that of sage Vishwamitra, who, in spite of all his great sadhana, often landed into this or that abyss of emotional disaster. And why? That was simply because his senses were not under the wraps as one would expect from a sage.

The good Lord cautions that even if you think that you have controlled your senses, be wary of being near objects of temptation, for they will drag you away from yourself and make a slave of you. Have you seen how people who vow never to fall in love ever again after a loss, fall into the pit soon enough?

Oh yes, Swamiji. In fact, I always encourage people to stay in company after a loss.

That is worldly wisdom, but it also shows how the malady of seeking company continues even after any number of hits.

Saying this, we moved onto the next slabs, where Swamiji's face beamed with joy.

Genesis of anger and the ruin caused by it

My favourite verses from Gita are on anger, and they also sum up the human psychology that Freud and Adler have talked about.

Excuse my saying this, but have you read them? My surprise was palpable.

Not extensively, since their views can be summed up in these two verses of Gita.

ध्यायतो विषयान्पुंसः सङ्गस्तेषूपजायते सङ्गात्सञ्जायते कामः कामात्क्रोधोऽभिजायते |
क्रोधाद्भवति सम्मोहः सम्मोहात्स्मृतिविभ्रमः स्मृतिभ्रंशाद् बुद्धिनाशो बुद्धिनाशात्प्रणश्यति

Thinking repeatedly of something, one develops attachment for them. Attachment leads to obsession, and from that arises anger, which leads to the clouding of judgement. This results in loss of propriety, and that is when the buddhi gets destroyed, resulting in one's ruin. (II.62–63)

Very often, we start liking something and then keep thinking about it for long. This creates a powerful mental association with the object or person, which results in a desire to possess it, even though in most cases that might be harmful and even dangerous. When we face obstruction in acquiring what we want, we get frustrated. This is the genesis of anger.

You know, most storms are preceded by a gentle wind. Likewise, every act of anger begins with a soft desire to have someone or something, which might be as innocent as your 'self-respect', 'self-esteem', etc.

While saying this, Swamiji clearly gave me the mischievous smile of the innocent, as if hinting at something for me to note.

And, what about the progeny of anger? Well, anger clouds your power of judgement. You cannot then tell right from wrong, and thus you tend to get abusive, short-tempered, unaccommodating, intimidating, insulting even towards those who need to be respected or cared for. That is when your downward journey towards ruin begins.

You lose self-control, develop psychosomatic problems, need counsellors and medications, and possibly you don't recover even then, since the root cause of the trouble continues untreated.

Once your buddhi is compromised – which means that you've let go of all that you learnt from your elders, teachers, society and books about the rightness of action – you are ruined, scattered to the winds. This is what has been happening to the collective wisdom of this nation for many centuries. Believe me.

Quite disturbing, I thought. I said so.

The way to peace

रागद्वेष वियुक्तैस्तु विषयानिन्द्रियैश्चरन्, आत्मवश्यैर्विधेयात्मा प्रसादमधिगच्छति ।
प्रसादे सर्वदुःखानां हानिरस्योपजायते, प्रसन्नचेतसो ह्याशु बुद्धिः पर्यवतिष्ठते ।

The self-controlled persons, moving among objects with senses under restraint, and free from attraction and aversion, attains tranquillity that destroys all sorrow. (II.64–65)

नास्ति बुद्धिरयुक्तस्य न चायुक्तस्य भावना, न चाभावयतः शान्तिरशान्तस्य कुतः सुखम् ।
इन्द्रियाणां हि चरतां यन्मनोऽनुविधीयते, तदस्य हरति प्रज्ञां वायुर्नावमिवाम्भसि ।

An undisciplined person neither has buddhi nor focus. One who is not focused on higher values – there can be no peace for him; and how can one be happy without peace? Just as a strong wind sweeps a boat off its course on the water, even one of the senses on which the mind dwells, can lead one's intellect astray. (II.66–67)

If you keep grazing across the quicksand of sense pleasures, you are bound to sink to your doom. It is like a boat getting caught in a storm. Stay away, man, stay away from sense pleasures. Leave that for the untrained and uncultured. Be wise and stay away from the tempting minefield of sense pleasures. There simply is no other way to peace and happiness.

To stay away from sense objects, it is imperative for you to be rooted in some higher values of life. Be creative, learn to serve, dedicate yourself to learning, or give yourself to God fully – do any of these and you will have the right mooring to weather the storm. Of these, spirituality is the best mooring.

Don't waste your life running after money, relationship, fame or pleasure. Have some values to live by. Don't let your precious life go to waste.

Awake in wisdom

Was I relieved that the lesson was coming to a close? Indeed, yes.

Swamiji continued, One problem with us is that we don't like to struggle towards the higher. How can you know if you are avoiding a struggle? For that, simply remember that a person needs a hundred reasons not to do a thing, but only one reason to do it. Analyse yourself, and you will be surprised to see how you rationalize not doing something with fabulous reasons.

I laughed loudly, remembering how I, like others, had come up with wonderful excuses for not going to school in my young days.

An ideal in life saves you from a lot of garbage, bhai. Take up an ideal, live up to that, and you will be surprised to see how smoothness slides into your life.

या निशा सर्वभूतानां तस्यां जागर्ति संयमी, यस्यां जाग्रति भूतानि सा निशा पश्यतो मुनेः |

That which is night to all beings, in that the perfect beings stay awake, and that in which all beings are awake, that is night to them. (II.69)

A common person finds peace and solace in worldly objects, which are like day to them, while spiritual reality is like night to them. For the sthitaprajna, it is just the opposite! They stay ever-asleep to enjoyment and ever-awake in God-consciousness. You must have noted how people who succeed in life do the same – they are always awake in their area of activity and ever-asleep in everything else.

And fulfilment!

Swamiji concluded with:

आपूर्यमाणमचलप्रतिष्ठं समुद्रमापः प्रविशन्ति यद्वत्,
तद्वत्कामा यं प्रविशन्ति सर्वे स शान्तिमाप्नोति न कामकामी |
विहाय कामान्यः सर्वान्पुमांश्चरति निःस्पृहः,
निर्ममो निरहङ्कारः स शान्तिमधिगच्छति ||

Just as an ocean remains undisturbed by the flow of waters from rivers merging into it, likewise the blessed ones remain unmoved amidst the world of objects. It is they who attain peace, and not those who run after desires.

They alone are at peace who are free like a bird, giving up all desires, and without the sense of 'I' and 'mine'. (II.70–71)

Yes bhai, this state of God-consciousness, born of realization of oneself as consciousness, is the ultimate state, which cannot be disturbed by any force of nature. Be great, be whole, be complete – be so full from within that neither love nor hatred can unsettle you. That's it.

It was night when I completed my notes on that day's discussion. It was all so new to me – unexpected, unsettling, unpleasant. But as Swamiji said, one can learn only what one does not know yet. I think I need to hear more from him.

III

KARMA YOGA

We had been together for barely a few days and yet I felt as if I had known him for ages. Every morning when I saw him waiting for me, I felt joy bubbling within me – much more than when I had made my first billion, and even more than when I got married. Probably because these were expected events, and a result of my way of life, so my happiness had been measured.

Over the years, the problem of plenty had wormed inside me and had made me want unselfish joy, which was like looking for pulse in a dead person. It is easy to say that I will give away my wealth in exchange for happiness, but those who have lived in poverty, illness and insecurity, know what it means to feel the fire of hunger in their belly. Even though wealth often comes at the high cost of inner joy, for us, it is worth the price.

Personally, I don't believe that Gita is meant for a hungry belly, unless that hunger is for a higher purpose, as with the sannyasins of older times. Gita – taught by the king-maker Sri Krishna to the would-be king Arjuna – who will believe that it can be understood by the weak or hungry? No, it is meant only for the brave, aspiring for fulfilment in life. The weak and needy can only recite by rote in anticipation of whatever, which is never going to come.

Swamiji never seemed excited to see me, which was quite disappointing for me. But why should he feel excited? After all, he had many students, while I had only one teacher.

On my way back the previous day, I had stopped at one of the religious bookstores and purchased a fat copy of Gita, then tried understanding it over the night. Was Swamiji really speaking from the same book? Nothing seemed familiar except for the verses.

When I mentioned that to him, he said, Every great work is explained by many, and every generation must have its own interpretation.

I suggested that he write an explanatory work on it. He said, Gita is essentially a spiritual work, so I will always go by what Acharya Shankara has to say about the verses. As for the common man, there are many who are doing that; while for me, I have to stick to what I stand for – spirituality. Conversation is alright, but coming up with an explanatory work is a strict no-no for me.

Perform action as yajna

After we had reached some distance, Swamiji started talking about the third chapter of Gita.

In the second chapter, Lord Krishna talks about Karma yoga but does not elaborate. Instead, he explains the qualities of a jnani. This creates confusion in the mind of Arjuna who asks, 'Since knowledge is superior to action, why do you then engage me in this terrible war?'

Not Karma yoga again, Swamiji!

He smiled broadly and said, Have you ever noted how the masters teach people what they lack so that they can improve their lot? That is why Jesus taught love to a bloodstained society, and Prophet Muhammad taught brotherhood to the divided Arab people. Interestingly, the words of these masters are for the future, too, since the fault lies in the societal gene.

That was funny, Swamiji! You mean to say that we Indians lack the initiative to work properly and hence receive repeated teaching of Karma yoga?

That is correct, he said. As we discussed earlier, India has this tendency to get into a wormhole of inactivity, claiming that to be a higher spiritual state. But that is only *tamas* – inertness. That is why action is required, and that is why work has been prescribed as the first step to realization.

As you can see, Arjuna wanted to enter the state of tamas, posing that to be *sattva* – the high state of the mind. But Sri Krishna, being his teacher, stopped him from doing so.

In response to his question, Bhagavan then expounds the rationale, philosophy, psychology, utility, and the obstacles in the path of Karma yoga. He says that the Knowledge of the Self dawns upon those who have attained a higher state of understanding by purifying their mind through Karma yoga, which essentially means getting rid of inertness and selfishness.

Swamiji then read out from the next stone plaque on the parikrama path.

न हि कश्चित्क्षणमपि जातु तिष्ठत्यकर्मकृत्, कार्यते ह्यवशः कर्म सर्वः प्रकृतिजैर्गुणैः |

No one can remain without action even for a moment. Indeed, all beings are compelled to act by their nature. (III.5)

There is simply no way to stop your body and mind working continuously, he said. Even during sleep, you stay active. So, why not convert your natural strength into your visible strength?

His choice of words!

Do you know why Gita focuses so much on action?

I had no idea.

It is because there have been two philosophical streams in India, in which the major space has been gobbled up by pseudo Vedantis who focus on self-realization by giving up all action. But that is extremely dangerous for those who are not yet ready for spirituality. In fact, that is the reason why Indians became prone to thrashings by any invader who wished to do so.

Swamiji, that way, India is waking up now. Do you think that the present generation is superior to their parents?

Of course, he said. At least the new generation has woken up the country from *ghor tamas* – intense sloth. This is why we need Gita today much more than ever, since it will teach our new generation how and when to accelerate, brake and steer the great vehicle of the nation, which otherwise was immobilized with a breakdown that lasted centuries.

That sounds quite positive!

I am neither positive nor negative, I am only a realist rooted in idealism.

He continued, In this chapter, Gita teaches how to outgrow selfishness by spiritualizing our acts. It then explains who can give up work altogether, but that is not our topic of discussion.

To harmonize work and spirituality, Gita guides us to perform every act as sacred yajna, like the worship of the divine. You don't need *vigraha* (idols) and priests to be performing these yajna – you would be the priest and the *yajaman,* your acts will be the oblation, and your endeavours will be the sacred fire in which you will make the offering. The reason for it is explained as follows.

यज्ञार्थात् कर्मणोऽन्यत्र लोकोऽयं कर्मबन्धनः, तदर्थं कर्म कौन्तेय मुक्तसङ्गः समाचर |

Work must be done as a yajna, otherwise it creates bondage. So, perform your acts without being attached to the results. (III.9)

The spiritual consciousness of India comes from the four Vedas, from which the Brahmins worked out ways to perform yajna, in which the priest, fire, oblations and gods played major roles, among others. The goal has been to get favours from the gods in the form of material gain, pleasures or a great life in heaven. But all this belongs to Mother Nature, so you continue to be in bondage even after performing rituals, worship, yajna, sacrifice, etc. However, all such acts, if done with the idea to purify one's mind from the obsession of lust and wealth, lead a person towards spiritual freedom.

Gita takes it one giant step forward and says that all your acts – cooking, washing, brushing your teeth – anything, should be done as a yajna. In fact, in Japan, making of tea is a great ritual.

Oh yes, I had seen that during my visit there. I told him this.

Your everyday acts, job, pleasure-seeking, relaxation – everything should be a yajna, an offering to the Lord. Do this and you will become a powerhouse. The reason? A detached mind is a powerful mind. You hit best when the swing is free of any restraint; you work best when there is no expectation! This happens because those are the moments when your mind becomes powerful due to freedom from attachment.

Wonderful! I exclaimed.

The ideas like 'work with passion', 'do what your heart says', 'work till you drop dead' – all these are for philosophically challenged persons, said Swamiji. Those who want to make their life integrated have to treat work as yajna. There is simply no alternative to that.

Strive for mutual interest

देवान्भावयतानेन ते देवा भावयन्तु वः, परस्परं भावयन्तः श्रेयः परमवाप्स्यथ |

By your sacrifices, the gods will be pleased, and by cooperation between humans and the gods, great prosperity will ensue. (III.11)

The offering in a yajna was made in anticipation of favour from the gods. Sacrifice, in some form or other, has been a set belief in every religion.

But the important idea to note here is that of 'cooperation.' A company can truly grow well if the bosses and employees strive to satisfy each other. Same with a nation. For a country or a society to be great, the mutual interests of the leaders and the followers must be considered at all times.

Bhai, you only have to look at the list of companies that failed because one of the parties became too demanding, and thus failed to honour the interests of the other. Do you know why Hindu society is under threat today? It is because the people of the upper caste did not look after the welfare and equality of those whom they considered lower in social hierarchy.

Well ... My brain cells were all fired up. I had to make immediate changes in a lot of things in my company and family. I was probably failing everybody. How I had missed this wonderful idea in life, I wondered. No more mistakes, I muttered under my breath.

I then asked, Swamiji, how do you come up with such unheard-of interpretations? Is it because of your meditation?

Meditation is not applied to trifles, bhai. It has only one purpose – to fix the mind on God. There might be some by-products, but that is inconsequential. Incidentally, I had heard this interpretation from a senior monk when I was a novice. That is when I had realized how intertwined Gita is with daily life.

Be a role model

He continued. Do you realize how we all act as role models for at least some people at some point of time in our life?

Parents for their kids, teachers for their pupils, bright students for their peers, leaders for their followers, and likewise. There are also national models and historically great ones whom we like to emulate.

It is a wonder that we do not develop a split personality disorder!

He ignored my comment and said:

यद्यदाचरति श्रेष्ठस्तत्तदेवेतरो जन:, स यत्प्रमाणं कुरुते लोकस्तदनुवर्तते |

Actions performed by the respected are copied by the common folks, and the standard set by them becomes the measure for all. (III.21)

The founders of a religion may have spoken the highest spiritual truths, but the practitioners always try to shape themselves in the mould of the life of those greats. You might have heard of the book, *Imitation of Christ*. The very idea of imitation in it shows how important the role of the noble is for the society. If you rise higher up in the society, people will emulate you, so be careful. Even if you do not rise up, there will always be some who will be copying you simply because they love you.

Do you know that the Hindu religion does not run on any texts? Mahabharata, the great anthology of dharma, says, 'The way is that which has been taken by the greats', meaning that dharma is defined by how the great ones lived their life.

Know this, and then get set to be a role model for society. Make money, acquire fame – do whatever you like – just remember to be an ideal role model, since people will walk in your wake, even if you do not want it, as your success grows.

I started breathing heavily. It was probably the climb up the parikrama.

Don't be preachy

न बुद्धिभेदं जनयेदज्ञानां कर्मसङ्गिनाम्, जोषयेत्सर्वकर्माणि विद्वान्युक्तः समाचरन् |

Do not unsettle the faith of others. Be with them, behave as they do, and then lead them gently upward. (III.26)

Knowledge is a wonderful thing because you then want to convert others to what you know. Watch a child talk about what they have just learnt. Parents go crazy listening to them. There are also people who believe that their religion is the only correct one, making them chop off heads instead of engaging in a meaningful dialogue, since they believe that they alone are knowers of truth, without realizing that if God has chosen someone to stay ignorant, they can safely be left alone. Holy war, crusades, jihad – even God may not know what horrible things people do in His name. All this simply because some nitwits think that what they know is the only correct thing.

If you really want good of others, then follow what the verse says, and behave the way grandparents behave with their grandchildren – lead them softly towards the right way of things. Abruptness only destroys.

Change is a slow process

सदृशं चेष्टते स्वस्याः प्रकृतेर्ज्ञानवानपि, प्रकृतिं यान्ति भूतानि निग्रहः किं करिष्यति |

People act according to their nature; restraint does not work in controlling what one is born with. (III.33)

Our immediate past actions determine our birth, and also our future actions. Being the immediate cause, the tendencies with which we are born are extremely powerful, and so, it is nearly impossible to overcome them. Our nature is not merely the template, as it is usually assumed to be. We are what our nature is – we are made of it. A snake, tiger, scorpion, cow, mosquito – name any creature or object – none can forget its nature. Because of their evolutionary success, human beings have all these traits in varying proportions, and so we, too, cannot escape our nature.

To change, one has to work on it continuously for a long time. It is a long-drawn process, and may even require many births. That is why it is not easy to be religious or spiritual.

This also means that you should not waste your breath correcting someone. God has not made them that way, rather it is they who chose over innumerable births to be like that, and hence it is not easy for them to change.

Once again, abruptness does not work.

Yes, Swamiji. In an interesting story from the Mahabharata, when the Pandavas were walking barefoot in the Himalayas for their ultimate journey, *mahaprayan,* the brothers started dropping dead one by one. When asked, Yudhisthir spoke out the innate character faults of each of the brothers, and also Draupadi. But he had stayed silent about these all his life, knowing well that if he told them about their faults, they would never be able to overcome them, and instead would hate him for pointing out the truth.

A team comprises members with inherent faults. Never point those out.

I needed to reorient myself, I thought with worry. We had been trained to do exactly the opposite during our management training.

It does not mean that we do not have a choice in life, added the Swami. The choice is all ours – we chose to be in this plight for births. In the same way, we can choose to be whatever we want for future.

I naturally objected. What rot, Swamiji! Why would someone choose to be poor, sick, handicapped, etc? At times, Hindu dharma truly appears to be hocus-pocus.

Haven't you ever enjoyed watching tragic or horror movies? What about war movies – don't you like them? And remember that you willingly paid to be scared or to shed tears! Life is quite similar – choice plus its effects makes us what we are. No one else is to blame for your plight – not even God.

That's disturbing, I thought.

The robbers in life

Life would have been so smooth if lust and anger were not there to torment us, said Swamiji. As we learned in the second chapter of Gita, and will find again, desires are the root cause of all our trouble.

इन्द्रियस्येन्द्रियस्यार्थे रागद्वेषौ व्यवस्थितौ, तयोर्न वशमागच्छेत्तौ ह्यस्य परिपन्थिनौ |
काम एष क्रोध एष रजोगुणसमुद्भवः, महाशनो महापाप्मा विद्ध्येनमिह वैरिणम् |

The senses and their objects have a natural bond, so be careful and do not come under their influence, for they are like robbers in life and great enemies. (III.34)

Desires and anger are the reason for all sins. These are the all-devouring enemy in the world. (III.37)

Desires are natural since these are born due to the contact of the senses with their respective objects. Also, we grow through our desires in the world, and become spiritual when we outgrow them. But they are also like an inner conflagration that can devour all if not kept under control. They need to be tended like fire. If you are careful about it, you can attain heights, but if you let them become wild, you can't imagine what consequences may befall you. Gita compares lust and anger with highway robbers ready to attack if you are not well-protected.

Do you know about the thugs who were eliminated by Lord William Bentinck?

I had heard of them, but not in detail.

These thugs – at least that is what the British say about them – used to loot and kill travelers by first becoming friendly with them. There are quite interesting narrations and books about them. The senses are like those thugs – they become friendly and then they finish you off.

The books that he had read!

I asked him if he believed in the ideas of sin, the original sin and other such medieval ideas.

Sin, as it is conceived of in Abrahamic religions, is an alien idea for us, he said. For them, sin is related to violating the command of God, implying that we are separate from God. But for us, God is our true nature, and so we can never go against Him or His command. For us, sin implies a kind of detour on our way to self-realization. The more you take the detour, the possibility of your suffering increases that much. The choice to leave your goal is yours and only yours. However, sooner or later you will surely be back on the path. So, there is no eternal damnation in the Hindu religion.

By your very nature you are pure and immortal, so how can you ever be doomed, let alone be damned!

No track changes, please

So bhai, the gist of Karma yoga is to be natural about your dharma, duty and way of life. Do not run after something simply because you find it appealing.

श्रेयान्स्वधर्मो विगुणः परधर्मात्स्वनुष्ठितात्, स्वधर्मे निधनं श्रेयः परधर्मो भयावहः |

Perform your own duties, even if they appear to be lacking merit. It is preferable to die discharging your own dharma, than to follow the path of another. (III.35)

But Swamiji, this verse seems directly applicable to varna-ashrama dharma, which is obsolete. Why go for it now?

I don't disagree with you. However, think of a student whose dharma is to study. Is it fair for them to get into worldly pleasures or politics during their student days? I don't think so.

What Gita says is to be clear about your duties once you take them up, and as expected by society, and then stick to them. Dharma and duty are not only meant for job satisfaction; they need to be discharged in the interests of the society. I feel that India seems to be forgetting the importance of sticking to one's dharma. We may have to pay a heavy price if we don't reorient ourselves.

Have you always been true to your dharma? asked I.

I am ashamed to admit that I have failed in that quite a few times and have thus let down those around me by not sticking to my duty. However, I can proudly say that I have got up after every such stumble and moved on with a greater resolve.

Wonderful to know that you, too, had stumbles, Swamiji.

The greatest of charlatans are those who claim not to have ever stumbled on their path of dharma, he said, and ended the lesson.

I feel that Swamiji could have explained more verses, but he refrained from doing so to keep it simple for me. At night,

I compared the notes that I had made with the Gita book that I have. What surprised me is how Gita stresses on the importance of work and yet, as Swamiji repeatedly said, we, the people of India, have been the great shirkers of our responsibilities.

Is religion to be blamed for this? Well, that is what I had thought till date, but the reality appears to be something else. An edifice of my preconceived notions seemed to have crumbled that day.

I said goodnight to myself, musing over what I may hear the next day.

IV

KNOWLEDGE LIBERATES

Do you know how to kill a society?

Swamiji and his questions! Often these questions seemed so innocent, but it was difficult to guess how his answers were going to hit me. So, I generally preferred to stay silent. As for this question, I had only killed mosquitoes in life, so how could I say how to kill a society!

It is not through hunger, nor through bloodshed that you kill a society, Swamiji said, for if that were the case, India would have died long ago. To finish off a society, starve it of knowledge, since knowledge frees you from physical wants, emotional needs and spiritual bondage. If you have knowledge, you are the emperor of the universe, king of your mind and the master of people. It is because of knowledge that God is the ruler of the universe, and it has been because of knowledge that the Brahmins became supreme in India. In spite of all the social justice that we talk about in India, even the political masters coming from the have-nots of society possess superior knowledge as compared to their kindred who continue to be in darkness.

Why spiritual knowledge is the highest

What the people of the four varna did in the past has been completely taken over by knowledge today. Learning, warfare, business, labour – everything requires specialized knowledge instead of mere skill, which was the norm till some years ago. And now, with the natural growth of artificial intelligence, everything that our mind can do, will be doable by machines, and so only spirituality, the eternal one, will remain our sole preserve, since it is not the product of mind. Human society will attain superior spiritual power and its effects will rule the world in future. Mark my words, bhai!

Obviously, I am not someone who can be rattled easily. But Swamiji! How come I had not come up with this idea regarding artificial intelligence! Indeed, it made sense that no amount of artificial intelligence can overrun us because of the spiritual knowledge that we are capable of possessing, and which no machine can ever possess. I was glad that he was not in our field, for who knows, he would have beaten us hollow or it may be that he would have been a big flop. After all, a great wrestler is not a great scientist, and vice versa.

Swamiji then added, Anything that is not a product of the mind is eternal, since mind, world, time, space, these are all produced together. Spiritual knowledge is the highest – the one who has it will always rule the universe.

One small question, Swamiji. Both our conversation and other floating statements that I have come across put spiritual knowledge on a higher pedestal. But I can't help but think of the story of 'nothing like leather'. According to this story, when a kingdom was attacked, the king asked for suggestions to protect it, to which a cobbler suggested that the entire city be covered with leather, since there's 'nothing like leather'. It suggests that what you know best, you consider to be the best. What is your take on this?

It is not as difficult as it appears to be. Knowledge means to know the truth about a thing, which every living being does to varying degrees. But in most cases, such knowledge is based on deduction. It is for the human beings to analyse things and then make predictions. Greek philosophers were very good at this technique, which has now been taken over by modern science.

While all this is good, a far better form of knowledge is that which unites two apparently distinct objects. In a word, the knowledge that tends towards exclusiveness is inferior to that which takes you towards inclusiveness. For example, the general belief was that the sun, moon and stars move independently of each other, but Newton showed how all such motions of heavenly bodies are products of one force – gravitation. In the last couple of hundred years, scientists have come up with equations that relate work and heat, magnetism and electricity, and other such independent forces. And then there has been the great Einstein who showed how matter and energy are same.

You may not know this, but just before Einstein, Nicholas Tesla – who knew Swami Vivekananda and used to hear his talks regularly – had attempted to mathematically show the unity of matter and energy. After some days, he backed off, saying that it cannot be done. This shows how difficult it is to find the unity between distinct entities.

In the present times, there are scientists who are trying to find the unity between matter and consciousness. Of course, by consciousness they mean aspects of the mind only. Having suckled on the dualism of Abrahamic religions from the first days of their lives, it is nearly impossible for Westerners to understand the true nature of consciousness. If you can let go of the ideas marketed by Western science, you will realize mind, matter and consciousness are three distinct entities in the world, from which all living and non-living things appear.

Here he goes again, turning my world upside down, I thought. Mind? Consciousness? Cause of creation? Not effect? What's coming next? But by then I knew better than to ask.

Swamiji continued, Most schools of Indian philosophy accept that mind and matter are related, which leaves us with mind and consciousness. You will be surprised to know that this is where Vedanta eclipses all – it kills all dualities, and shows through arguments, the words of sages, and direct knowledge gained in samadhi, the greatest of all unifications: *sarvam khalu idam brahma* – Brahman (Consciousness) alone is all this (that appears).

Just like $E=mc^2$, the famous equation of unity, Vedanta shows *aham = brahma* (I = Brahma). And the way it was difficult to accept the theory of relativity by the scientists for a long time, it is nearly impossible for even the most intelligent to accept the great Vedantic truth of unity! Unification, bhai, unification makes spirituality the highest of knowledge.

My head was reeling.

This is where science meets Vedanta, he said. It is impossible to bring science and religion on the same platform to those who have grown up with a firm belief in the Cartesian division of mind and matter. If you indeed want to do that, you have to come to Vedanta, which unifies the two logically. And yet, you will be surprised to know how even great saints, philosophers and scientists get uncomfortable with the idea of the oneness of everything.

That may be because their business model will be doomed if they accept divine oneness, he added with a twinkle in his eye.

Knowledge is eternal

All knowledge comes from within, whether of the world, nature or God. What comes from the outside is sense-born information that acts like blows to awaken the knowledge within. So, neither the entertaining words of the preachers marketed by the glib, nor reading any number of books is going to make you spiritual. To be spiritual, you have to read the book that is within you! This means that real knowledge, about the Divine as well as the principles of life, is eternal, and hence no book or prophet can claim to have an exclusive right over these.

Hindu dharma is called *sanatan dharma* because it narrates the principles that are eternal, and states that its applications will vary in space-time. As a mark of respect, our sages declared these eternal principles to have come from Brahman itself, since these are not a product of verbal dysentery.

Scathing!

And yet, Swamiji said, the great spiritual truths get diluted in practice, as you can see all over the world. The spiritual masters, either as an avatara or as sages, give us the purest of truth, but because of the followers, whose lust for the world remains high, the yoga of spiritual wisdom gets diluted. It is then that the Lord has to come again or send someone powerful to cleanse society and re-establish dharma.

एवं परम्पराप्राप्तमिमं राजर्षयो विदुः, स कालेनेह महता योगो नष्टः परन्तप |

The science of Yoga, as taught by the Lord, continuous through tradition, but with the passage of time, it gets diluted. (IV.2)

Why God incarnates

Swamiji walked down some steps and then proudly stood in front of a stone carving, smiling tenderly. He read out aloud for me to hear:

यदा यदा हि धर्मस्य ग्लानिर्भवति भारत, अभ्युत्थानमधर्मस्य तदात्मानं सृजाम्यहम् |
परित्राणाय साधूनां विनाशाय च दुष्कृताम्, धर्मसंस्थापनार्थाय सम्भवामि युगे युगे |

Whenever there is a decline of dharma and a predominance of adharma, then I manifest Myself for protecting the good, destroying the evil, and for establishing dharma. (IV.7–8)

These two verses are quite well-known all over India because of their direct message. People also love them in the hope that the society's evils will get cleaned up by God. With that he chuckled. We lazy Indians! We always hope that someone else will clean our garbage, as if God has nothing better to do. No wonder we have suffered so much for thousands of years, despite having the best of spiritual religion.

I asked, I have heard some people say that Sri Krishna alone is God. This verse, too, says something similar. Do you agree to that?

Swamiji looked annoyed and replied in a terse voice, These newlings to religion! They will degrade the majesty of Hindu dharma to be at par with the Abrahamic belief system. Sri Krishna is not the only God, but God came as Sri Krishna. The difference in these two statements may appear trivial but is actually huge. To say that your God is God is perfectly fine, but to say that your God is the only true God, is at best funny and at its worst, fanaticism. God, whatever form He may take, teaches us the highest spiritual truths directly or through some sage.

As for us, we Hindus have forgotten that God comes to not just destroy adharma, but to also re-establish dharma. We have fixated on the former aspect of Puranic stories in which Bhagavan assumes an Avatar to kill the demons. This is fine for instilling values in our kids, but these Puranas and other scriptures also carry deep wisdom on how to create order in a society and ascend to the higher pursuits of inner growth. When the grown-ups of the day ignore these aspects, know then that dharma has indeed degenerated.

How to approach God

God doesn't kill on your behalf; he only teaches you directly. This is the whole of spiritual science. Approach Him in any way and He will respond. After all, He is your soul!

ये यथा मां प्रपद्यन्ते तांस्तथैव भजाम्यहम्, मम वर्त्मानुवर्तन्ते मनुष्याः पार्थ सर्वशः |

As is one's attitude towards Me, likewise do I provide. Everyone follows My path only, knowingly or unknowingly (IV.11)

Whatever you do is God's will; whatever your way of your life, it is by God only, since He is your inner self. The problem with the single-birth theory (or YOLO) of the materialists and some religions is that this noble truth cannot be explained in that limited timeframe. For the Hindus, this is the most natural thing to accept since we live for eternity. When you look at life on a larger scale, you realize that indeed all is God's will.

It is not at all clear, Swamiji, I said.

It is simple. If you love eating meat, and you are obsessed with it, then the human body will not suit you, and so you will have to take up the body of a carnivore. Your other mental outlooks will determine whether you are born as a tiger or a fox or a bird of carrion! So, a fox is a fox, and a lion is a lion by their own choice. Though all this comes from the paths laid down by The Creator only, He is not directly responsible for making a fox a fox! So, be careful about what you do and what you wish for.

I felt jolted. For the first time in my life, I suddenly woke up to the possibility of my next birth. That could be bad for me, I thought. Even though this wonderful truth negated the ideas of the eternal hell about which I used to hear from some of my friends who had assured me of my place there simply because I was born a Hindu, the truth about rebirth was big shake-up.

Umm, do you think there is a way to avoid rebirth?

Ha, ha, ha. He laughed heartily and said, I was waiting for you to ask that ... That is what Gita is indeed all about. Listen to the verses carefully and you will then learn how to avoid hell, as also rebirth.

How did he know that I was thinking about hell?

Think divine to be divine

The first step towards spiritual wisdom is to perform all your acts – physical, verbal, mental – as an offering to God, in which every related item is Brahman, or God.

He then added, we monks begin our eating with this mantra, since eating is also a form of yajna.

Eating as yajna! He would probably explain how drinking wine can be a yajna, I thought. Sure enough, he did just that during one of our talks.

ब्रह्मार्पणं ब्रह्म हविः ब्रह्माग्नौ ब्रह्मणा हुतम्, ब्रह्मैव तेन गन्तव्यं ब्रह्मकर्म समाधिना |

The oblation is Brahman, the spoon is Brahman, the act of offering is Brahman, the sacrificial fire is also Brahman, and the result of the act is also Brahman. (IV.24)

For a spiritually illuminated person, everything around him is Brahman. So, when they perform any action, they see the instrument of action, the doer, the result and the action itself as Brahman. This kind of sacrifice does not produce any binding result and is known as *jnana yajna* (knowledge sacrifice). So, you need to treat all your acts as divine, as also the objects that you use. The catchline is: Think that you are divine, and you will become divine; think that you are matter, and you will end up being as dead as matter! The choice is yours.

He then turned towards me and said lovingly, Bhai, if you can get a quality product for the same price, then why should you settle for the ordinary?

So true, Swamiji! But how does that help us in our daily life? Will that help me make more money?

Not directly, but indirectly yes. As I said before, knowledge frees you and once you are free you can achieve anything, including wealth and fame.

He then continued: Every act of ours, including breathing or reading, can be treated as a yajna. Try doing it and you will see how uplifted you feel in no time.

Importance of spiritual knowledge

However, the ultimate goal of spiritual knowledge is to burn down all that has saddled us for so long. It is explained beautifully now.

यथैधांसि समिद्धोऽग्निर्भस्मसात्कुरुतेऽर्जुन, ज्ञानाग्निः सर्वकर्माणि भस्मसात्कुरुते तथा ||

As the blazing fire burns wood to ashes; similarly, the spiritual knowledge reduces all bonds of Karma to ashes. (IV.37)

What else would one want, bhai? It is not you who wants money, but it is your wants that want wealth. Know that you and your wants are different, and you will be free of this ghoul that drives you like a slave.

Who can have spiritual knowledge?

What you say is good but appears so impractical and unrelatable, I said.

The same objection again! Why do you say that?

Well, I'm trying to think of how 'thinking Divine' will apply when I'm dealing with an under-performing employee, or a worker caught stealing.

How do you deal with an under-performer now?

The usual. Try to motivate him, point out where he's going wrong, and show the shtick about consequences of continued failure. What else?

Can you be a bit more imaginative about the same situation? Instead of thinking of him as a problem and hindrance to your work, can you choose to approach him as an opportunity to practice seeing divinity everywhere? To view him as a child of the Divine who is under-performing, and not label him automatically as an under-performer?

Hmm ... what will that do?

Look ... this is not a management coaching session. But when you change your attitude towards a person from 'here is someone who is cheating or failing me' to 'Okay, God wants me to deal with this now, how can I best serve as His instrument?', which one is likely to produce more valuable outcomes for you, your business and your employee?

I made it clear in the beginning itself that the knowledge of consciousness, which actually means to be one with it, is completely subjective. So, yes, it cannot be reduced to labs and tests and equations. That may make it appear unrelatable. But once you choose this path, you can begin to train yourself to align your thoughts and words and actions with the premise of all-pervading Divinity. This is the sadhana of spiritual growth, and to expect to get it without practicing it is like expecting to taste the ice cream without putting it in your mouth.

Also, unlike other subjects, one must have deep shraddha – a complete change in one's outlook, soaked in faith – if one wants to acquire spiritual knowledge.

अज्ञश्च अश्रद्दधानश्च संशयात्मा विनश्यति, नायं लोकोऽस्ति न परो न सुखं संशयात्मनः |

The irrational, the faithless and the disbeliever cannot attain this knowledge. There is neither this world, nor the world beyond, nor happiness for such people. (IV.40)

Strong words, I agree. Unfortunately, that is the reality. You can test your spiritual teacher as much as you want, but once you accept him as your master, just hold on to what he says in matters of religion. The growing unhappiness all around is directly related to a lack of spiritual knowledge and practice in society. Learn this or perish. Your choice. Period.

That 'period' again. I've realized when he says that word, the subject is truly complete for him!

Swamiji then recited:

तद्विद्धि प्रणिपातेन परिप्रश्नेन सेवया, उपदेक्ष्यन्ति ते ज्ञानं ज्ञानिनः तत्त्वदर्शिनः |

Acquire this knowledge from a spiritual master through reverence, sincere inquiry and service. (IV.34)

How does one find the right teacher?

Ah! How many times have I been asked this question!

As I said, all knowledge comes from within. Even the great master can only ignite what is already there within you. So, pick any teacher, acquire what he has to offer, and then God Himself will guide you to the right master if you need one.

Incidentally, do you know that Swami Vivekananda had visited many teachers before he could reach Sri Ramakrishna?

No, I did not.

You will get the teacher that you are fit for. Once you outgrow his knowledge, God will take you to a better teacher. Period.

As I completed that day's note, I felt that there was substance in what Swamiji was saying, but it was truly difficult for people like me to grasp – those whose gaze was fixed on maximizing pleasure in this world. If I can take a few or even a single idea from all these discussions, my way of life will surely improve, and I may be freed from my self-imposed emotional sty.

V

GIVING UP ALL

We were walking on the parikrama path when our steps were interrupted by a call from a friend since our nappy days.

Friends. Such a wonderful breed of humanity! I doubt that any other species has this kind of bonding with its members, that remains intact even if one stays disconnected for years. Unlike herd mentality, friendship thrives on the idea of oneness, and thus bears the stress and strain of our good and bad without complaint. I had read somewhere that one can attain God through friendship. Though I did not believe in God then, I firmly believed in the power of friendship that stays true even when one keeps committing wrong acts. Good acts are appreciated by all, but your bad acts are accepted as part of you only by your true friends. I was lucky that way.

A little birdie has whispered in my ear that you are in the company of a monk. Is that true? Since when did you start getting ensnared by the pseudos? What about your rationality? Are you okay? Do you need help? Should I come down?

It is all fine. Don't you worry, I said.

Are you planning to become a monk? Look buddy, it is alright to go for meditation and tantric kundalini but be careful about becoming a monk with a shaven head looking for nothingness. Or Buddha! Don't hesitate to let me know if you have landed in some kind of emotional soup.

He and his words! I loved him for who he was and what he meant to me, but friends can, at times, be annoying, too. This was one of those moments.

No, I said, I have no intention of becoming a monk. I have no empire to give up yet. Now hang up.

With a little more of his verbal therapy, he hung up.

Friends!

As soon as the call ended, Swamiji asked, What was he saying about becoming a monk? You know bhai, people think that it is easy to give up all, and that a monk is a loser who escapes his responsibilities. But no, a monk gives up the small to embrace the universal. In fact, the stretch of the parikrama where we are standing right now is about the ideals of monkhood.

Who is truly a monk?

He then quoted from the stone tablet that was a few steps ahead.

ज्ञेयः स नित्यसंन्यासी यो न द्वेष्टि न काङ्क्षति, निर्द्वन्द्वो हि महाबाहो सुखं बन्धात्प्रमुच्यते

An ideal monk neither craves nor hates anything. That is how they gain knowledge of the Supreme. (V.03)

This chapter is a favourite of mine, the Swami said. Partly because it is about the ideals of being a monk and partly because this is the first chapter that I memorized.

You mean all these stone carved verses have been carved in your memory? Incredulity oozed from my words.

You can say that, he said with a smile. He had a good sense of humour.

What a waste of your time and brain power, Swamiji. You could have put that power to better use. Rote learning is such garbage.

Better use like what?

Thinking, writing, reading, speaking ... anything.

That is the problem with you lazy ones, he said. You people just ape anything that comes from America! Know that memorizing never diminishes the brain power; rather it increases one's capacity to hold information. I have known monks who could've repeated word-for-word what you said just now, but I am yet to come across someone who made a great use of their time by not memorizing. And how much time does it take to memorize one verse every day? A mere five minutes. Even if you look at this as an investment, it is a good investment.

I had no intentions of making any such investment, so I let it go. Even otherwise, I was a better achiever than Swamiji. He was the one who lived off charity, and I was the one who made such charity possible. I liked him, so I walked with him, but that did not mean that I was going to put time or money into what he suggested.

To become a monk, he resumed, you first need to know what you are aiming for, as described in the second chapter.

The next step will be to work hard to burn down your laziness, and then you will have to give a spiritual orientation to all that you do. It is only when you have gone through these preparatory stages that you can aspire to be a spiritual being whose living ideal is a monk.

Forgive me for saying this, but I do not think that being a monk is the highest ideal of spirituality or anything. I know many householders who are far better than monks. Serving your parents and serving society is a far better way of life than taking up the *gerua* (saffron) cloth.

Your life, your choice, Swamiji said. What you are saying is theoretical, while my words are from experience. When someone goes abroad for work, you don't complain; when someone lays down their life in the line of duty, you don't complain; when you park your old parents at an old age home, you have no issues. But when a person wants to become a monk for the greater good of himself and the society, you start cribbing. Why?

Even then ...

Even then what? Do you know what your problem is?

Ah, I said to myself. There he goes once again!

You never want others to grow, whether academically, financially, socially or spiritually. You think you are the best, and that no one should progress from where they are. And for some person presuming to be better than monks, remember that even a beggar does not like to give up his bowl. To give up means to embark on a journey that is truly difficult to complete. The armchair spiritual is usually lazy, and at best a good person, but to be truly spiritual, you will have to give all up. Have you ever thought that giving up, too, is action, and that it requires effort to give all up? Withdrawal is more difficult than engagement, bhai! Ask anyone who's given up any physical addiction – liquor, cigarettes or drugs. Even these are child's play compared to mental and emotional addictions.

Was he getting personal? I was not sure, so I kept my scorching words on the topic to myself. The experiences one has in a business empire teach you some good things, you know.

He then went on to explain the idea of virtue and vice, which, according to many, was because of one's acts or due to God's will. That is how one went to the heaven or hell. I did not believe in all that hocus pocus, but I admired words like, 'Heaven and hell are here on this earth only.'

How a monk works

An ideal monk, Swamiji said, offers all their acts and thoughts to God, and thus becomes blessed. Try doing it even as a lip service and you will find the difference in your life. This idea has been put beautifully as:

ब्रह्मण्याधाय कर्माणि सङ्गं त्यक्त्वा करोति यः, लिप्यते न स पापेन पद्मपत्रमिवाम्भसा |

One who does all work as an offering to God, remains untouched by any form of virtue or vice, the way a lotus leaf never gets wet by mud. (V.10)

This is the ideal of Karma yoga. The reason being that whatever you do, speak or think leaves an impression in your mind, which sprouts fully when a similar situation comes again in your life. That is how you become tempted by certain things and feel dislike for others; and that is how, when practised to the extreme, criminals become criminals and saints become saints. But when you offer to God all your acts – physical, verbal or mental – they do not leave any impression on your psyche. The acts of such persons do produce results, but without leaving any residual influence on the mind. You can compare this with the burning of camphor, which leaves no ash.

Such a wonderful truth, and what a great ideal for all! Try doing it, bhai, and you will become a great businessman. The problem with the world is that they are so locked up in their narrowness that they refuse to accept the higher ideals that will liberate them. Fear of freedom is a very dangerous fear! You can see that when a bird keeps returning to its cage, even when the door is open.

I had always thought that fear of bondage was the worst, but here he was!

God does not take your good or bad

Do you know that whatever your offering may be to God, He neither takes your good nor bad?

That was shocking for me! How could that be? This is unbelievable and unacceptable.

Yes ji, God does not goad you towards good or bad, and nor does he accept your sin or virtue. Thus, the idea of Jesus taking the sin of his followers can be contested from the standpoint of Gita.

So, who is right, Swamiji, Christian believers or the followers of Krishna?

Why bother, he said. Take any of these beliefs and grow from where you are. Your sincerity will take you forward, and if need be, God will show you the right path. When you are studying a sacred book, you should stick to it closely, or else, you will end up being a mass of confusion.

But I don't believe in God.

He stopped walking, turned and looked at me, eyes boring into the innermost caverns of my mind. That is your problem. Sacred books are not meant for people who do not believe in life continuing in some form after one's death. Let such people enjoy and suffer birth after birth, acquiring small bits of *punya*, virtue in each birth. Through this there will be some awakening in them that will mark the beginning of their zig-zag journey to spirituality.

To sum up, you can outgrow your involvement, and thus get rid of your suffering by knowing the truth – that through detachment or by offering the results of your acts to God, you can keep your mind free of the ensuing impressions. Do that and be free. It is so simple.

It was not, I thought.

He explained:

नादत्ते कस्यचित्पापं न चैव सुकृतं विभुः, अज्ञानेनावृतं ज्ञानं तेन मुह्यन्ति जन्तवः |

The Lord does not take the responsibility for the good or evil deeds of anybody. The veil of ignorance covers the Self-knowledge, which makes people deluded. (V.15)

The responsibility of good and bad lies squarely with us. This is not speculative wisdom, nor idle wishful thinking, but the truth that is realized when one gains knowledge of the Atman in samadhi.

Why worship God then, as can be seen all over the world?

You love yourself, don't you? We all do. We love God for the same reason. God is our essence, our truth. We love Him only because of that and not for any other reason. That is the message of Indian spirituality.

The results of spiritual wisdom

The consequence of this spiritual wisdom is astounding, as you can see in this verse:

विद्याविनयसम्पन्ने ब्राह्मणे गवि हस्तिनि, शुनि चैव श्वपाके च पण्डिताः समदर्शिनः |

An enlightened person looks at a person of learning and humility, an outcast, a cow, an elephant or a dog as having the same spiritual reality. (V.18)

Wait a minute, Swamiji. You are saying that there can be no discrimination based on caste, gender, class or anything else. And yet, look at the reality. India has been, and continues to be, the land of discrimination. What is the use of big words if a precept cannot be walked the last mile? Just tell me, what is the use of it?

No need to get animated. The higher the ideal, the greater is the chasm in its implementation. Who wants to accept that the Sun does not rise in the east, or that energy and mass are the same, or that the quantum world is a reality? We, the ordinary mortals, live in our small world shaped by our fears and aspirations, and so it is natural that when we face the knowledge of reality, we either get frightened away or fail to practice that knowledge. In response, we often go in the opposite direction, particularly if it concerns our social life. The keyword is enlightened. Such persons are rarer than pearls in the beach sand.

Blame not the ideals for failures, but blame our own limitedness, bhai. I was once talking to a Marxist friend who was trying to convert me to his philosophy by saying, 'We believe in the equality of men', to which I replied, 'How wonderful! And we believe in the divinity of all.' You should have seen his face! Tell me, how do you think Marxists fared when their philosophy was applied to the society? The answer is there for everyone to see. Look at any other system that preaches brotherhood or equality, and you will see how they all failed to bridge the chasm between the philosophy and the practices. So, do not blame Vedanta for the gap. As for me, if I have to choose an ideal, I will always go for the best, highest and most inclusive. Do not lower the ideal simply because people cannot practise it. Even if one person can practise the highest, then the ideal is worth it.

Even then, I replied grumpily.

Achieve here and now

Moreover, whatever we have to achieve, has to be done here and now. Unlike other religions that promise heaven in the afterlife, Vedanta emphasizes on the importance of attaining spiritual enlightenment right away, in this very body. Can you think of a better positive outlook?

इहैव तैर्जितः सर्गो येषां साम्ये स्थितं मनः, निर्दोषं हि समं ब्रह्म तस्माद् ब्रह्मणि ते स्थिताः |

Everything is accomplished in this very life by them whose mind is set in equanimity because he has realized the supreme state, which is without any imperfections. (V.19)

Do you know why we suffer? Swamiji asked.

I was happy to see that he did not mention it as a problem. Like anyone else I, too, had my share of suffering, but unlike many others, I knew how to keep it hidden in the closets of my psyche.

Pain takes you forward

Pain takes you forward, Swamiji said, but it is misery that bogs you down. People often confuse the two, and so they fail to get rid of misery, and also fail to make use of pain to get ahead. Nature gives you pain to say that you need to let go, but misery comes when you get obsessed with pleasures related to the senses, and you cannot even think properly. Fire burns your finger to let you know to be careful about the power of burning, but a morbid person won't withdraw from it, would they?

ये हि संस्पर्शजा भोगा दुःखयोनय एव ते, आद्यन्तवन्तः कौन्तेय न तेषु रमते बुधः |

Sense pleasures are the source of all misery. Every such pleasure has a beginning and an end, so the wise stay away from these. (V.22)

Come on Swamiji, what is there in the world other than enjoyment? After all, we have only one life.

See how you are still trapped in the same philosophy of 'You only live once!' We have already discussed whether or not you want to get out of miseries and suffering. If you want to get freedom, then stay away from bringing your senses in contact with the respective sense objects. The choice is yours. Every mother knows how her baby feels miserable if its favourite toys and food are taken away. That is what happens to us, too, when our favourite things are taken away from our lives. Now the question is do you want to continue being a mustachioed baby all your life? Probably not. Then you better listen to what Gita has to say about it.

You will be ready to explore the subtler layers of existence only when you are out of sense entanglement. If you think that you are fine living the life of a brute, then who can help you? So, wake up to the brighter realities of life and get ready to make the great leap which can be made only by a few. Be a yogi!

That night, I sat thinking. I surely did not want to be a yogi, but what Swamiji had said about pain – its genesis and consequences – was definitely true. Whatever my suffering, it was all due to my entanglement with sense-objects indeed.

Was my fig-leaf of scientific objectivity dropping away? I could not be sure.

Walking the last mile, as I had accused Swamiji of not doing, now seemed so true for me!

VI

MEDITATION

'Baba *savdhan*!' One of the devout on the parikrama path shouted at us, and came running with his stick raised. Savdhan in Hindi is a call to attention. Naturally, I was startled. The journey from pranam to savdhan with a raised stick had been pretty quick, I thought wryly.

During our walk I had seen notices that advised the pilgrims to carry sticks with them, and to travel in groups so as to stay safe from the wild animals. I had also noticed small groups of monkeys sitting here and there in anticipation of food from the pilgrims. Unlike zoos, where feeding animals is prohibited, religious places allow it. Due to this, the monkeys of Vrindavan, Ayodhya and innumerable such pilgrim centres have become extremely demanding and dangerous.

Lost in our conversation, I had failed to notice how one of the monkeys had stalked us and was about to catch hold of Swamiji's pocket. The gentleman had shouted to catch our attention. The very next moment a tug-of-pocket between man and monkey began! Well, I feel ashamed to admit that the scene was so funny that I laughed out aloud with, The monk and the monkey! Bravo! But the sight was juicy.

The devotee reached us in time with his stick and a banana, and succeeded in shooing the monkey away. Initially taken aback, Swamiji was his jovial self in no time. He then narrated how Swami Vivekananda had once been chased by a group of monkeys in Varanasi, when he was advised by a sadhu in a loud voice to 'Face the brutes!' He turned around to face the monkeys, who then turned back. Later, he would mention this many times to highlight the inherent message of how to face the world.

'Face the brutes!' That is the central teaching of Gita, bhai. Face the challenge that comes to you in the form of life, duty, dharma, problems, etc. That is the only path to growth. Problems and temptations will come, but stick to your way of life, that is, dharma. In case of conflict, face it and move ahead. But keep the highest philosophy of life in sight at all times.

Wonderful, I thought. Life mostly brings brutes before us, whom we try to tame in various ways, but mostly unsuccessfully. Now I could see what had been missing almost every time: 'Face the brutes!' must be the backbone of every such taming.

It also occurred to me that learning is a lot like crystallization – you put the substance in a solvent, heat it up to put more of it, and finally put a pure crystal in it. And lo! A large, beautiful fresh crystal is produced. Exactly like that, if you want knowledge, then you must take in words from various sources, and heat yourself up through intense activity centred on that field to make your mind more receptive to ideas. It is then that the super saturated mind is ready to create the crystal-like knowledge. That is how great poets create poetry around what they see, while we fail to scribble even a line. Indeed, exposure and activities – these are the twin forces that make learning possible.

I had always understood the importance of facing the brutes, but it was only when I heard Swamiji that this knowledge crystallized within me.

Interrupting my musings, Swamiji asked if I had ever gone for any course on meditation. No, I told him. But I knew some guys, and some helpless friends who went for the seemingly exalted.

Who is meditation for?

Meditation is not about giving a break to the mind, but about uncovering the divine within us, Swamiji said. Nowadays, what is passing off in the name of Vedantic or Buddhistic meditation is a mere mockery of Vedanta, yoga and meditation. Why can't they change the name to something catchy, without soiling the sacred? These gurus!

He then explained who can go for meditation and yoga.

आरुरुक्षोर्मुनेर्योगं कर्म कारणमुच्यते, योगारूढस्य तस्यैव शमः कारणमुच्यते |

Unselfish activity purifies the mind of inertness and cravings. It is only then that one can go for meditation. For those who have attained such purity, self-control is the way to yoga. (VI.3)

Meditation brings focus to the mind, which gives it immense power. So, unless a person cleanses the impurities of the mind – lust, greed, laziness and other such vices – through intense activity, one cannot and should not try meditation, for it will then become counterproductive, as seen in the stories of the *asuras* and *rakshasa* (those with selfish motives) who got unbridled power through meditation, which became the cause of their downfall and destruction.

The only goal of meditation is to become the divine that you already are. Meditation leads to massive concentration of mind, which if not pure, will become an infinitely powerful amplifier of the defects that one has. What to say of the demons, even the sages who deviated from the path of pure spiritual goals had to face severe consequences. Viswamitra was one such sage. He is also my favourite. He was such a maverick, and so focused on outpacing sage Vasistha that whatever power he got through meditation, it leaked out through his anger, sense of power and lust. In one of his last problems, he had an amorous tryst with Menaka, the apsara. The sage got so massively entangled with her that it resulted in the birth of Shakuntala. Consequently, he lost all his virtues. Of course, he grew up from that tremendous fall by realizing that he had to become spiritual; Viswamitra then set about his goal with single-minded focus. And that is ultimately how he and his descendants came to contribute some very important sections of the Veda, including the Gayatri mantra.

So, before one goes for meditation, it is important to do intense work as a way of purifying oneself. Since we are good at using our body, it is easier to perform activity than to sit idle and try to focus on some hocus-pocus. The samskara, impressions born of unselfish activities, destroy the sloth and selfish tendencies like laziness and cravings. This state of pure mind is known as *sattvic* – pure or serene. It is only then that a person becomes fit for meditation. But who will caution these gurus?

You know bhai, we monks are always in danger of falling prey to lust and other such vices, simply because of the impurity that might have lingered inside us. Meditation is like unleashing the atomic energy – it can ruin you, and it can also take you beyond the sky.

So, shouldn't you monks be yoked to work?

Well, I work a lot; but what can I say about others, he said. Maybe they should study Gita more thoroughly to understand their problems. But rarely does anyone feel that they have problems. Swami Vivekananda had cautioned the country with, 'Be strong, my young friends; that is my advice to you. You will be nearer to Heaven through football than through the study of Gita.' Meditation and Gita are meant for the strong; not for physical, mental and emotional weaklings. Period.

You alone are your friend and enemy

He then took up the next verses, saying: One of the greatest takeaways from Gita is the importance of self-dependence in life. Depend on none, lean on none – know that you are your only friend and only enemy in this world. Know that not even God in any external form can help you.

उद्धरेत् आत्मनात्मानं नात्मानम् अवसादयेत्, आत्मैव ह्यात्मनो बन्धुरात्मैव रिपुरात्मनः |
बन्धुरात्मा आत्मनस्तस्य येनात्मैव आत्मना जितः,
अनात्मनस्तु शत्रुत्वे वर्तेतात्मैव शत्रुवत् |

One has to uplift oneself by their self, so one should never degrade oneself. You are your best friend if you have self-control, and you are your greatest enemy if you don't have that. (VI.5–6)

What is true for life is true for the spiritual life, too – make yourself your best friend, or else there will always be the danger of you becoming your worst enemy. There is no middle way in that, bhai. You are born alone, enjoy or suffer alone and die alone. Your family and friends are just fellow travellers in this journey of life, who will move to their own destiny soon enough. So, know that whatever you have to achieve, you have to do that yourself. You are what your achievements are, so train your mind to behave if you want to achieve anything in life. Give the mind license, and it will behave like the monkey we met a while ago. Men may or may not have evolved from the monkey, but our mind will surely become a monkey if not kept under check.

You were wondering if Gita has anything for people of the present times. What better message would you want than to stand on your feet! I can tell you from my own experiences that indeed nothing and no one can help you better than you yourself.

Essential habits to be a yogi

We walked silently for a while, lost in our respective thoughts, when some verse caught his attention. It was about how to sit for meditation and concentrate. I was not interested in it, so I let it go. But what I gathered from his words about how to meditate appeared good. I had often seen my grandfather sit straight on an *asana*, with his eyes closed and doing *japa*. I liked his sitting posture and copied it. It is because of him that I always sit and walk straight. My spine, physically and metaphorically, stays straight all the time.

Swamiji then explained:

नाति अश्नतस्तु योगोऽस्ति न चैकान्तम् अनश्नतः,
न चाति स्वप्नशीलस्य जाग्रतो नैव चार्जुन
युक्ताहारविहारस्य युक्तचेष्टस्य कर्मसु, युक्तस्वप्नावबोधस्य योगो भवति दुःखहा |

A yogi does not eat too much or too little; and they neither sleep too much nor too little. Yoga destroys all sorrow for them who are moderate in eating, recreation, working, sleeping and waking. (VI.16–17)

This yoga stuff is not meant for me if these are the essential conditions to be a yogi, was my immediate thought. I was a passionate worker – I believed in working till you drop dead. My well-wishers always cautioned me regarding that, citing examples of some of my acquaintances who had started developing lifestyle diseases, which made my doctor friends and counsellors pay more income tax.

So, was this verse the solution to the many lifestyle problems that lay siege on the successful? Should we be moderate in place of being passionate? The words of Gita appeared convincing, but not enough to convert me. At least not yet.

Swamiji put brakes on my racing thoughts with, What is true for us is true for you, too. Life in the world and spiritual life are not set at right angles. For Hindus, life is a continuous whole that includes artha, kama, dharma, moksha – the four possible goals of life. Each of these has freedom as the purpose. Wealth frees you from bodily wants, enjoyment frees from emotional wants, dharma frees you from inferior rebirths and moksha frees you from all kinds of wants and troubles forever. The problem with you people is that you do not even know what you want, and why. Once you realize this, you will have no issues with adopting the life of moderation.

Do you have any idea of how complicated life has become, Swamiji? It is not the same kind of life that our ancestors lived. They went for toilet in open fields, but we need a water faucet; they ate in private, but we eat in public; they waited for trains, but our cars wait for us. The list goes on. And for all this we need money, which has to be earned. Today if we are not in the race of meeting the deadline, we will be centrifuged away.

Of course I know, he said. As I told you, I am a regular at management and technical institutes, and so I know what is happening in society. The problem that you are talking about is famously known as *ninnyanbe ka chakkar* – 'the trap of ninety-nine'. According to this story, a poor couple got ninety-nine silver coins magically. To make it a round figure, they worked hard to add money to the money bag, but that magic bag still had only ninety-nine coins. The story is so popular that you hear various versions of it.

There is no rat race, no compulsion, bhai; it is only your insatiable urge to convert ninety-nine into hundred, which will actually never happen. Be moderate; have a regulated life and be your best – try it, and you will find how life becomes uncomplicated and yet full of majesty!

Nah, I was not going to try it. At least, not yet. I was in my money-making phase, so moderation could wait for a while.

What is concentration like?

Swamiji continued with his explanation of the verses of Gita that he felt would interest me. Explaining the ultimate of focus and concentration, which we all should have in our life, he read out:

यथा दीपो निवातस्थो नेङ्गते सोपमा स्मृता, योगिनो यतचित्तस्य युञ्जतो योगमात्मनः |

The way a lamp in windless spot does not flicker, exactly so the mind of a yogi does not waver when they practise concentration. (VI.19)

You know, Swamiji, when I work I am also focused like what has been described here. So, in what way is your moderation and meditation technique superior to what we do?

Bhai, a *paanwala* is a businessman and you, too, are. It is something like comparing your concentration with that of a yogi! Work of any kind requires and results in concentration – even a simple act like chopping a vegetable needs concentration. Our education system is not only about giving information and knowledge, but also about gaining higher levels of concentration. But that is not *dhyana*, since focus requires external aid, while a yogi does not require that for meditation – they focus their mind on the mind itself. Try doing it, and you will know how difficult that can be, he said with a mischievous smile.

I laughed loudly at what Swamiji said, remembering how I was once trapped into going for a meditation course by one of these mushrooming yoga schools. It was a seven-day course with no external contact, etc. I am not sure what they were promising in lieu of my forced silence, but after some hours of that crazy routine, I wished them well and made my escape from what seemed to me like a silent black hole. I still wonder what good people gain by sitting silently, practicing to be like another Buddha. My philosophy is that if you want to relax, go to the Himalayas on a trek, or to some seaside, and enjoy the silence. There has to be a way and method to everything. But, no! These silence-seekers need guidance even in doing that. They had probably refused to be guided in their learning days and so they made up for the loss by getting guidance for silence and sleep! Crazy world it is!

How not to be destroyed

We were standing near the Kedareswar temple on the parikrama route. Swamiji entered the temple to worship Lord Shiva, and I stood outside looking nowhere in particular.

An elderly gentleman approached me with, You must be Baba's chela. I also want to spend some time with him to gain some wisdom. Will you kindly help me in that?

Me a chela! Could there be a bigger insult? Being friendly does not mean being a disciple. However, I did not want to be rude with the elderly, so when Swamiji returned, I gave him a quick dekko of the situation. He, unlike me, behaved in the most familiar way with that simple villager who wanted words of wisdom from him. Swamiji looked around, and read out:

यो मां पश्यति सर्वत्र सर्वं च मयि पश्यति, तस्याहं न प्रणश्यामि स च मे न प्रणश्यति |

He who sees Him (God) in all things, and sees all things in Him, he never becomes separated from God, nor does the Lord ever become separated from him. (VI.30)

This is the whole of religion, and the magic mantra of life, he said, looking at the elderly gentleman. Stay united with the ideal and one day you will realize the ideal. The truth is that we are always residing in God, and He in us – only we don't know that, and hence all our suffering.

He then turned towards me and said, The problem is that you people neither know what your ideals are, nor do you care to grow. Ideals need to be impersonal. For example, it is good for you to run companies, but it will be better if you engage in wealth creation for society. Similarly, it is good to have a degree, but it is better to acquire knowledge. You can take up any impersonal ideal and then devote yourself to it with all your strength and thought. The personal aspect of it will automatically come under control with extra perks.

How to concentrate

As you know very well, it is grand to parrot around the ideals, but very difficult to practice them. Gita raises this problem as a question from Arjuna amidst the word of the Lord, to which he replied:

असंशयं महाबाहो मनो दुर्निग्रहं चलम्, अभ्यासेन तु कौन्तेय वैराग्येण च गृह्यते |

The mind is indeed very difficult to restrain, but by practice and detachment it can be controlled. (VI.35)

Success knows many failures. You know, we cry too much over failures without realizing that these were the training grounds for success, which when accomplished looks back at failure with gratitude, realizing that it helped build muscle to gain the glory of success. As they say, 'failures are the pillars of success'.

So, we should regularly cogitate over what to give up for our growth and then keep practicing that. We, monks, are often approached by young minds to teach them the art of concentration, without their knowing what that is. Concentration is the art of giving up the comfort zone to move to an uncharted area, and to make that the new comfort zone! People have no difficulty in concentrating on movies and games, so the general problem is not of concentration at all but of coming out of the comfort zone. The word for that in Gita is *vairagya* – detachment, which is a wide term implying withdrawal and outgrowing. Learn the art of detachment and you will be the master of the world. Want to be one, bhai?

I was happy the way I was.

The village gentleman was still listening to Swamiji with folded hands, which made me quite uncomfortable, but I tolerated the intrusion.

Rebirth of the failed

Breaking from the old topic, he asked, Do you believe in rebirth?

No, I said emphatically. I believe in Karma and some of its derivatives, but rebirth is a strict no-no for me. Why believe in something that is not scientific?

My comment kicked Swamiji once again into combat mode. He asked, What is science or scientific temperament? Science is about finding pattern in the data that is available through perception or reasoning, isn't it? It is also about finding a cause-effect relationship in events. As for cause and effect, why do you then accept the theory of probability or quantum physics about which the great Einstein had said 'God does not play dice with the universe?' The problem with you pseudo-scientists is that you only go by the philosophy of convenience. You neither have philosophical outlook nor a scientific temper; you are only convenience seekers.

Strong words, Swamiji! I protested.

He ignored that and continued, And, as for finding a pattern, why do you overlook the words of the masters who have repeatedly talked about rebirth, and hundreds of such cases reported every year from all over the world with meticulous documentation? Why this selective application of scientific investigation? You know what, one thing that I have understood of science and scientists is that they first decide what they want to prove, and then choose data to suit their theory.

Come on, Swamiji, you are going too far with that.

Not at all. You are into money-making, so you may not be keeping a track of all this. But you only have to study the history of twentieth century science to know how data is picked up selectively. Worse, how many of those who swear by science understand it? They are dazzled by the technology, which is a mere by-product of science. They don't even realize that when science was not there, technology was. 'I believe in science' is a mere truism for the scientifically blind.

Very strong words, Swamiji!

But he was unstoppable. Ignoring me, he continued, If you believe in the inviolability of Karma, then by extension, you have to accept rebirth, since not all Karma done by you can be exhausted in one birth, which automatically results in appropriate circumstances suitable for exhausting that Karma in the next birth. And, if you believe in the science of cause and effect, then also you will have to accept rebirth since not all causes get worked out in one life. And this further exposes the common lie that 'all men are born equal', which is a ridiculously false statement.

What to say of this logic? I thought.

Bhai, the verses regarding rebirth of a failed yogi have been great source of sustenance for me. These verses explain who I was and what I will be.

प्राप्य पुण्यकृतां लोकानुषित्वा शाश्वतीः समाः, शुचीनां श्रीमतां गेहे योगभ्रष्टोऽभिजायते |
अथवा योगिनामेव कुले भवति धीमताम्, एतद्धि दुर्लभतरं लोके जन्म यदीदृशम् |
तत्र तं बुद्धिसंयोगं लभते पौर्वदेहिकम्, यतते च ततो भूयः संसिद्धौ कुरुनन्दन |
पूर्वाभ्यासेन तेनैव ह्रियते ह्यवशोऽपि सः, जिज्ञासुरपि योगस्य शब्दब्रह्मातिवर्तते |

The yogis who fail to attain liberation, get reborn in the house of the pious and prosperous. Some lucky ones are born in a spiritually advanced family.

Having worked out the karma that caused the birth, they regain the knowledge acquired in the previous life and strive again to achieve perfection which they had left midway for whatever reason. In the current birth, they get instinctively carried towards God by virtue of the practices of previous lives. (VI.41–44)

What is true of yogis is true of you, too, and of all those who are striving towards attaining something. It is just that most people are 'born like corns and die like corns', as the *Katha Upanishad* says. Every story of success is preceded by a series of failures that may extend to many births. If you are successful today, it is because you have failed many times in previous births! It is a fact, and like any other truth of life, it is so full of positivity.

Be positive! This is what Gita teaches and Hindu dharma practises. You may fail but your efforts will be carried forward in the next birth.

Thus, there is no sudden conversion in Hindu dharma; every spiritual aspirant is actually a product of a slow transformation, accumulated over many lives. The stories that you hear about the sudden transformation of, say, Buddha, may sound seductive, but the fact is that his spiritual evolution must have taken hundreds of births, as narrated beautifully in the *Jataka Katha*.

So, said he, your act of listening to an explanation of Gita, performing parikrama, going to the temples – your past lives have built you up to this level of introspection, and now these acts are all adding to your virtue drop-by-drop. Who knows, in some birth you may be walking on this path and giving your gyan, or as you said hawa gyan, to some budding aspirant!

Wasn't that scary?

The elderly gentleman made pranams to Swamiji and left silently.

It was deep in the night that I completed my chores, and then wrote my note for the day. I think I enjoyed the day's chapter, for it seemed to convey 'moderation' and 'positivity'. And yeah, I have to admit, the eternal thread of cause and effect across lifetimes answers many questions that otherwise face either the dead-end of an indifferent and random universe (which is contrary to my personal experience), or an all-controlling, vengeful God who is constantly playing judge, jury and executioner in everyone's life.

VII

KNOWLEDGE AND BEYOND

Omkareswar is a hot place, made hotter by its rocky terrain. So, walking on the trek was draining and I loved it whenever we got shade of any kind. The lifestyle of our times demands an air-conditioned environment even in moderate climates, making me wonder if our brains evolved in some cold climate. In the heat of Indian plains, brain-work is impossible – the grey matter seems to melt and leak out as sweat. Maybe the climate was more congenial in earlier times, which helped our ancestors create literary masterpieces, compared to which the later works are a major retardation.

We stood in the shade, cooled by the trees, when I expressed my dislike for people touching the feet of the so-called holy persons. How can you permit such regressive practices, Swamiji, when you seem to belong to our century?

What is wrong in that? he countered. If shaking hands and kissing can be used to express camaraderie, why can't a believer touch the feet of someone who reminds them of their spiritual ideal?

It appears regressive and humiliating.

If you think deeply, you will realize that it is regressive to not be spiritual, as our monkey ancestors were. To be spiritual means to be humble. There is absolutely nothing wrong in bowing one's head as a mark of humility. You people do that all the time in different forms with your 'Good morning, sir' or 'Thank you, honey', but you have a problem if others do something that you don't do. And you consider yourself rational!'

Even then!

There is no 'even then'. It's a meaningless door-closer you use when you don't have a valid response. It is only the stubbornness and prejudice of you English-speaking elite, who consider every traditional practice of your own land regressive. Have you ever tried criticizing the practices of other religions?

I am a Hindu. My responsibility lies with my religion.

So true! But do you have no duty towards your religion as well? You don't read your own scriptures; you know nothing about your religion, and you want to discharge your responsibility of criticism? Great!

Seeing him being so combative, I let the topic go. One needs to give space to others during a conversation, as we, in management, know well.

It is difficult to be spiritual

One good thing about Swamiji was that he could compartmentalize his acts. Once a topic was over, he never broached it again. This is the one thing I learnt well from him and now tell my staff to practise it all the time – 'compartmentalize' and 'no spill-over from the previous action'.

Breaking off from the earlier thread, he began, One reason for our misery is that we do not know who we truly are, and what our relation is with the world. At best, we have a vague sense of the mind-matter relationship, which seems to interact somehow. The reality, however, is far more deep and subtle, so Lord Sri Krishna explains the layers of existence that are with us all the time.

The first thing to know is that God is real and is reality itself. But it is nearly impossible to believe this, what to say then of realizing this truth! So, the Lord says:

मनुष्याणां सहस्रेषु कश्चिद्यतति सिद्धये, यततामपि सिद्धानां कश्चिन्मां वेत्ति तत्त्वतः |

One, perchance, in thousands strives for perfection; and of them rare someone knows Me the way I am. (VII.3)

If you believe in the notice 'Beware of dogs', you become careful. Won't you be similarly careful if you believe in God? Won't you become kind towards all – even towards those who don't have the same set of beliefs as you? The truth is that we believe that we believe in God. So, you can easily see how difficult it would be to be spiritual, when the first condition is to have a firm belief in God, in whatever form.

Swamiji, do you yourself believe in God?

I told you earlier, too, that I believe in scriptures and in their words, the way you believed who your father is, simply because your mom said so. The world runs on beliefs. Rare few go beyond words to probe the reality.

The example that Swamiji gave was good but reeked of being personal.

Creation

The relation between God and creation confounds nearly all, since it is very difficult to answer how consciousness produced inert matter. That is why the answers offered by theologians sound so naive that rational minds scoff at them.

Why is it difficult to unravel the mystery of creation? The Vedas have put it beautifully: 'No one knows the mystery of creation, since none was there then'. How can there be an explanation of what happened before the human mind came into existence? Even the explanations offered by physics fail miserably to explain creation. They have expressions like 'singularity' to tell us in a dignified way that they have no answer to the mystery of creation.

And Gita has an answer? I asked mockingly.

Every philosophy and outlook on life has to explain human existence, which means explaining the universe – its origin and dissolution, and the nature of human beings, their origin and ultimate destiny. There are uncountable theories to explain these, which range from gross materialism to the ultimate divine nature of all. So, it is in the rightness of things that Gita, too, would explain creation to us. After all, the goal of spirituality is to get out of the cage of creation, and hence one has to know what creation is and how it came into being, before one can take up the long journey beyond.

When you go deep into meditation, as explained in the previous chapter, the layers of matter start getting peeled away. You then realize that whatever the nature of an object, you can know it only through your five senses, and consequently, you can know only five of their properties as permitted by your five senses. These properties are the nature of five immediate constituents of all matter that abound the universe, and are known as earth, water, fire, wind and space. Do not confuse these with the terms that we use in our daily life; these are technical terms, which imply constituents of matter with the properties of smell, taste, sight, touch and hearing.

Kya Swamiji! All this is so confusing.

No, it is not. Your forefathers knew all this well and lived their life in a dignified way. But you brainwashed money-chasers have let all this go in just one generation. If you want to know a subject, you have to know its technical terms. 'Bit' in English and in computer language has different meanings, doesn't it? Same is the case here. The terms like earth, fire, etc. in Hindu philosophy mean different meanings than when they are used in common speech.

They should have come up with specialized terms.

He laughed and asked, Have you read the works of Immanuel Kant?

No, I had not.

He was very good at coining terms and explaining their meaning in detail. At times, he also used common words to mean something special. All this leaves the readers totally confounded. Hindu philosophy, that way, is far better and simpler.

God, being the reality of all, creates, sustains and dissolves the universe. Why and how this is done cannot be answered, since there was nothing at the time of creation other than God, the pure consciousness. To say 'time of creation' is also absurd, since time itself did not exist then. This is impossible to express in any human language, which takes time for granted, so we have to make do with indicative references.

What is known is that the act of creation is achieved by His divine power, called variously as Prakriti, Shakti or Maya, which has been described as being composed of three qualities which are neither mind, matter nor energy but pure quality – something like the 'redness' of red. It is from these qualities that the cosmic mind, worlds, beings and the individual mind is created. The five elements mentioned earlier were among the last to be produced.

I wanted to have a little fun and so I asked, Swamiji, does a fruit fall on the ground due to gravity or due to God's will?

He laughed at my impertinence and said, Religion and science may be at war for some belief systems, but for us, science is a part of religion. The laws offered by science are a subset of the universal laws of God, known as *ritam*. So, laws of gravitation are part of God's will. The fruit falls on the ground by God's will, carried out in accordance with the laws of gravitation.

Clever! I thought.

As for the theory of creation that I explained, if you meditate, you will actually see the layers that envelop matter. And, as you peel each layer, you will have yogic powers related to the truth of existence as perceived there. It is through this principle of 'knowledge is power' that yogis and spiritual persons get power. Patanjali's *Yoga Sutras* detail all this wonderfully.

The subject of discussion was beyond me. But so was quantum physics that talked about quarks and what not! I can be no judge of who is right or wrong.

Swamiji continued, The combination of these five cannot create the universe, since the consciousness part is missing. And that comes from God Himself, as the higher nature of the universe. So, whatever we see around us, is indeed permeated by God.

भूमिरापोऽनलो वायुः खं मनो बुद्धिरेव च, अहंकार इतीयं मे भिन्ना प्रकृतिरष्टधा |
अपरेयमितस्त्वन्यां प्रकृतिं विद्धि मे पराम्,जीवभूतां महाबाहो ययेदं धार्यते जगत् |
एतद्योनीनि भूतानि सर्वाणीत्युपधारय, अहं कृत्स्नस्य जगतः प्रभवः प्रलयस्तथा |

Bhumi (earth), ap (water), anala (fire), vayu (air), kha (ether), mind, intellect and egoism are the eight-fold lower nature of Brahman. The higher nature that sustains the universe is Consciousness. These two natures are the cause of all beings. God is the origin and dissolution of the whole universe. (VII.4–6)

While making a note of all that I had heard about creation at night, I was laughing to no one in particular! I intend to send this note to my physicist friends who will surely think that I have gone nuts. Or better still, I should send it as a memo to my staff. They might think that I am torturing them before firing them from their jobs! But honestly, I am enjoying my conversations with Swamiji. At least, I am paying my homage to my respected ancestors who came up with all this and maintained it with sanity and sanctity. The highlight, however, was the part about creation mentioned earlier.

God runs through everything

Swamiji completed the talk on creation with a one-line relation between God and His created beings:

मत्तः परतरं नान्यत्किञ्चिदस्ति धनञ्जय, मयि सर्वमिदं प्रोतं सूत्रे मणिगणा इव |

There is nothing outside Me (God). Whatever is there is in Me like pearl strung in a thread (of a necklace). (VII.7)

Think of anything in the universe, and know that God is present in it. Sri Krishna explains it in the next verses.

बलं बलवतां चाहं कामरागविवर्जितम्, धर्माविरुद्धो भूतेषु कामोऽस्मि भरतर्षभ |

Of the strong, I am the strength devoid of desire and passion. I am desire in beings, unopposed to Dharma. (VII.11)

So, bhai, your strength is God Himself, provided you stay away from passion and selfishness. It is the same with your desire for wealth and other things. Thus, you can have anything you want in this world; just know that God alone has become all your activity and its outcome.

Hmm. So, God is exclusive? He is present only in what is unselfish, right? How are then the followers of Abrahamic religions wrong in saying that the non-believers will go to hell?

No, no. Not at all. God is not and cannot be exclusive. It was said so earlier, too. But for a beginner it is said that God is in virtue, this being the simpler path of growth. Know that non-virtue also leads to God in the end, after the individual exhausts all their energy and will for non-virtuous pursuits. But we will not go into that since the discussion here is about the seekers, who, as they advance, realize that there is neither good nor bad – God alone is everything. This fact may be terrifying for those professing dualism, but for Hindus, it is common knowledge.

Who loves God?

You know, bhai, when I was young, I had selective devotion towards God like anyone else of that age. I used to pray only when I was facing some problem or anticipating one. What sincerity I had during my prayers, ah! And innocence! How I wish I had such intensity and innocence now! I am sure that you too must have gone through that phase of growth.

Yes, I had. I smiled at the naiveté of my childhood.

Most people fail to grow out of their childhood and so continue to pray in anticipation of something, or out of fear. Does God answer those prayers? I am not sure. If He did, a lot many schoolteachers would have been dead by now. I myself would have been the cause of many deaths, and experienced multiple deaths, since I have been into teaching for a long time.

I smiled. I, too, would have blood on my hands if God answered all my prayers. I asked, Why do people pray then?

That is partly because most people suffer from childhood syndrome, and because they like to have a shoulder to cry on. However, God takes care of only those who have surrendered their all – their very 'I'-ness to Him. The prayers that get answered otherwise are probably mere coincidences, since there is nothing called 'God's miracle' in the Hindu dharma.

Why pray then?

The first reason is that there are times when we might have exhausted all other resources. The second one is that God being our essence, it is our birthright to pray to Him. That, of course, does not mean that our prayers will be answered.

Then, according to your words, only saints can have the grace of God. But is it possible for a common person to give up all for God and become a saint?

There have been innumerable cases when a person gave up all support and took shelter in God, while for many others, the process was gradual. Remember, saints do not drop from heaven but are made here on the earth by working constantly on their virtues for many births.

What about you? How did you give up all?

Mine was a gradual process. In fact, I am not a believer in sudden conversion.

He then read out the two verses that discussed types of devotees.

चतुर्विधा भजन्ते मां जनाः सुकृतिनोऽर्जुन, आर्तो जिज्ञासुरर्थार्थी ज्ञानी च भरतर्षभ |
तेषां ज्ञानी नित्ययुक्त एकभक्तिर्विशिष्यते, प्रियो हि ज्ञानिनोऽत्यर्थमहं स च मम प्रियः |

Four types of people worship God – those in crisis, the curious, the favour seeker and jnani, that is, those who know God. Of them, jnani are the best. They are dear to God, and God is dear to them. (VII.16–17)

One cannot become a supreme devotee through a lukewarm effort. It takes many births to develop true love for God to become a jnani, the best among the devotees.

बहूनां जन्मनामन्ते ज्ञानवान्मां प्रपद्यते, वासुदेवः सर्वमिति स महात्मा सुदुर्लभः |

It is only after the efforts of many births that one becomes a jnani by realizing that God alone has become all this. Such souls are rare. (VII.19)

Swamiji, anyone can see in these verses that God is partial towards the jnani, and that it requires such huge effort to become a true devotee that it is not worth it for us. Don't you agree?

Of course, God is partial, he said with a wink. The fact is that everyone loves only themselves, that is, their Self. People love their spouse, children, wealth, etc. because they see their Self in all that. But a jnani sees only God as their Self, so they will naturally love God the best, and vice versa.

God is Atman, and Atman is God – it is obvious that God will love those who know themselves to be pure Atman!

I wasn't sure what to say to that. However, I felt good. It all seemed so logical.

Can one worship other gods?

He continued, It is important to know that God accepts the devotion of all and fixes their faith in what they worship. That is why you find so many religions, and even fanaticism.

यो यो यां यां तनुं भक्तः श्रद्धया अर्चितुम् इच्छति,
तस्य तस्याचलां श्रद्धां तामेव विदधामि अहम्|

Whatsoever form a devotee seeks to worship God, He makes that devotion unwavering. (VII.21)

There is nothing wrong in worshipping any god, demi-god or God. Till one has devotion towards the worshipped, all is well. With time, God will take care of such devoted persons. So, condemning others in the name of religion or God is a strict no.

It is difficult to know God

That is the reason why we should promote the learning of scriptures. Otherwise, people will pick up wrong ideas peddled by the semi-learned, and get lost in the maze of semi-spiritual ideas.

अव्यक्तं व्यक्तिम् आपन्नं मन्यन्ते मामबुद्धयः,
परं भावम् अजानन्तो मम् अव्ययम् अनुत्तमम् |

The ignorant regard Sri Krishna (or any such incarnation) as coming into existence like any common person, even though He remains un-manifested all the time. Such ignorant people do not realize that God is always infinite, unchanging and transcendental. (VII.24)

Even when God incarnates, Swamiji said, He is not a being in the way we are. Sri Rama, Sri Krishna and every other avatara are mere appearances, like waves in the ocean. We, the ordinary folks, think God to have become manifest, and to have been born or to have a body, but in fact they are always the infinite. This act of God – the infinite appearing in a finite human form – is a divine mystery that can be fully understood only after a lot of contemplation, or after the realization of God.

I can't say that I comprehend all that you are saying.

Bhai, spirituality is a technical subject, and like any technical subject, one has to prepare oneself for it before one can wade deeper. Spirituality is not what the elites of metro cities pick up in a parlour or in a spiritual camp as a part-time hobby; it is a deep subject that requires purity and perseverance for a long time.

For your convenience, let me end this chapter with a beautiful verse that compares the knowledge of the knower (God), with that of the known (us).

वेदाहं समतीतानि वर्तमानानि चार्जुन, भविष्याणि च भूतानि मां तु वेद न कश्चन |

God knows fully the beings of the past, present and the future, but the beings cannot know Him. (VII.26)

We, limited as we are because of our minds, can never know God, the infinite. After all, how can the finite know the infinite? But God knows us – always, everywhere. Thus, you cannot know God; you can only be one with Him by letting go of your 'I'.

Hmm. God takes everything, right?

Right! Swamiji answered.

That day's walk and talk had been good, exposing me to more new ideas.

Once more, as I lay on the edge of sleep, was that feeling of something waiting to be re-discovered ...

VIII

THE WAY TO BRAHMAN

Swamiji, are you married? I was not familiar with the ways of modern-day monks, so I asked.

He was startled and responded with an emphatic no. I was not sure why he put so much stress in his negation.

But the sages in the past used to marry, didn't they? I have heard of sages going astray to taste lust. I have also heard quite a few names of female sages from my grandfather, who in his old age was given completely to spirituality.

There is a difference between sages and monks, he said. However, from the viewpoint of their respective spiritual attainments, it is difficult to feel the difference. The sages had one leg in the society, but the monks were like warriors in the open, fighting their way out of the world with swords of detachment in both their hands. There are also special rituals connected with becoming a monk.

As for slipping on the path, it is quite natural. As Swami Vivekananda had famously said, 'The road to the Good is the roughest and steepest in the universe. It is a wonder that so many succeed, no wonder that so many fall. Character has to be established through a thousand stumbles.' (CW: VIII.383)

Why didn't you marry? You would have saved your chance of fall!

Nice question. But let me first ask you why you got married. And what guarantee is there that you will not go astray?

I didn't like his asking me about 'going astray' but realizing that I had started the conversation, I didn't protest. I gave the usual answer of marriage being the normal practice, and then added the importance of bodily needs, the need for companionship, etc.

No, all these are like flowers covering the carcass. The real reason is that 'Marriage is for the weak and celibacy for the strong.' Those who are vulnerable or with desires, which are forms of weakness, go for marriage; those who aspire for freedom at all costs, go for monasticism. Actually, we are all moving towards freedom – some with the help of crutches, and some others without those. Marriage and companionship, call them by any name, are the crutch of the emotionally impaired.

Swamiji, many of these Gen X or Gen Z people say that they do not believe in marriages and that they want to stay free. Your words seem to echo their views.

No way, bhai. I emphatically stressed on the dangers of 'freedom of the senses', and the importance of 'freedom from the senses' in life. I hope you remember that. Even if you forget everything that we discuss, do please try to remember that Gita teaches the importance of 'freedom from the senses' over 'freedom of the senses'. This is directly related to 'focus on work' and not 'focus on results'.

What these young people want is 'freedom of the senses'. They want the licence to behave like animals – eat, sleep, roam, mate freely – without taking on the responsibilities of society. The security of these very people is maintained through the sacrifice of others. They demand responsibility from parents, teachers, police, military, monks, politicians, but they themselves will never do what is expected of them.

The young ones are coming up with expressions like 'my life, my choice' or 'my body, my choice'. But the fact unknown to them is that they are developing severe personality issues. Give them the charge of the country for a few years, and we will be slaving for our enemy nations even before their period of rule ends.

Freedom can indeed be granted to those demanding it, but will they promise to keep our society safe for all? They would never do that – these spoilt, irresponsible brats reeking of their parents' money! My take on it is simple: behave the way you want to, but for that go to a desert or to some cave as your ancestors did millions of years ago. Do not poison society with your demonic desires.

Strong words indeed!

Continuing the thread of the discussion, he said, this contentious issue of the ultimate in spirituality has been an age-old problem. Householders wish to have enjoyment in the afterlife, too, with their loved ones, while the freedom worshippers want to be what they are – absolute Consciousness, known as Brahman, Atman, God, Nirvana, etc. The eighth chapter of Gita brings out these issues for both types beautifully. It is quite technical, so I will give you an overview of it, and then explain some of the verses that lie before us on our parikrama path.

Supreme spirit, soul, karma

Arjuna wanted to know the meaning of some technical terms of spirituality. And, as you can guess, Gita proposes questions not because Arjuna had asked them, but to maintain a storyline while discussing an otherwise intense subject. Sri Krishna explained those terms so that a *sadhaka* may understand these terms and then differentiate between the imperishable (*akshara*) and the perishable (*kshara*) to move ahead in their spiritual journey to the imperishable without meshing in the perishable.

1. *Brahman* – The Imperishable Supreme Reality that rules over everything, forever.
2. *Adhyatma/Svabhava* – Atman, the Reality (*tattva*) that exists in everyone as the innermost Self. In truth, the Adhyatma is Brahman itself.
3. *Karma* – The process of making an offering during a sacrifice. It requires giving up (by pouring the offerings) and is thus responsible for the welfare of those who perform this. This term should not be confused with ordinary work, or the law of Karma.

4. *Adhibhuta* – Every form of matter has an origin and dissolution, and hence is different from the non-perishable Atman. And yet, these are dependent on Atman (the consciousness) for their existence, and hence are known as adhibhuta. The whole range of products of Nature (prakriti) is kshara, and hence is adhibhuta.
5. *Adhidaivata* – Literally, the entity existing on the divine plane. This is God, in the form of Hiranyagarbha, who resides in the Solar Orb and sustains the organs of all creatures.

    According to Vedanta, every sense organ has a presiding deity that makes it function. The deity of a particular sense organ is also present at the cosmic level in the external world. Thus, the sun god is in the solar orb and is also the presiding deity of vision in beings. All such deities are the manifestation of Purusha (the Universal Self) in His subtle aspect known as Hiranyagarbha.
6. *Adhiyajna* – God sustains all the Vedic sacrifices and hence is called adhiyajna. All the bodily functions are like sacrifices (explained in chapter IV) and so, as the inner controller of the body, God is the adhiyajna who directs all the physical functions of the body.
7. *Attaining God at the time of death* – Those who remember God at the time of death, attain God.

All this was pretty technical for me. After all, we were discussing the practical aspects of Gita. But, as Swamiji had made clear, spirituality is an integral part of our daily existence, and so I guess we should know about its foundational terms to lead a meaningful life.

The last thought before death

Do you have any idea where you will go after death? he asked.

No, Swamiji, as I told you, I think my existence will cease once I am dead.

That is good, he commented. But where do you think your grandfather might have gone?

This was disturbing. I was not such a confirmed materialist to think that my grandfather, whom I loved so much, had vanished into thin air. O Culture, what a cruel thing you are! You train us to think the unthinkable and then laugh at our vulnerabilities! I could accept that I would cease to exist after my death, but to think the same for my son made me nervous. Our savage ancestors, who knew nothing about all this, were probably better off. Or even animals. But is it okay to wish to be an animal for such a small thing? I don't think so.

The set belief with us, said Swamiji, is that we become what we think of at the time of death. However, you can only think of your most fundamental thoughts at the time of death, which means you would most likely be thinking about your family, their well-being, your own suffering, and other such things, if you have been deep into these concerns all your life. That is why we Hindus have this tradition of singing *kirtan-bhajan* when someone is about to die, in the hope that devotional words may enter them and make them think of God. However, I am not sure if that works.

अन्तकाले च मामेव स्मरन्मुक्त्वा कलेवरम्, यः प्रयाति स मद्भावं याति नास्त्यत्र संशयः ।
यं यं वापि स्मरन्भावं त्यजत्यन्ते कलेवरम्, तं तमेवैति कौन्तेय सदा तद्भावभावितः ।

He, who at the time of death, meditating on God leaves his body, attains the state of God. A person becomes what their last thoughts are at the time of death. (VIII.5–6)

What one thinks at the last moments of their life determines the next birth. This means that one should always be absorbed in the thoughts of God, or else they won't be able to remember God at the time of death. This kind of absorption is possible only through constant practice since the mind has the tendency to be swayed by the inputs from the senses and memories.

Swamiji, you have spoken about rebirth many times, and as a Hindu I have also heard of it since my childhood. However, it somehow does not jell with modern thought. It does not seem logical.

Indeed, you cannot believe something that you have not experienced. So, knowledge about God, heaven, hell, rebirth and all such things have to come from the spiritual greats, since these can neither be proved nor disproved through usual arguments. In passing, may I ask whether you would dare question the validity of belief in God to followers of other religions? No, you won't. But when it comes to Hindu dharma, you are an Einstein of criticism. Why, bhai? Why this duplicity?

I mumbled this and that, which Swamiji ignored.

Since every religion accepts continuity of life after death in some form, the idea of rebirth is the most logical and profound explanation. After all, you cannot be in an eternal heaven or in eternal damnation for your acts committed in one life, howsoever bad those might be. It defies reasoning and sensibility. More importantly, hundreds of sages have confirmed this, so why should we unnecessarily get into a catfight that is not going to lead us to any meaningful conclusion?

Seen from the prism of philosophy, there are three ways of looking at what happens to us: blind chance, God's will, or Karma and rebirth. If chance and chaos were the ultimate truth, then we are indeed in a cruel, monstrous world. It sounds so painful, pessimistic and pathetic. If it was all due to God's will, then our miseries are due to God's whims. This sounds equally hopeless. The little positivity that we get in life is from the idea of Karma and rebirth, according to which you are free to change your destiny anytime you want.

Makes sense, Swamiji. But I don't find it acceptable.

Who cares! he said.

Freedom from rebirth

He then explained how one can attain Brahman, the supreme consciousness through sadhana.

ओम् इत्येकाक्षरं ब्रह्म व्याहरन् मामनुस्मरन्, यः प्रयाति त्यजन्देहं स याति परमां गतिम् |

One who gives up his body while remembering God, and chanting the sacred Om, attains the supreme spiritual state. (VIII.13)

The state of Brahman is attained by those who have self-control, are free from dualities, have conquered their passions, and constantly meditate on God. At the time of death, these greats withdraw their senses from everything else, focus their mind only on God, and then give up their body while uttering Om. These high-souled beings reach God and become freed from the cycle of birth and death.

Swamiji, why do you say attaining Brahman instead of knowing or seeing Brahman?

Knowing, seeing or any such act requires the medium of the mind, he said. But the real knower within us is the atman – the individual consciousness – which is beyond the mind's grasp. So, when individual consciousness realizes its true nature as universal, it attains what it was all along. Naturally, there can be no knowing or going or whatever else for the Self. When you wake up after your sleep, you do not know yourself afresh, or attain yourself – you continue to be what you are.

Excuse me, Swamiji, but just now you said that a yogi attains Brahman. Isn't there a contradiction?

Indeed, there is a contradiction, bhai. But this is being said from the perspective of those great souls who fail to know their real nature while leaving their body. These people, by meditation on God, attain that state at the time of death. Honestly, it is just a figure of speech.

He then continued.

आब्रह्म भुवनात् लोकाः पुनरावर्तिनोऽर्जुन, मामुपेत्य तु कौन्तेय पुनर्जन्म न विद्यते |
सहस्रयुगपर्यन्तम् अहर्यद् ब्रह्मणो विदुः, रात्रिं युगसहस्रान्तां तेऽहोरात्र विदो जनाः |
अव्यक्ताद् व्यक्तयः सर्वाः प्रभवन्ति अहरागमे, रात्र्यागमे प्रलीयन्ते तत्रैवाव्यक्तसंज्ञके |
भूतग्रामः स एवायं भूत्वा भूत्वा प्रलीयते, रात्रि आगमे अवशः पार्थ प्रभवति अहरागमे |

The dwellers of all the worlds – up to and including the world of Brahma, the creator – are subject to the miseries of repeated birth and death. But, after attaining God, one does not take birth again.

The knowers of the mystery of creation realize that the duration of creation lasts a thousand yugas (roughly 4.32 billion years) and that the duration of destruction also lasts as much.

All manifestations come out of the primal seed during the creative cycle, and they merge back into it during the destructive cycle.

The same multitude of beings comes into existence again and again at the time of the creative cycle; and merges back at the arrival of the destructive cycle. (VIII.16–19)

Everyone, except for the yogis who attain liberation directly or by meditating on God at the time of death, has to be reborn after death. Even those who, by the virtue of their meritorious deeds, reach the highest heaven must be reborn after a time. It is believed that the inhabitants of the highest heaven, known as Brahmaloka, enjoy the day of Brahma (9,58,81,60,000 human years). However, during Brahma's night (same span of time) they all disappear, only to reappear again during His next day. Thus, the cycle continues. Those who have not attained the Lord keep on evolving and involving in this vicious cycle.

Those who attain *atma jnana* (realize who they are) while alive, become free instantly, but the other types of yogis ascend to higher heavens through one of two paths:

1. Those who meditate on *Saguna Brahman* (God with form) take the solar path to reach Brahmaloka. At the end of the

cycle of Brahma (His hundred years, 30,91,73,76,00,00,000 human years), they get liberated.

2. Those who perform meritorious work like ritualistic actions, sacrifices, charity and other noble activities, take the lunar path, enjoy in various heavenly spheres and then are reborn on this earth to continue with their spiritual journey.

How do we know all this, Swamiji?

Don't take all this literally as many proponents of Hindu dharma have started doing in the present times. The idea is to impress on the mind of people that if they do not realize who they truly are then they are going to suffer for a long time.

The glory of yoga

परः त्स्मात्तु भावोऽन्यो अव्यक्तो अव्यक्तात् सनातनः,
यः स सर्वेषु भूतेषु नश्यत्सु न विनश्यति |
अव्यक्तो अक्षर इत्युक्तः तमाहुः परमां गतिम्, यं प्राप्य न निवर्तन्ते तद्धाम परमं मम |

(Nature is supreme) But there is another transcendental existence called Eternal Being that does not perish when all created beings perish. This is also known as the Supreme Abode. Those who attain that, do not take birth again. (VIII.20–21)

If you ever study the Upanishads, you will come across the teaching that just as the nave of a wheel does not move with the motion of the wheel, those who reach the nave of creation, that is, God, do not have to be born again. This state of no more motion is known as *Param Pada* – the supreme state.

A yogi who understands the terms explained at the beginning of this lesson, and also knows about these two paths, can never get deluded by the play of Nature that one sees everywhere. Such a yogi transcends everything, and thus reaches the Supreme Abode.

I gave a sigh of relief. Thank God it was over!

As I completed my notes, I had no idea what to make of them. But perhaps, as Swamiji said, life gains meaning only when you realize that it continues after death, and that life makes us whirl and twirl through endless births and deaths till we realize our divine nature, away from the material nature with which we identify.

Maybe he is right. After all, these are not products of his brain waves – they are mere explanations of what the sages have given us, and continue to give.

IX

THE ROYAL KNOWLEDGE

It had now become routine for me to join Swamiji on his morning walk of around seven kilometres, and then go back to my hotel for a bath, visit the temple, and conduct my affairs online. In the evenings I often went to the banks of Narmada where I watched the flowing water, and occasionally threw pebbles into it. At times I used to laugh remembering how tossing one of these stones had affected the trajectory of my life. Indeed, I was not becoming a convert – and even otherwise, conversion is an alien concept in our religion. Nevertheless, the essence of Gita had started seeping inside me very softly, like the falling of dew during winter nights.

Creation cannot be explained

That morning, Swamiji began with, Do you know how creation came into being?

Yes, of course. You described it while explaining the seventh chapter.

In that case Hindu dharma will become like an Abrahamic religion, with one God, one book, one theory of creation!

This is something funny about Swamiji. He would ask a question, and even if you answered with his own words, he would either contradict you or render it conditional.

Irritated, I said, But how can there be more than one theory of creation? That is irrational, confusing and unacceptable.

There is a beautiful hymn in the Veda, *Nasadiya Sukta*, that states why creation cannot be explained. This is the general idea that we Hindus accept. However, since there has to be some model to explain creation and its process, the Hindu spiritual tradition filled up the void not by one or two but with hundreds of theories of creation, some of which are meant for the masses and some for the learned. It is similar to having millions of gods to depict one infinite God who cannot be grasped by the mind and so cannot be expressed in words.

According to Vedanta, which is the most popular philosophy of the Hindus in present times, creation is a product of Maya.

Before he could proceed further, I cut him with, You know Swamiji, I admire this concept of Maya neither because it is a grand concept, nor because I have heard about it since my childhood, but because I love how you people can prove anything with its help. It is like the number zero in mathematics, which can be used with the numbers to do any kind of juggling! Use it in multiplication and all numbers become like a socialist state – equal without being equal!

Use it in subtraction and numbers become like a capitalist state – keep what you have; use it in addition and numbers become like a welfare state, where nothing changes in spite of the doles by the Government; use it in division and you have the infinity of the mythical kingdoms! Tell me Swamiji, can't you people come up with anything better than Maya?

Swamiji's laughter! Ah! His trim belly shook heavily, revealing how innocent he was. If one has to judge a person by their laughter, the richest will end up at the south of the graph. As for me, I was not going to give up my riches only to laugh freely. Nah!

Managing to stop his laughter, Swamiji said, A fool and his wealth soon part ways. So, it is not surprising that you are able to create and hold on to your wealth, bhai. But with due respect to your objection, I must reiterate that Maya is the only way to explain the process of infinite appearing as finite. As you rightly pointed out, a number divided by zero will throw up strange results. So, to avoid getting swamped by strangeness, we use the term Maya, which actually means the phenomenon of a thing appearing as something else, often with opposite nature. It is like mistaking a rope for a snake in darkness.

Swamiji, don't you people get bored using the same snake-rope theory again and again?

No, we don't. Actually, every religion has to contend with this problem of the infinite becoming finite, but none of them has succeeded in coining a term for it. Abstract thinking used to be the forte of the Hindus, and that is how we came up with the concept and coinage of zero. It was due to the same power of comprehending the abstract that we came up with the concept of Maya, which gives a rationale as to how the infinite appears as finite.

We have previously discussed how creation, as an act of God, is actually Maya only. Why? It is like a mirage in a desert. The desert is real, but the water of mirage is real only till one comes to know of its true nature. The universe, with all its beings, is actually God only, but it appears as having a different identity. The fact is that there is nothing in this universe that can be called matter or unconscious or mind – it is all pure consciousness. The universe is something like water becoming ice and getting various forms and shapes while retaining its nature as water at all times.

Who will believe all this, Swamiji?

Why bother about who will believe the truth? When Galileo was prosecuted for saying that the earth revolves around the sun, he had to apologize to save himself from punishment from the church. While coming out, he had muttered, 'Nevertheless, it revolves around the sun!' We all now know the truth.

Is God the Creator?

He then continued, The magical transformation of consciousness appearing as mind and matter is affected due to Prakriti, which is the mother of all energy. But the real source of power comes due to the presence of God behind It.

मयाध्यक्षेण प्रकृतिः सूयते सचराचरम्, हेतुनानेन कौन्तेय जगद्विपरिवर्तते |

It is due to the presence of God that Prakriti produces all this, the moving and the unmoving. And it is because of God that the world wheels round and round. (IX.10)

This verse explains many things. It implies that anything that has motion is not conscious but belongs to the realm of energy. Since the mind has motion, it too is a kind of energy-matter. Thus, consciousness as understood by the Western world is not same as what we know. To be spiritual means to get out of all motion and be what you are – consciousness.

Also, the relationship between God and creation is not direct, meaning that God does not create the universe, and hence He is in no way responsible for its defects. To understand this, imagine a transformer with primary and secondary coils. The primary coil is powered by the powerhouse, which induces current in the secondary coil. The supply that we get from the electric companies is not direct but induced. The defects of a transformer, wiring or a fused bulb are local problems, and these have nothing to do with the powerhouse.

What if the powerhouse itself generates the wrong voltage?

Do not take examples literally. God being Absolute consciousness, there can never be any kind of defect or variation. Similarly, the functions of the secondary coil and the local supply do not affect the manufacturing unit in any way. Likewise, our acts do not affect God in any way. But remember that this is just an example to make things clear. It also shows how we all are dependent on God and yet we appear to be independent. Get out of this fake independence and be free. This is the whole of religion. In short, you are divine, and so you better start behaving like that.

God: the divine father, mother and sustainer

Swamiji broke off the thread of conversation and asked me, Have you ever loved anyone?

Of course, Swamiji! What kind of question is this? Can life run without the love of father and mother? Can we continue living without –

Before I could finish what I was saying, he interrupted with, I asked whether you have ever loved someone.

Of course, I asserted with a smile. Swamiji had stressed exactly like this when he had answered my question in the negative when I asked about his marriage. How the tables had turned. Throw of dice, you resemble life so much!

God alone is love, he said. You love only what you know, and you know only what exists – even if that be your imagination or memory. Since God alone exists, He alone is knowledge and love. So, what we experience as love is actually God. Moreover, He being the creator and sustainer, He alone is the real provider of all that you have. He alone is our real father, mother, friend – everything. This is now explained.

पिताहमस्य जगतो माता धाता पितामहः, वेद्यं पवित्रमोंकार ऋक्साम यजुरेव च |
गतिर्भर्ता प्रभुः साक्षी निवासः शरणं सुहृत्, प्रभवः प्रलयः स्थानं निधानं बीजमव्ययम् |
तपाम्यहम् अहं वर्षं निगृह्णामि उत्सृजामि च, अमृतं चैव मृत्युश्च सत् असत् चाहमर्जुन |

I (Lord Krishna as God) am the Father of this world, the Mother, the Sustainer, the Grandfather, the Purifier, the (one) thing to be known, sacred Om, and also the Rik, Saman and Yajus. I am the Supreme Goal of all living beings, and I am also their Sustainer, Master, Witness, Abode, Shelter and Friend. I am the Origin, End and Resting Place of creation; I am the Repository and Eternal Seed. (As sun) I give heat: I withhold and send forth rain; I am immortality and also death; being and non-being am I, O Arjuna! (IX.17–19)

Swamiji, please don't mind my saying this, but God sounds like a narcissist. I am this, I am that; I can do this, I can do that! Don't you agree?

He offered me an indulgent smile and then explained the idea behind these verses. He said, Let us go back to the example of the primary coil, secondary coil and electrical gadgets. Now imagine, just imagine, these all having a conscious personality. Now if a gadget wants to know its relation with the powerhouse, won't it say something similar? For instance, 'I am the light of the bulb, I am the sound of the speaker, I am the flicker of the cursor!'

You have a point there, Swamiji.

Everything that is within our ken – secular or sacred – including the Vedas, their divisions and content as mentioned in these verses, are God alone. There is nothing that is not God Himself. It is due to our limitedness that we see objects and persons as separate from God.

God shoulders the burden

It all sounded logical, but it indeed had drawbacks, so I asked, Hasn't such an outlook made people weaklings in India? Knowing that God does everything and is everything, a person is bound to become lazy, the way we Indians have been. What would you say to that?

Indeed, you are correct. However, the idea that God is the provider holds only for those whose minds are totally absorbed in God, and who care nothing for themselves. These are the people who have grown beyond selfishness and self-identification to be dependent on God the way a baby depends on her mother. God as a provider is relevant only for them, as is expressed wonderfully in this verse.

अनन्याः चिन्तयन्तो मां ये जनाः पर्युपासते, तेषां नित्याभियुक्तानां योगक्षेमं वहाम्यहम् |

Those who always think of Me and are in constant devotion to Me, whose minds are always absorbed in Me, I provide them with what they lack and preserve what they already have. (IX.22)

The phrase योगक्षेमं वहाम्यहम् – *yoga kshemam vahami aham* – caught my attention. I asked him whether this is the phrase used by the Life Insurance Corporation of India – the famous insurance company. He nodded his assent.

Yes, we are still fortunate enough to have Sanskrit phrases and names in our premier programmes and projects. Who knows? Someday all this may go for a toss!

God takes care only of those who have the traits I have described. In that case, who provides for people like you who do not even give two hoots for God? Well, God provides for them, too, but through fruits of their labour. You get what your efforts have been, and your results do not go to someone else, since God is the *vidhata* (superintendent) of all. So, the spiritually lazy will only get a big naught, and the spiritually conscious will get the bare minimum of what they need. For more, we all have to labour!

I loved that, believe me!

This verse reminds me of a traditional story, said he. Would you care to hear it?

Of course, said I.

There was a poor but learned Brahmin who had been starving for some days due to lack of provisions at home, as was the norm in earlier times. Disgusted with this verse, he corrected the expression to *dadami aham*, meaning 'I give', instead of *vahami aham*, meaning 'I carry', in his manuscript, and then went to some other village in the hope of getting some dana, financial help. During his absence, Lord Krishna, dressed like a poor village boy, came to the lady of the house, carrying a huge basket of provisions, and said that her husband had sent them. The lady then noticed red marks on the back of the beautiful young boy. When asked, he said that her husband had beaten him up for not carrying the load. The lady could not believe him, knowing well how tender her husband was. So, when the Brahmin returned empty-handed in the evening, she scolded him for being a brute to have beaten up a young boy mercilessly. When he heard the whole story, he realized that the boy was Lord Krishna himself who had carried the provisions for his devotee, and that the corrections made by him were the red marks on his body. He started crying piteously and erased the corrections, with profuse apologies to the Lord.

Quite a touching story, Swamiji. But do you really believe it?

Who am I to pass my judgement on the veracity of a popular story? The lessons from such stories and myths are the subtle ideas that cannot be grasped by human minds in the usual ordinary way. Myths are neither true nor false – they are simply myths to convey a profound and subtle idea. We in India have a huge number of myths related to God for the same reason, that is, to take people from the gross ideas about God to the subtle reality.

Oh!

Incidentally, did you ever realize that you can know the soul of a society by the myths that it tells its children?

No, I had never thought along those lines.

Fairytales, Aesop's fables, *Harry Potter*, the folktales from *One Thousand and One Nights* – all these are the voices of the culture that speak about their soul. Compare these with the stories of the divine in India, and you will know why we are the true religious country.

I needed to sit down.

Rituals to worship God

Do you know what rituals are?

Of course, I knew what rituals were. I was at Omkareswar, and the temple itself was bathed in rituals. Another nearby temple town, Ujjain, probably had many more rituals which began with *bhasma arati*. More importantly, who in India does not know about rituals? After all, we in India breathe rituals from one morning to the next, and bathe in it from birth to death. If there is something that India can export easily, it is rituals. In fact, many non-resident Indians have started carrying rituals to other countries; perhaps we will invade the world with our rituals soon.

Rituals are philosophy in action. Be that of religion, schools, military, society – wherever you see ritual, know that it is the concretized version of the philosophy practiced by that group. It is through rituals that cohesion and unbreakable bounds are created among the members of a group. Rituals also help the learners and the learned form a mental structure that helps them move from one state of being to another.

I don't think I understand, I said.

You might have noticed how, during your school days, when the bell rang to mark the end of one period, it shattered the continuity of the class, whether absorbing or boring, and prompted you to wait for a change. This is detachment; this is compartmentalizing. The ringing of a bell is a ritual that marks the end of something, and the beginning of something else which may not be connected with the previous act. This is how the mind gets trained to face the world, and how our armies train recruits to face enemy bullets. A wonderful thing these rituals are, bhai! Blessed are those who follow rituals in their daily life.

I was taken aback. Did some of my problems stem from a lack of rituals in my daily life? I was not sure.

In religion, rituals play a similar role, in which a person cuts themselves off from the world and engage their mind with the Divine. There is always the fear of rituals becoming extra luggage, but you cannot let a wonderful instrument go waste simply because of some ignoramus acting silly. Indeed, in Hindu tradition, prayers and worship to idols play a very important role.

But Swamiji, people these days prefer calling themselves spiritual instead of religious. Shouldn't you heed to popular sentiments and reduce rituals?

Well, new ads are regularly produced to market the inferior. The same is true with religion. Some spiritually challenged and intellectually impaired people have attempted to import regressive ideas and force them down the throats of the people of the fertile lands of the Indian subcontinent. Take my words, they did not succeed in the past, nor will they ever see a sliver of success in the future. To be spiritual means to start with rituals. Otherwise, you end up with a big fat vacuum both inside and outside. Just look at Buddhism and its love for rituals and ritualistic meditation in the hope of getting the enlightenment of void! If even the void requires rituals, how much more rituals would the realization of the 'whole' require, since God is whole?

Swamiji, you can be scathing!

Why should I be scathing? I told you earlier how I am a realist rooted in idealism. I won't prefer any other noun or adjective for myself. The rituals of the Hindu religion have been quite elaborate since the Vedic period, that is, at least for 10,000 years. This can be daunting for ordinary folk.

More importantly, a true devotee does not require elaborate rituals – they can go into the depths of their being in an instant. So, the gracious Lord says

पत्रं पुष्पं फलं तोयं यो मे भक्त्या प्रयच्छति, तदहं भक्ति उपहृतम् अश्रामि प्रयतात्मनः |

Even a leaf, a flower, a fruit or water offered to Me with devotion is enough to please me. (IX.26)

A word of caution here! Do not confuse Sri Krishna with a personal God but know that God came as Sri Krishna. So, wherever Gita says 'I', its direct meaning is God.

The best offering to God is when one offers all that they do, think or speak to Him.

यत्करोषि यदश्नासि यज्जुहोषि ददासि यत्, यत् तपस्यसि कौन्तेय तत्कुरुष्व मदर्पणम् |

Whatever you do, whatever you eat, whatever you offer as oblation to the sacred fire in a yajna, whatever gift you make, and whatever austerities you perform, do them as an offering to me. (IX.27)

All our pains, miseries, fears, greed, expectations and other such limiting qualities are with us simply because we think ourselves to be the ultimate in the universe. We behave like a dog in the manger, trying to grab all that can be snatched, but failing to do so simply because there is too much to take from this world.

If you want peace in life and want to grow, then offer all your acts and thoughts to God. Offer your food, veg or non-veg; drinks, soft or hard; smoke, plain or weed, to God before you let them enter inside you, and you will change forever. In the Tantra tradition, this kind of offering played a very important role to sublimate one's base desires. And the weed smokers used to worship Lord Shiva, imagining that He did so, too!

I could not suppress my laughter at the absurdity of God smoking weed.

Yes, we have this strong tradition in India of offering all that we love to God before enjoying it. Try it yourself, and you will see the impact. In fact, you can extend such feelings towards your wife and children, too.

Wife and children, I repeated. Something stirred deep within me. I went silent.

Swamiji instantly felt what I felt but did not mention it. Instead, he read out the last part of the penultimate verse.

Spirituality in one sentence

अनित्यमसुखं लोकमिमं प्राप्य भजस्व माम् |

Realize that this world and existence here is transitory and lacking joy, and then love God with all your heart. (IX.33)

What more needs to be said about this verse? It sums up the essence of spirituality, life, happiness, meaningfulness, mindfulness – name anything and this half-verse sums that up.

There was a massive tenderness in Swamiji's voice and words when he said this. He was probably honouring my feelings or maybe he himself was stirred with devotion.

He continued, The earlier verses here explain how anyone, irrespective of gender, class, learning, nationality and other such distinguishing factors, can have devotion for God, without worrying for any limiting adjunct that the society may have put on them. God is for all, but the society is for the privileged even in a democracy. Whether you are a meat eater or a wine drinker – such discrimination belongs to the society and the world. But God is beyond all this. In fact, I refuse to bow before a God who discriminates on any count. You can go on shouting that your God is like father, merciful, delivering justice and all other such big words, but I will never ever bow before the God who discriminates and keeps upgrading hells for the non-believers.

Oh God!

What is needed in life is to love God and God alone. And how can you love God when you are still entrenched in the pettiness of the world? What is this world but a bazaar of trinkets? We, like immature kids, love to play with these trinkets to find happiness in how they look and sound. Worse, we make even God a plaything, so how can we ever feel the sheer joy of loving God? To do that, you first have to realize that you have surrounded yourself with the breakable toys of the world, and that you need to let all those go if you want to love the real amidst the unreal.

Swamiji had become passionate, but he calmed down and said something wonderful.

Bhai, you might wonder about my life, achievements, purpose and other such things. It so happens that after being a monk for many years, and knowing this verse for decades, one day I was hit by the enormity of what the phrase was conveying. I now have one and only one goal, path and support: *anityam asukhamlokam imam prapya bhajasva mam*. I will feel blessed and fulfilled once I am established in the truth conveyed by it, he said and went silent.

After I had finished writing this paper in the dead of that night, I cried copiously.

X

GOD EVERYWHERE

A noisy group of college students overtook us on the parikrama path. They were on some kind of religious adventure of which running, jogging, shouting and singing seemed to be essential rituals. We were around halfway through the trek, and the group needed a bit of rest after their creative nonsense. They sat down, chattering and aping the primates hovering around, discussing silly nothings.

Guru and chela, one commented. It was not even a hint but a direct assault.

Let us put a bet on who is trying to extract from whom? Does the chela want blessings for success, or does the Guru want to lighten the chela's purse?

Last night's pain got converted into annoyance, and so I walked up to them and asked if they wanted to know more about us, to which one young lady retorted, You seem to have the sensitivity of irritant dermatitis. Don't we have the freedom to talk among ourselves? If you are so self-obsessed then you better stay glued to your office cubicle.

I breathed hard and fought the temptation to tell them who I was. But I paused. One good thing about being a high achiever is that you outgrow the need to wear your success like a badge. Still, I wished to say something unpleasant to the unbridled, when Swamiji called me back and turned his back on the group whispering, Never argue with a mixed group. They may even tear their own clothes simply to blame you. I have seen such cases. Just let it go.

I breathed deep to feel at ease. The group made more remarks and jogged away.

Swamiji, what are you people doing to educate the future generation? Of what use are your Upanishads and Puranas and even Gita when you cannot take care of the young? These very people may someday end up on the wrong side of drugs, sex, harmony and tranquillity. Do something for them.

My emotions were throbbing within my calm words.

Wah! It is your society and your children, and you expect us to do the cleaning and washing of the blunders that you parents have been committing? Society has come to such a pass that there can be no discipline at home, school, college – nowhere. So, who will tame the wild? The onus then falls on the court or the police to instil discipline in these value-challenged folks. Many of them will end up at the clinic of a shrink or at some Babaji's ashram, hoping for the miracle that will never come. Mark my words, India will soon be ruined unless society takes it upon itself to discipline their young.

I once heard a lady proudly proclaim that she was the best friend of her daughter. I wanted to ask her, who will then play the role of the child's mother? A child needs all kinds of relations to grow up. That does not mean that you will roll up all those relations into one person. In the name of modernity, you people are only parading stupidity. Remember that training hastens perfection. Training is like putting a hedge around young plants to save them from the attacks of the wild. But no, you people, claiming to be GenZ or whatever rot that might be, would rather be ruined than disciplined. What a price this liberalism demands!

As for me, I see these young ones taking the longer path to spiritual perfection, as I told you earlier. Indiscipline is like taking a long detour to your goal. God is everything – the good and the bad. So, even when you are going wild, you are with God only, but on a longer path of knowing God as God.

In fact, the tenth wonderful chapter of Gita shows how God has become everything – even secretive acts and cheating.

Moving beyond the taunts of the raucous group, Swamiji started explaining how God is present in everything.

God alone is virtues and shortcomings

He said, Every creature and human being has various qualities and attributes which distinguish one from the other. Qualities like intelligence, strength, speed, knowledge, wisdom, fear, courage, cunning and honesty have a common source of origin, since these cannot have an independent existence. We believe that these all come from consciousness. Do not confuse this consciousness with the activities of the mind, since even those activities have consciousness as the basis.

And what is consciousness? It is God. So, whatever special quality that you see, personified or impersonal, is God Himself.

Interesting, said I.

Once you realize that the qualities and achievements that you consider your personal possessions are actually from God, you will become humble instead of being vain. Similarly, the shortcomings of your personality, too, are from God. Nay, they are God Himself. If you realize this then you will never feel dejected. Instead you might want to outgrow your defects and be one with God, the repository of all qualities. You will also learn to accept your impairments with dignity. This is what this chapter is about.

Also, it is not possible for a simple-hearted person to accept God as being vicious, so it is customary to focus more on the nobler things that one sees in society. Sri Krishna thus says:

बुद्धिर्ज्ञानम् असम्मोहः क्षमा सत्यं दमः शमः, सुखं दुःखं भवोऽभावो भयं चाभयमेव च |
अहिंसा समता तुष्टिस्तपो दानं यशोऽयशः, भवन्ति भावा भूतानां मत्त एव पृथग्विधाः |

Intellect, knowledge, non-delusion, forbearance, truth, restraint of the external senses, calmness of heart, happiness, misery, birth, death, fear, as well as fearlessness, non-injury, evenness, contentment, austerity, benevolence, good name, (as well as) ill-fame, etc. arise from Me alone. (X.4–5)

Swamiji, what will anyone do with these qualities? Can these get us money? Or happiness? Or security? Will I be able to run my business with these? Do you know how much debt today's students have to take on to complete a degree?

Will these values help them? Why do you people keep talking about values, values and values? Aren't these as outdated as religion itself?

Bhai, Jesus had famously said that a man cannot live by bread alone. He meant to say that there are higher things in life beyond your belly and bread. If Gandhiji is admired today in the world, it is only because he was established in certain values. People are respected in society for their values and not because of the loot that they have amassed. Do you respect the match-fixers? Do you respect the inside traders? Do you respect the fakes? That is because the practice of values helps you become a real super-achiever. Try practising these in your business and someday you may thank me for guiding you to greatness. If Gandhiji could practice these in politics, which is the nest for you-know-what-kind of people, why can't you practise these in your business? The problem is that you don't have the courage and patience to practise these. Blame not values for sheepishness in men but your own weakness in implementing these.

I wanted to protest, but he cut me short with, Our society evolved from the level of apes in millions of years, and simply because some of you want to go back to the state of being animals, that cannot be made the philosophy of all. Even otherwise, do you people have any philosophy of life other than 'eat, sleep and mate'? Be an animal if you want to, but do not drag down those who want to remain human.

You are getting personal, Swamiji!

There is nothing personal about what I said. Regardless, when you are in a discussion, you have to be ready to be addressed personally, too. It is typical of you people to argue in the vein of: 'I will eat my cake and keep it, too'. Wah, bhai wah!

I maintained an angry silence.

He continued.

The enumeration of qualities here is not exhaustive but merely suggestive. But once you realize this fact, you become spiritual, and not until then. That does not mean that you will go all out for God, but there will always be some fortunate ones who do, after understanding that they would want to be in the nearness of God, as explained in the next verses.

Also worth noting here is the mention of ill fame coming from God! Just see how everything comes from God – all good and bad. Actually, both good and bad have roles to play in our lives. When adversity due to our bad habits hits us, it makes us move upward towards God, and when things are favourable, we feel the temporary respite of rest.

Wait, Swamiji. Do you mean to say that success is like a resting place?

Indeed, yes. The only purpose of our existence is to move towards knowing who we are. Adversity helps us more in that journey than the favourable. Swimming against the current gives you more powerful muscles than floating with the current.

Do you mean to say that we should choose suffering and adversity to be spiritual?

No, no. Choosing pain is as bad as choosing pleasure. The goal is to let things come to you on their own in life.

Imagine yourself swimming in a river. When you move downstream, there may be various things floating around you, of which you can choose what to surround yourself with. Thus, you can push a carcass away from you, and float freely with, say, flowers. But if you are swimming upstream, then you won't have the choice of being with this or that. When you start accepting things as they come, know that you have grown internally.

Buddhi Yoga: How God blesses a devotee

मच्चित्ता मद्गतप्राणा बोधयन्तः परस्परम्, कथयन्तश्च मां नित्यं तुष्यन्ति च रमन्ति च |
तेषां सततयुक्तानां भजतां प्रीतिपूर्वकम्, ददामि बुद्धियोगं तं येन मामुपयान्ति ते |
तेषामेव अनुकम्पार्थम् अहम् अज्ञानजं तमः, नाशयामि आत्मभावस्थो ज्ञानदीपेन भास्वता |

Those, who stay absorbed in me and who find pleasure only in talking about Me, the God, to them I give that Buddhi Yoga which destroys the darkness of ignorance by the luminous lamp of knowledge, and thus they attain Me. (X.9–11)

God does not bless you by sending you to some heaven or by sending you camel loads of wealth. What He does is make your intellect firm in the understanding of spiritual matters. Once you have that, you can attain anything that you want. This is known as *Buddhi Yoga* – the divine knowledge – which removes every trace of worldliness from the mind forever.

This happens only to those who are constantly into God, as the verse explains.

God has become all

अहमात्मा गुडाकेश सर्वभूताशयस्थितः, अहमादिश्च मध्यं च भूतानामन्त एव च |
आदित्यानामहं विष्णुः ज्योतिषां रविरंशुमान्, मरीचिः मरुतामस्मि नक्षत्राणामहं शशी |
वेदानां सामवेदोऽस्मि देवानामस्मि वासवः, इन्द्रियाणां मनश्चास्मि भूतानामस्मि चेतना |

I am the consciousness in all beings; the beginning, the middle and the end of all. Of the Adityas, I am Vishnu; of luminaries, the radiant Sun; of the winds, I am Marichi; of the stars, the Moon. I am the Sama Veda of the Vedas, and Vasava (Indra) of the gods; of the senses I am mind, and sentience in living beings am I. (X.20–22)

These and all such verses only show how God alone is the essence and the basis of everything. This is best appreciated when you look at the best of a group.

प्रह्लादश्चास्मि दैत्यानां कालः कलयतामहम्, मृगाणां च मृगेन्द्रोऽहं वैनतेयश्च पक्षिणाम् |

I am Prahlad amongst the daityas; amongst all that controls I am time. Know me to be the lion amongst animals, and Garuda amongst the birds. (X.30)

Daityas and *Adityas* are two classes of divine beings who were born of Sage Kashyapa but of different mothers – Diti and Aditi, who were sisters. Although co-brothers, these two groups have always been at war with each other.

अक्षराणाम् अकारोऽस्मि द्वन्द्वः सामासिकस्य च, अहमेवाक्षयः कालो धाताहं विश्वतोमुखः |
मृत्युः सर्वहरश्चाहम् उद्भवश्च भविष्यताम्, कीर्तिः श्रीर्वाक्च नारीणां स्मृतिर्मेधा धृतिः क्षमा |

I am the first alphabet 'A' amongst all letters; I am the copulative compound (dual word) in grammatical compounds. I am the endless Time, and amongst creators I am Brahma. I am the all-devouring death, and I am the origin of those things that are yet to be. In women, I am kirti (fame), sri (prosperity), vak (refined speech), smriti (memory), medha (intelligence), dhriti (courage) and kshama (forgiveness). (X.33-34)

The feminists may object to the idea of women having special qualities like *kirti*, *sri*, *vak*, *smriti*, *medha*, *dhriti* and *kshama*, but the facts cannot be negated. This idea of women having special qualities is so prevalent in India that these qualities have become names.

So, you agree that the Hindu outlook goes against gender equality? The critics of our religion have been saying this for decades.

Who are these critics? Can you specify them? Whosoever they might be, remember that they are never specific about their criticism of the philosophy and outlook of Hinduism. Also, look around and tell me which system in the world that has run for so long is perfect? Just look at socialism. What happened to ideas of social equality within a hundred years? The poor going up in smoke and the powerful becoming billionaires! And, as for Hindus, we believe in gender speciality, which goes way beyond gender equality.

That was a blast from Swamiji – 'gender speciality'. I had never come across this expression. Nice!

To add to that, the moment you use the word 'gender', you admit to inequality and division. To be gender neutral would mean to get rid of the very term. Think over it, young man, and you will realize how you people are simply big on words and hollow on ideas.

However, find one culture – just one society or culture – that treats women as special keepers of the unmatchable qualities mentioned in these verses. Women have been treated as second-class citizens all over the world, but it is only the Hindu race that has cherished them with utmost respect. Note it!

But Swamiji, just see what is happening in our country to women. There is no equality. Isn't religion responsible for that?

The problem with you people is that you compare the grandiose principles of an impractical system with the worst practices of our society. Just now you were talking about me getting personal. What are you doing now? Why are you bringing in practices while discussing Hindu ideals? Learn to be fair during arguments by comparing ideals with ideals, and practices with practices. Do not behave like the opposition parties in a Parliament. Know that if our forefathers failed to implement the ideals, blame that then on their helplessness, and not on the scriptures.

Considering everything, Gita has the highest ideals and outlooks that have been practised by many Indians. The failure of some cannot be claimed to be a collective failure of the society or religion.

God in gambling!

A stocky silence ballooned between us. We waited in silence for a while, and then he got up, patted me, and read out the verse that stood before us.

द्यूतं छलयताम् अस्मि तेजस्तेजस्विनाम् अहम्,
जयोऽस्मि व्यवसायोऽस्मि सत्त्वं सत्त्ववताम् अहम् |

I am the gambling of the cheats and the power of the powerful; I am the victory of the victorious, the resolve of the resolute, and the virtue of the virtuous. (X.36)

Cheating, of all types, is merely an obedient subject of His Majesty – gambling! And God is that! Empires have changed hands in India due to gambling, and Gita, which you are hearing from me right now, is the finale of cheating in the gambling match between the Kauravas and the Pandavas. Indeed, gambling is the king of all cheatings, and that verily is God!

God is in every glory

He then concluded that morning's discussion with:

यदत् यत् विभूतिमत् सत्त्वं श्रीमत् उर्जितमेववा, तत् तदेवावगच्छ त्वं मम तेजोंऽशसम्भवम् |

Whatever you see as splendid, glorious or powerful, know that to be a spark of My splendour. (X.41)

So, I can clearly see the presence of God's splendour in your success and riches, he said mischievously. In turn, you, too, should learn to see the Lord's presence wherever you see beauty, success, love, knowledge or strength. Every success and every quality that you see anywhere is the glowing presence of God. Know this and become blessed.

Near midnight, after my work for the day was over, I completed my notes. Thinking over the day's conversation, I found it amusing that my achievements are not mine, nor God's grace, but the presence of God's *vibhuti* – the divine splendour. If Swamiji had stuck to the idea of God's grace, I might have contested him fiercely, but the content of this chapter instead appeared so fresh and soothing!

Most importantly, revolutionary.

XI

GOD'S COSMIC FORM

We were going to discuss Chapter XI of Gita that day, which has been made famous by J. Robert Oppenheimer, the great scientist who quoted from it when the first atomic bomb detonated under his supervision. I mentioned that to Swamiji, who, as expected, knew about it.

What are spiritual visions?

In turn, he asked me how I would react if God appeared before me, and in what form I would like to see Him.

I was taken aback by the abruptness of the question.

Swamiji, I have no idea about this, so I can't comment. Moreover, my belief in God is sketchy at best. But since you ask, I may expect God to appear as Sri Rama or may be as Sri Krishna, or Shiva.

He asked, Does it make you wonder how a Christian will see God?

Interesting. I have never thought along those lines. But I wonder whether it will be impacted by their belief that their God alone is true.

They would indeed be correct if God were to be a finite something with a defined form. But God is infinite, so He can appear before you in any form. Isn't it?

True.

To think that here we are in this physical world and then there is the infinite God, with nothing in between, is quite irrational. There must be layers of existence, varying in their subtleness. So, the popular projection that the soul departs from the body at death and lands in some fixed heaven with this and that luxury is simply ridiculous.

Maane? I broke out in Hindi, and then added, But science does not believe in the description of the universe that you are giving!

No doubt that science does not believe in all that, said he. But it does believe in people having different kind of talents as compared with animals. It also believes in people having an affinity for numbers, words, colours, music, abstraction, etc. Do you know that there are people who see the numerator and denominator of a fraction in different colours?

No, I did not know that.

There are also people who can grasp things very quickly while others take a lot of time to understand even simple matters. The terms we use for those who grasp a subject quickly are intelligent, talented, prodigy, genius, etc. However, we in India often use the expression *sukshma buddhi* to denote the grasping power of a person, although we do not know why some people have that buddhi and others do not. But the idea that the power of perception varies from person to person is universal.

Our senses and organs are actually quite opaque, like glazed glasses, and so these can only perceive the physical world in its crudest form and thus allow us to live the simplest way of life, like reptiles that live only for bare survival with their rudimentary brain. However, many of us have incisive intellect that can pierce through the layers of an object and see things that usually do not meet our eyes. All great scientists have such power.

Beyond this kind of intelligence, there is a different type of talent that can make people see through the covering of the physical to unravel their subtle nature. Actually, as explained many times earlier, the real power of knowing is through the Atman since it alone is conscious. When it looks at the universe through the senses, it is like looking at things through semi-opaque lenses. When the Atman frees itself from its identification with the physical body, it looks at the universe with a different set of senses that belong to our subtle body. We, the ordinary, have no idea about this body but the yogis know about it well, and it is through this body, senses and mind that most spiritual knowledge is acquired. The spiritual visions about which you might have heard are invariably experienced through this subtle body.

If a person, through meditation or otherwise, can acquire the power to detach themselves from the physical body, they can then move effortlessly from the subtle world to the physical. You may wonder if that is acceptable. Well, had there been only one such person with this kind of knowledge, we might then have treated that as an aberration, but history is so full of persons with this special talent that the existence of the subtle world, percolating the physical, cannot be overlooked. This is what I mentioned earlier. The subtle universe with different kinds of existence and folks envelops us.

It was all Greek to me. If spirituality is about all this, then I will never be a successful student of spirituality.

More special than people having this kind of power are those who can impart the power to perceive the subtle universe to a potentially great spiritual person by a mere touch or word.

Is that possible, Swamiji? This sounded interesting, almost like acquiring a magical wand.

Should you search for the perfect Guru?

Let me narrate to you a famous incident that took place between Sri Ramakrishna and Swami Vivekananda, who was then known as Narendranath. At their very first meeting, Sri Ramakrishna realized the potential of the future world-mover, although Narendranath felt nothing special about his would-be Guru.

You know, this simple incident shows how you should never try to find the right Guru for yourself, since you will never be able to know the greatness of a person even if he stands in front of you. To judge a person, you have to be greater than him. So be happy with anyone who teaches you spirituality. If you are sincere, then God will send other teachers to you if you need them. In fact, it took years of bumbling around for Narendranath to accept Sri Ramakrishna as what he was – God.

Sri Ramakrishna encountered Narendranath on different occasions to give him glimpses of the subtle world. It was through such awakenings and his own sadhana that Narendranath became what he became – Swami Vivekananda.

There is no reason for us to doubt these incidents. Even Jesus gave such powers to his disciples. The problem with us is that simply because we do not have the competence to be spiritual, we discard all such incidents summarily.

If you can understand the transmission of spiritual power from God on earth to his chosen to be divine visions, you will understand how Sri Krishna showed his divine form to Arjuna as described in this chapter.

Swamiji, how does it matter what Arjuna saw something some thousand years ago? Is it relevant in any way for us? No matter how much money the richest person in the world has, I have to create and preserve my own wealth.

The chapter and the vision described in it are indeed important for all, as you will soon realize. To start with, our scriptures lay a lot of emphasis on meditation. Not the kind of pop-meditation taught to the bored, but the real, actual, deep meditation on God that helps you develop the power to see beyond the physical.

Meditation on the Lord can be done in one of the three ways: *rupa chintana* (meditating on the form), *lila chintana* (meditating on the episodes of His life) and *guna chintana* (meditating on His divine qualities). The previous chapter gave a glimpse of guna chintana, while this chapter is on rupa chintana, which describes how God with form may look like, so that we can meditate upon such forms.

I wondered if all this was going above my head, but looking back, I can say firmly that it was no rocket science.

Swamiji then explained the premise. Sri Krishna being God, it was obvious that he would have a cosmic form which could only be seen by yogis in their meditative state, or those blessed with a special mind power as explained earlier. So, Arjuna prayed to the Lord to show him the cosmic form. Realizing that Arjuna was no yogi, the Lord gave him divine eyes so that he could see His subtle form. Just to remind you, it is one of the infinite forms in which God can appear.

Swamiji, does that mean that one has to wait for a gift of this kind before one sees God or His form?

No, not at all. As explained just now, the usual path is through meditation, by which one can get rid of experiencing the world through the gross senses. It is then that they can have some form of vision, which will, in all probability, not match with anyone else's vision. God is not finite, and so the visions will be different. In fact, if you have similar visions to anyone else, then probably you are faking it.

Strong words, Swamiji.

Bare truth, bhai.

Presence of all in one

In the form that the Lord showed Arjuna, there was One in the many, and the many in One, which explains the apparent contradictions of the relative world. It also reconciles the opposites of the spiritual world – justice and mercy, fate and free will, suffering and divine love, and so on.

Such a vision of God, or contemplation upon it, removes all doubts and perplexities that cloud us. It is only after we have seen such a form that we are able to observe the relation and unity in the apparent diversity of the universe, and spontaneously surrender to the will of God; it is then that we are able to see the most hateful and the terrible things of the world as the divine manifestation of the Lord; it is only then that we can accept the world with joy and perform every task as the Lord's work.

Baba! I uttered under my breath.

इहैकस्थं जगत्कृत्स्नं पश्याद्य सचराचरम्, मम देहे गुडाकेश यच्चान्यद्द्रष्टुमिच्छसि |

See Arjuna, the entire universe, with everything moving and non-moving, assembled together in My universal form. Whatever else you wish to see, observe it all within this universal form. (XI.7)

What Arjuna was about to witness was so unique that Sri Krishna cautioned him beforehand.

The cosmic form of God

From this point on, let me narrate the vision in English as composed by the poet Edwin Arnold, instead of translating and explaining verse by verse.

Saying so, Swamiji brought out a small book from his pocket, leafed through the pages, and read out from

Arnold's translation, which I would later find out was highly respected as a work of art.

अनेकवक्त्रनयनम् अनेकाद्भुतदर्शनम्, अनेकदिव्याभरणं दिव्य अनेकोद्यतायुधम् |
दिव्यमाल्याम्बरधरं दिव्यगन्धानुलेपनम्, सर्वाश्चर्यमयं देवमनन्तं विश्वतोमुखम् |
दिवि सूर्यसहस्रस्य भवेद्युगपत् उत्थिता, यदि भाः सदृशी सा स्यात् भासस्तस्य महात्मनः |

All the splendour, wonder, dread, of His vast Almighty-head.

Out of countless eyes beholding, out of countless mouths commanding,

Countless mystic forms enfolding, in one Form: supremely standing

Countless radiant glories wearing, countless heavenly weapons bearing,

Crowned with garlands of star-clusters, robed in garb of woven lustres,

Breathing from His perfect Presence, breaths of every subtle essence

Of all heavenly odours; shedding, blinding brilliance; overspreading –

Boundless, beautiful – all spaces, with His all-regarding faces;

So He showed! If there should rise, suddenly within the skies

Sunburst of a thousand suns, flooding earth with beams undeemed-of,

Then might be that Holy One's, Majesty and radiance dreamed of! (XI.10–12)

It is this verse about a thousand suns in the sky that Oppenheimer is said to have quoted when he saw the bright light of the atomic explosion.

God's Cosmic Form

Arjuna's prayer to the Lord

What Arjuna saw, he then described to the Lord.

पश्यामि देवांस्तव देव देहे सर्वान् तथा भूतविशेषसङ्घान्,
ब्रह्माणमीशं कमलासनस्थम् ऋषींश्च सर्वानुरगांश्च दिव्यान् ।
अनेकबाहु उदरवक्त्रनेत्रं त्वां सर्वतोऽनन्तरूपम्,
नान्तं न मध्यं न पुनस्तवादिं पश्यामि विश्वेश्वर विश्वरूप ।

Yea! I have seen! I see! Lord! All is wrapped in Thee!
 The gods are in Thy glorious frame! The creatures
 Of earth, and heaven, and hell, in Thy Divine form dwell,
 And in Thy countenance shine all the features
 Of Brahma, sitting lone, upon His lotus-throne;
 Of saints and sages, and the serpent races, Ananta, Vasuki;
 Yea! Mightiest Lord! I see, thy thousand arms, and breasts,
and faces,
 And eyes, on every side, perfect, diversified;
 And nowhere end of Thee, nowhere beginning,
 Nowhere a centre! Shifts –
 Wherever soul's gaze lifts –
 Thy central Self, all-wielding, and all-winning! (XI.15–16)

वक्त्राणि ते त्वरमाणा विशन्ति दंष्ट्राकरालानि भयानकानि,
केचिद्विलग्ना दशनान्तरेषु सन्दृश्यन्ते चूर्णितैः उत्तमाङ्गैः ।
यथा नदीनां बहवोऽम्बुवेगाः समुद्रम् एवाभिमुखा द्रवन्ति,
तथा तवामी नरलोकवीरा विशन्ति वक्त्राणि अभिविज्वलन्ति ।

The Kings and Chiefs drawn in, that gaping gorge within;
 The best of both these armies torn and riven!

Between Thy jaws they lie, mangled full bloodily,
Ground into dust and death! Like streams down-driven
With helpless haste, which go, in headlong furious flow
Straight to the gulfing deeps of th' unfilled ocean,
So to that flaming cave, those heroes great and brave
Pour, in unending streams, with helpless motion!

The real nature of Sri Krishna

Swamiji closed the book by Arnold and asked if I liked his presentation. I replied in the affirmative. He then continued.

Quaking with terror at the sight of this cosmic form of God, Arjuna asked in trembling voice who Sri Krishna was and what was the purpose of all this? To this, the Lord replied:

कालोऽस्मि लोकक्षयकृत् प्रवृद्धो लोकान् समाहर्तुमिह प्रवृत्तः,
ऋतेऽपि त्वां न भविष्यन्ति सर्वे येऽवस्थिताः प्रत्यनीकेषु योधाः |
तस्मात्त्वम् उत्तिष्ठ यशो लभस्व जित्वा शत्रून् भुङ्क्ष्व राज्यं समृद्धम्,
मयैवैते निहताः पूर्वमेव निमित्तमात्रं भव सव्यसाचिन् |
द्रोणं च भीष्मं च जयद्रथं च कर्णं तथा अन्यानपि योधवीरान्,
मया हतांस्त्वं जहि मा व्यथिष्ठा युध्यस्व जेतासि रणे सपत्नान् |

The Lord said: I am mighty Time, the source of destruction that annihilates the worlds. Even without your participation, the warriors arrayed in the opposing army shall cease to exist.

Therefore, arise and attain honour! Conquer your foes and enjoy the unrivalled dominion. These warriors stand already slain by Me, and you will only be an instrument of My work.

Drona, Bhishma, Jayadratha, Karna, and other warriors have already been killed by Me. Therefore, slay them without being disturbed. Just fight and you will be victorious over your enemies in battle. (XI.32–34)

You might be wondering how all this description is significant for anyone. The answer lies in the fact that Hinduism accepts God in totality, meaning He is the Creator, Preserver and also the Destroyer. So, Hinduism has no need for a Devil who appears to undo all the good that God creates. Since every new creation requires the destruction of the old, we accept destruction to be coming from God, and thus see *Kala,* Time, as a manifestation of God that devours all. For the same reason we have reverence for both Brahma (the Creator) and Kali (the Destroyer).

The Lord says that He is the world-destroying Kala, there to annihilate the warriors there, implying that even without Arjuna's intervention, all those warriors were going to die. So, the best course of action for Arjuna was to stand up in the battlefield and win glory by becoming an instrument in the hands of the Lord.

This verse explains that none can resist the divine will. Sri Krishna reminds Arjuna that he has been appointed by the Lord as an instrument on account of his past good Karma. The reward for his present actions has been determined by the divine will in the form of glory for him. Now he only had to make his own will one with the divine will by performing his duty.

As for us, continues Swamiji, the best thing is to perform our duties, as expected by society and accepted by us. This is known as *varnashrama dharma*. And to be spiritual, duty has to be coupled with a complete surrender to the divine will. If one of these is compromised, a person becomes like a maimed bird with one wing only – helpless in the storm of Nature.

Needs thinking, Swamiji.

Let me add a personal note to this. The line *nimitta-matram bhava savyasachin* – 'Be thou an instrument in the hands of the Lord' – is my favourite from Gita. I was once advised by a senior monk to practise it in life, and I try to do so all the time.

Have you succeeded?

Not really. But I have not given up.

Anyway, coming back to Gita ... overwhelmed, Arjuna then broke into a prayer to the Lord and asked for his forgiveness for having treated him merely as a friend.

The ultimate prayer

नमः पुरस्तादथ पृष्ठतस्ते नमोऽस्तु ते सर्वत एव सर्व,
अनन्तवीर्य अमितविक्रमस्त्वं सर्वं समाप्नोषि ततोऽसि सर्वः |
सखेति मत्वा प्रसभं यदुक्तं हे कृष्ण हे यादव हे सखेति,
अजानता महिमानं तवेदं मया प्रमादात् प्रणयेन वापि |
यत् च अवहास-अर्थम् असत्कृतोऽसि विहारशय्यासन भोजनेषु,
एकोऽथवा अपि अच्युत तत्समक्षं तत्क्षामये त्वाम् अहमप्रमेयम् |
पितासि लोकस्य चराचरस्य त्वमस्य पूज्यश्च गुरुर्गरीयान्,
न त्वत्समो अस्ति अभ्यधिकः कुतोऽन्यो लोकत्रये अपि अप्रतिमप्रभाव |

GOD'S COSMIC FORM

तस्मात्प्रणम्य प्रणिधाय कायं प्रसादये त्वाम् अहमीशमीड्यम्,
पितेव पुत्रस्य सखेव सख्युः प्रियः प्रियायाः अर्हसि देव सोढुम् |

Salutations to You from the front and the rear, indeed from all sides! You possess infinite valour and might and pervade everything, and thus, You are everything.

Thinking of You as my friend, I foolishly addressed You as, 'O Krishna', 'O Yadav', 'O my dear Friend'. I was ignorant of Your majesty, showing negligence and undue affection. And if, I treated You with disrespect, while playing, resting, sitting, eating, when alone, or before others – for all that I pray for forgiveness.

You are the Father of universe, of moving and non-moving beings. You are the most deserving of worship and the Supreme Master. When there is none equal to You in all the three worlds, then who can possibly be greater than You, O Lord!

So, prostrating my body in adoration, I ask for your forgiveness, Lord adorable! As a father forgives his son, friend a dear friend, a beloved one his love, even so you forgive me, O Lord. (XI.40–44)

Did you note the sweetness of Arjuna's words when he asks for forgiveness from the Lord? It is so sweet – forgive me the way 'a father forgives his son, friend a dear friend, a beloved one his love'. Ah! The beauty of devotion to the Lord! How I wish that we had such sweet relation with God!

These five verses are thus the ultimate of prayer, since we too trivialize God by asking for this and that or thinking silly things about Him.

To calm down Arjuna, the Lord then withdrew his cosmic form and appeared once again as the smiling charioteer, the role that he was performing before showing His divine form.

The message of the chapter is that whatever happens is the Lord's will. Does that take away our individual freedom? No, it does not. In essence we are Atman, which appears within us as the conscious principle known as the soul, and in the universe. It appears as God to which we pray and who answers our prayers. This easily sorts out conflicts between divine will and free will, destiny and effort, Karma and God's grace, justice and mercy, and all such conflicting ideas that abound in religious philosophy. It is we who pray, and it is our own higher self that answers it!

Also, the true conviction that God alone does everything comes only after one has seen a divine vision like this. Till then, every expression about God and His power is mere parroting of what one has heard from elders. These lead you nowhere.

Swamiji, the idea of my soul being the God who rules all seems far-fetched.

How true! The moment you use the expression 'my soul', you have limited yourself and then must pray to the almighty God who is *actually* Atman – the pure consciousness but seen through the glass of your mind. So, 'you' can never be God or one with Him. But as pure consciousness there is no you nor He – only the non-dual absolute!

The idea is not very clear.

Imagine an ocean which is partly frozen; say, in the South Pole. Also add to your imagination that everything there is conscious of itself. Now, if a ball of ice were to look at an ice mountain there, what would it see? It will see it as God.

However, if it were ever to realize that its true identity was not as a ball but as water, it will then know that it has no limitedness – it is the huge ocean, spreading everywhere; it alone has become the huge mountain from where infinite number of snowballs roll down and merge! Simple.

Know you are that and be free – this is the whole of religion, said Swamiji, concluding the topic.

What was there to write after what I had heard that day? It was all so overwhelming.

I stayed up the whole night thinking about how God had devoured my dear ones, and also made me what I am. Are the words of Gita indeed true? I don't know.

I kept tossing in the bed, waiting for the sunrise.

XII

BHAKTI, THE DIVINE LOVE

The Mandhata Parikrama, or parikrama path, as I have been calling it, is a wonderful experience with its temples, monasteries and gates meeting us at regular intervals. Nature, spirituality, religion, mythology, sculpture and archaeology are woven seamlessly on this route. As we walked, we crossed gates dedicated to the five Pandavas for whom the Kurukshetra war had been fought, resulting in the discourse of Gita.

We – Swamiji and I – had cycled through various moods – silence, discussion, understanding, argument, humour and a fat silence that indicated disagreement.

Breaking the lull, Swamiji asked, How did you feel when you experienced love?

I felt happy, full and on the top of the world, said I, remembering my days of folly.

That is how a dog also feels after a full meal, he said. I once saw a tiger after his meal in a zoo. It purred with such satisfaction, as if beyond any care in the world!

I mean, I felt a surge of power that could make me grab the world and pulverize it in my palms.

Every animal feels like that during its mating season.

I don't know what else to say!

Love is the state of your being, and not of becoming, said Swamiji. In that state, your identity dissolves and you become one with love; not with the object of love. You then want to give instead of wanting for yourself. Your love extends to all instead of one, and you become tender towards all. This is the subject matter of chapter XII, known as *Bhakti Yoga*.

Who are the best devotees of God?

Swamiji, most people in the present time prefer the formless aspect of God. This gives them a feel of being spiritual. There are also religions that lay stress on the formless aspect of God.

The great teachers of Bhakti have defined it as the 'supreme love for God', implying that of all kinds of love, the love for God is the supreme in which neither you nor God remain; instead, only love remains – love, also known as Brahman, or Consciousness.

It was discussed earlier how God is formless but may appear to a devotee in a form, so we can opt to love any of these aspects. The outcome in every instance will be the same, that is, unalloyed love. So, to think that one kind of devotion is superior to another is mere ignorance. This problem of categorizing love as superior or inferior, depending on which aspect of God you love, has been going on since ages.

As for your observation of the current fad regarding worshipping the formless, know that if popularity were to be the test of correctness, then stage performers would be the greatest God. Not just that, we would then change our God frequently. So, do not judge the correctness of truth by the number of its adherents. Gita settles the conflict about the correctness of path with its clear words and the reasoning.

मय्यावेश्य मनो ये मां नित्ययुक्ता उपासते, श्रद्धया परयोपेताः ते मे युक्ततमा मताः |

The best devotees are those who have their minds fixed on Me and have steadfast devotion for me. (XII.2)

The verse says that devotion to God, say, Lord Krishna, is the highest form of Bhakti. The reason will be explained later. But before that, let me tell you about an interesting incident from my life. Once, I met a Sufi saint in Kashmir who was famous in his area. Out of curiosity, I asked him how to have devotion to God. He replied sternly, 'The way one acquires zamindari (property).' The meaning is that you have to struggle and make efforts for having Bhakti, too. There can be no casual approach in spirituality – whatever your goal and path.

Impressive, I said.

I have never forgotten that meeting with him. Indeed, one has to slog a lot through ritualistic worship to acquire love for God. As you know well, it is difficult to get the affection of anyone without effort, so how can one expect to be the beloved of God just like that! But, once you reach that state of oneness where your being is only with God, you become the greatest monk, yogi, devotee, jnani ... or whatever you prefer to call such a person. There is no higher or lower in that love.

In worldly love, you can talk of oneness or use some high-sounding phrase, but the fact is that in any love between two persons, their individuality persists, which makes it nearly impossible for them to experience true love. That is the big reason for so many break-ups despite supposed bonding.

I had no reason to disagree with what Swamiji said. His words had such persuasive power that every now and then, I had to lock an idea in my mind for thinking over it when I had time.

Struggles in the worship of the formless

क्लेशोऽधिकतरः तेषाम् अव्यक्तासक्तचेतसाम्, अव्यक्ता हि गतिर्दुःखं देहवद्भिरवाप्यते |

The spiritual path is extremely tortuous for those who meditate on the formless, since it is difficult for those who are conscious of their body and senses to fix their mind on the formless. (XII.5)

Here is the answer to your supposition that *Advaita* sadhana, or worshipping the formless, is better. It is simply a momentary sensationalism.

Saying so, Swamiji slipped into silence with a distant look in his eyes. I wondered what might come out of the gestating silence. I waited without drawing him out from that state.

He finally spoke. We can only love what we are. There is simply no way that we can love what is not our true nature. Water mixes with water, and oil with oil. Likewise, those who have a body-sense can only experience material love, while those who have outgrown their attachment with their body can love the formless.

This outgrowing is quite difficult. Sri Ramakrishna used to say that such a person may cut their hand and bleed profusely, but insist that they are not hurt. Rather it is their body that is hurt. Believe me, it is difficult to reach this level of detachment from one's body. Those who talk of the worship of the formless or the idol breakers are a deluded lot. Indeed, your body consciousness makes you fit only for worshipping God with form.

Let me tell you a funny story. Once, a monk was to be operated upon. When the doctor was to administer anaesthesia, he refused it saying that he is not the body. So, the doctor applied the knife directly. The monk jumped up in pain, shouting, '*Arre, wo Gita mein hai!*'

I laughed heartily at the episode, even if it might have just been a made-up story.

Well, that sums up the situation. But know that, God with form and the formless God are one and the same. The difference lies in the path, which again is determined by your personality. So, it is meaningless to claim the superiority of one over the other.

God saves His devotees

The quest for spirituality begins only when a person becomes totally dissatisfied with the state of affairs around them. It is not a temporary disillusionment but a permanent disgust, and it is then that they want to hold on to the real amidst the unreal. Those who are quite satisfied with their life, having this and that fun, can never become spiritual. It is because of this that Jesus Christ famously said: 'It is easier for a camel to go through the eye of a needle than for someone who is rich to enter the kingdom of God.'

Once you are on the path of spirituality, you realize that the cycle of birth-death-birth is a real and inviolable law of life; once you are convinced of the viciousness of existence as a Ferris wheel in which you keep going up and coming down, you get desperate to get out of the cycle.

Yes, Swamiji! I am pretty scared to ride on such a contraption. But I am not sure about the cycle of birth and death.

He responded, Those who want enjoyment in this life or the next can never become spiritual – they are either materialists or at the best, ritualists in religion. Only when you want nothing to do with the physical existence – which only makes you whirl through the never-ending cycle of life and death – can you truly become spiritual. It is then that your real journey begins. Till then it is only a motion in the never-ending cycle.

God, the ever loving being that He is, takes His devotees out from this cycle and makes them spiritually blessed.

ये तु सर्वाणि कर्माणि मयि संन्यस्य मत्परः, अनन्येनैव योगेन मां ध्यायन्त उपासते |
तेषामहं समुद्धर्ता मृत्युसंसारसागरात्, भवामि नचिरात्पार्थ मय्यावेशितचेतसाम् |

Those who dedicate all their actions to Me, regarding Me as the Supreme, worshiping Me and meditating on Me with full devotion, I take them out of the ocean of birth and death, since their consciousness is united with Me. (XII.6)

Spirituality is not a part-time affair. In fact, this is true in the world, too. If you take up a way of life, you have to be fully into it. When a mother raises her child, she has to be fully into looking after her.

God is quite demanding that way. It is no wonder that people prefer to enjoy the world instead of going for God. You will find this note of complete surrender in the religious texts of every religion. After all, you cannot be yourself and someone else at the same time!

Struggle, struggle, struggle!

How and where to begin if one wants to love God? The next verses explain how the complete merging of 'I'-ness in God is the goal.

But not everyone can do that. Sri Krishna tells us what to do in that case.

अथ चित्तं समाधातुं न शक्नोषि मयि स्थिरम्, अभ्यासयोगेन ततो मामिच्छाप्तुं धनञ्जय |
अभ्यासेपि असमर्थोऽसि मत्कर्मपरमो भव, मदर्थमपि कर्माणि कुर्वन्सिद्धिम् अवाप्स्यसि |
अथैतत् अपि अशक्तोऽसि कर्तुं मद्योगमाश्रितः, सर्वकर्मफलत्यागं ततः कुरु यतात्मवान् |

If you are unable to fix your mind on Me, then practice Abhyasa yoga, which means, remembering Me with devotion at all times. If you fail in that, then perform all your activities dedicated to me. If you can't do even that, then practice offering the results of your actions to Me. (XII.9–11)

The crux lies in giving up!

The highest form of giving up is when one is immersed in God, the second is if one considers themselves to be the Lord's servant, and the last one, in which one retains one's individuality to a great extent, is to offer the results of one's actions to God.

Let me tell you an interesting story to explain the idea behind these verses. Sage Narada was a great devotee of Lord Vishnu. Once, Narada wanted to know who the Lord's greatest devotee was. So, the Lord took him to see a farmer who performed his daily duties and took the Lord's name only while leaving his home and on return. Narada found this unacceptable. So, Lord Vishnu gave him a jar full to the brim with oil and asked him to make a round of the place without spilling a single drop.

On completing the task, the Lord asked him how many times he had taken His name during his walk. 'None,' said Narada. 'After all, I was doing your work.'

'Just imagine,' said the Lord. 'The farmer at least takes my name twice daily, all the while doing my work!'

This shows how a struggler on the path of spirituality is as great as those who have arrived. A father equally loves his children whether they call him 'papa', 'dad' or a toddler's 'da'. As long as you are connected with God, even if you are struggling to move ahead, everything is fine with you in matters of spirituality.

India, the land of spirituality, once preached the practice of these ideals at every stage of growth, in every stratum of society. This was known as varnashrama dharma. It is all gone now. Forever.

I let out a deep sigh. This was all quite simple and yet so deep.

Virtues to have in life

I knew a monk, said Swamiji, who used to say that his only sadhana in life had been the practice of the XII.15 verse of Gita. Curious, I tried to understand what it implied, and I realized after a long time that it talks about the ultimate of inclusiveness in life. It is the state where no one can disturb you, nor will you ever disturb anyone.

यस्मात् न उद्विजते लोको लोकात् न उद्विजते च यः,
हर्षामर्षभय उद्वेगैः मुक्तो यः स च मे प्रियः |

I love those devotees who do not cause annoyance to anyone, nor get agitated by any. They stay steady amidst pleasure and pain, and they are free from fear and anxiety. (XII.15)

I was not going to let Swamiji off on this point. It is one thing to talk big but walking the talk is a different matter. I said, We have some employees who are so good that they are good-for-nothing – they do not even react to suggestions or condemnations. Would you call them great?

They are *tamasik* people, the inert ones. They mask their incompetence and lack of strength under goodness. A true spiritual person is extremely efficient and highly active. If they face a barrage of activities, they know what to prioritize and how. So, do not compare the greats with the dolts. You will find all these qualities described in this chapter of Gita.

Fine! But what about Jesus Christ, who was crucified for annoying his own people? What about the many saints who were persecuted, or killings in the name of religion?

To your many questions, I have one answer – what Gita says is correct. For every violent act against the saintly, there are thousands of cases when these saints brought solace even to the offenders. The statement about not antagonizing others is a general statement, since the nasty always itch for a fight. Do remember the words of Jesus who asked for forgiveness from God for those who were crucifying him.

And those who kill in the name of religion, their motivation is partly political and mostly ignorance. How can a man of God kill anyone? God who creates, and who has made this beautiful earth, can never ask anyone to kill or maim others. If He wanted, He would not have created the victims, or could have finished them off by His mere wish. It is simply illogical that God, the all-knowing and all-powerful, will create someone, guide them on the wrong path, and then send them to eternal hell for not following His instructions! Illogical and cruel!

I was not going to give up. Are you established in any of these virtues?

I don't think that I am perfect, but I try not to be a nuisance to people, which means that I try not to be demanding. Nuisance or annoyance is only caused by the demanding. For example, if you go to a hotel, you might expect a level of service, but even there you should not be over-demanding, treating the staff as slaves. As for me, I treat people with respect, and those who are lower on the social hierarchy,

I make them comfortable by paying a little extra care and concern.

I liked that. It is now one of the guiding principles of my life.

He continued, Do you know the qualities of a gentleman? They do not get perturbed easily, nor do they unsettle others. To be spiritual, you first have to become a gentleman. Compare the behaviour of a monk with that of a gentleman, add to that God-centric nature, and you will know if a person is a budding saint or not!

Wonderful, Swamiji! My spontaneous expression encompassed many emotions.

Similarly, a gentleman has to learn from a saint the qualities that need to be imbibed.

यो न हृष्यति न द्वेष्टि न शोचति न काङ्क्षति, शुभाशुभपरित्यागी भक्तिमान्यः स मे प्रियः |
समः शत्रौ च मित्रे च तथा मानापमानयोः, शीतोष्णसुखदुःखेषु समः सङ्गविवर्जितः |

Those who do not get excited on getting the favourable, nor feel dejected, who neither seek nor avoid, and have full devotion for me, are dear to Me. Those, who treat friend and foe alike, success and failure, cold and heat, joy and sorrow, and all such dualities with equanimity, are my favourite. (XII.17–18)

Ordinary people are like a weighing scale – add a little weight and it comes down, reduce the weight and it goes up. We, the ordinary ones, puff up if praised and feel squeezed if criticized. This happens simply because our personality does not have weight – we lack strength.

So, increase your inner strength, bhai. Make that the goal of your life, and some day you may thank me for giving you this advice!

Due to the immensity of their personality, born of identification with God, a spiritual person does not let praise or blame affect them. Even when you act humble when you achieve big, or when someone praises you, know that these are affecting you. A true devotee of God is beyond such humility or arrogance. Attain this state.

Later, I thought over all that Swamiji had said that day. First be a gentleman, then be religious, and then struggle to become spiritual.

It was interesting to learn the relationship between the qualities of a gentleman and a monk. We have grown up thinking of monks as otherworldly, unsophisticated and worthless. But the facts seem different now.

Now my worry is that I may start judging monks against the scale of the qualities described in Gita!

XIII

MATTER AND CONSCIOUSNESS

Having covered two-thirds of the chapters of Gita, I had started getting a drift of what this sacred scripture wanted to convey to humanity. Whatever my earlier prejudices, I now felt that the book was not at all sectarian or religion-bound – it could be used by all for growth and welfare. Most importantly, it was not about war or instigating others.

That day, Swamiji asked me if I knew why we were in such a mess. I cherry-picked several ideas related to it that I had gulped down over the years. Honestly speaking, I had nothing great to offer.

You are partly right, bhai. However, the fact is that we wanted the situation in which we are for ourselves. There is no other reason for it.

Surprised, I halted my steps and retorted with, It is cruel to say so, Swamiji. Coming from your mouth, I find it abominable. How can you say that the poor, wretched, sick, differently-abled – they all wanted a situation like this? The inequality, molestations, subjugation, exploitation – how can we be responsible for all this? Blame it on chance or on God, but us choosing it is a revolting idea.

Swamiji smiled and replied, It is the privilege of the irresponsible to get hyper without understanding an issue well. You don't have that privilege. Know that if the single birth theory was correct, as believed by many, then the responsibility for the mess would lie squarely with God, the creator, or with the blind Nature. But for us in India, life is a continuous process in which we, the soul, experience various sights offered by Nature. The good, bad, boring, ugly, pleasant are all mere sights that are experienced by us so that we can outgrow them.

Even then the idea of us wanting the mess is unacceptable.

Why do you say so? Don't you watch movies? What are movies, plays, serials and all such performing arts but a serving of various emotions embodied through certain characters and offered to you at some cost? If you can enjoy violence, pain, suffering, etc. in a movie, then why do you blame life for giving you the same experiences? Only, in the case of life experiences, you get all this for free instead of a fee!

I refused to budge, even though the phrase 'free instead of fee' had a nice ring to it.

Truth does not depend on your acceptance or refusal of it. The all-majestic soul wants to experience various sights of Nature, so it goes through it all. The saving grace is that since we got into it, we can also get out of it.

What is the way out? Spirituality?

Indeed. This is where spirituality scores over philosophy and religion. Philosophy is like a consultant that tells the why, what and how of mess without giving you a solution; religion teaches you how to pray so that you may get some relief; but spirituality shows you the way out so that you never again get in the mire.

Words!

Swamiji avoided my taunt and asked, Have you heard of modern sayings like 'The present is everything', 'Live one day at a time', and all such nonsense?

Of course, I had.

The solution to a problem lies in going a notch higher. You can never solve a problem while you are within it. You might have heard of Kurt Gödel's incompleteness theorem, which talks about the limits of mathematical logic: put simply, a consistent mathematical system cannot prove its own consistency. If you stretch this a bit, you will realize the importance of getting out of a system to find the right solution for a problem.

If mathematics can be used in spirituality, it surely sounds impressive. But I remain unimpressed.

The first rule of getting out of the mess would be to see life as a whole, and not in parts. Whatever your outlook towards life, if you look at the larger whole of it, you will be at peace. The second rule would be to get solutions from spirituality for the complicated issues in life, since it gives you a better perspective on life than when you are wallowing in the mesh of matters.

For example, take anger issues. Many people are preaching about how to manage one's anger. These solutions indeed help to some extent, but they do not work all the time. But when you look at life on a larger canvas, your anger issues will go down.

How?

When I was pretty young, I knew a monk who never got angry. Impressed, I asked him how he managed that. He said that when he was young, he was the complaining type. Whenever he went to his senior with a complaint about someone, he was told that the person had always been like that. Slowly he realized that *people* are like that, and so it was no use getting angry!

You can thus see how a larger perspective solved his problem irrevocably. This is true of fear, greed, hatred ... everything. The story of the monk and the solution that he got is just one example. A soldier is killed in the battlefield, a suicide bomber dies for their beliefs, noble persons die for their values, monks give up the joys of the world – all this because they have a larger picture of life before them.

You can have your own philosophy of life, known in German as *weltanschauung*. Whatever your outlook, try to put the pieces of your problems together, and you will be surprised to see how they fit. Even if you are a crass materialist who sees life as having no meaning or purpose, you will see adversities as products of blind forces hitting each other. Be honest with your outlook, and it will take away your agitation.

I needed a break to grasp the idea, and sat down on the side wall for a while. Swamiji, as was his wont, looked at distant sights and waited till I got up.

The largest canvas of life, he continued, shows two realities working within and outside of us. The first one is the ocean of matter-energy-mind, which are one but appear differently. The second one is the consciousness present in all living beings. The entire universe, explored and unexplored, is the interplay of these two realities. Understand the nature of both, and you will find yourself at peace. If you are lucky, you may also grow to be spiritual.

A bit rattled after the discussion, I asked, Why do you always seem to suggest the superior nature of spirituality over the world?

Well, you go to a doctor to know about medicine, to a mechanic for repairing your car, to an engineer for building a structure, etc. Just like that, you go to scriptures to know about the realities of life. There can be no exception to this. So, indeed, spirituality gives you solutions to your worldly problems.

The world of matter

This chapter begins with a description of what is matter and what is consciousness. I believe that everyone in the world should have a clear knowledge pertaining to matter, soul and God to make their life meaningful and dignified.

The body of any being is said to be the *kshetra* (lit. field, since it is through the body that one reaps the fruits of one's acts) and *kshetrajna* (the individualized soul, which is the knower of the respective field). Again, God Himself resides as the knower in all fields, implying that the individual soul is one with the universal God. Kshetra, the empire of matter-energy-mind, known as Prakriti, extends to all existence that we know, and its effects.

महाभूतानि अहंकारो बुद्धिः अव्यक्तमेव च, इन्द्रियाणि दशैकं च पञ्च चेन्द्रियगोचराः |
इच्छा द्वेषः सुखं दुःखं सङ्घातश्चेतना धृतिः, एतत्क्षेत्रं समासेन सविकारमुदाहृतम् |

Nature (Prakriti) is composed of the five great elements (smell, taste, sight, touch, hearing), the ego, the intellect, the avyakta (unmanifest primordial matter), the eleven senses (five senses, five organs of action, and mind) and the five objects of the senses (earth, water, fire, air, sky). Desire and aversion, happiness and misery, the body, sensations and the will – all these comprise Nature and its modifications. (XIII.5–6)

This chapter gives a complete picture of the empire of matter, so that one can move from here to freedom. Unlike the idea of matter as in Greek philosophy, matter is seen in Indian systems as having layers of subtleness, which extend from solid matter up to the subtlest mind and all its modifications, as also its activities. The activities of the mind, too, are included in this list, as enumerated.

By now, it has been explained many times how the idea of consciousness in the Western world is limited to the activities of the mind, which for us belong to the realm of matter – a philosophical chasm that is difficult to bridge. They will not accept the existence of something beyond mind, and we will never accept mind as non-matter!

Who can be spiritual?

To acquire the discerning knowledge between matter and spirit, we have to first know the qualities of those who can undertake this difficult voyage. To remind you, spirituality cannot be for the masses, and it definitely cannot be a fad, as you can see in these verses.

अमानित्वम् अदम्भित्वम् अहिंसा क्षान्तिः आर्जवम्,
आचार्योपासनं शौचं स्थैर्यम् आत्मविनिग्रहः |
इन्द्रियार्थेषु वैराग्यम् अनहंकार एव च, जन्ममृत्यु-जराव्याधि-दुःखदोषानुदर्शनम् |
असक्तिः अनभिष्वङ्गः पुत्रदारगृहादिषु, नित्यं च समचित्तत्वम् इष्टान् इष्टोपपत्तिषु |

Humility; freedom from hypocrisy; non-violence; forgiveness; simplicity; service of the Guru; cleanliness of body and mind; steadfastness; self-control; dispassion toward the objects of the senses; absence of egotism; keeping in mind the evils of birth, disease, old age and death; non-attachment; absence of clinging to spouse, children, home and so on; even-mindedness amidst desired and undesired events in life (are the primary qualifications to be spiritual). (XIII.7–9)

Some more qualities have been listed in the next verses, but for us this list is good enough, he laughed as if he was telling a joke. Maybe he was laughing at the neo-spiritualists and their simpleton followers.

Two words of interest here are *asakti* and *anabhishvanga*, which imply non-attachment of two different kinds. In the first, it is non-attachment from your own body and mind, that is, the internal detachment. In the second, it is detachment from the external objects that you feel to be your own, that is, external detachment. In simple words, get rid of 'me' and 'mine' to know the real 'I'. Tell me, how many of the modern-day Gurus can do this? So, you can very well imagine the kind of product that such assembly lines are coming out with!

Were you fed with honey when you were born, Swamiji?

He got the joke and laughed at it. This is the problem with you people. When I explain scriptures, the blame comes on me. Anyway, know the nature of consciousness.

How does all this help us in daily life?

Come on! When you know that fire burns, you make use of it very carefully, as during cooking. Similarly, when you know the nature of life, you treat it very carefully. Life is like fire. It will burn you down if you don't handle it carefully but will lead you to great achievements if you learn how to make a controlled use of it.

The nature of consciousness

According to us, consciousness is everything in the world – the source, sustenance, power, enjoyer, etc. Consciousness is God. The description of it in Gita is so beautiful that you will have to allow me to read out all the relevant verses, he said.

Who was I to object? He would have done that even without my consent.

ज्ञेयं यत् तत् प्रवक्ष्यामि यत् ज्ञात्वामृतमश्नुते, अनादिमत्परं ब्रह्म न सत् न असदुच्यते |
सर्वतः पाणिपादं तत् सर्वतोऽक्षि-शिरोमुखम्, सर्वतः श्रुतिमल्लोके सर्वमावृत्य तिष्ठति |

The Lord said: I shall tell you that which ought to be known, and by knowing which one attains immortality. It is the beginningless Brahman which lies beyond existence and non-existence. Everywhere are Its hands, feet, eyes, heads, faces and ears, for It pervades everything in the universe. (XIII.12–13)

सर्वेन्द्रियगुणाभासं सर्वेन्द्रिय-विवर्जितम्, असक्तं सर्वभृच्चैव निर्गुणं गुणभोक्तृ च |
बहिः अन्तश्च भूतानामचरं चरमेव च, सूक्ष्मत्वात् तद्विज्ञेयं दूरस्थं चान्तिके च तत् |

Though It perceives all sense-objects, yet It is devoid of the senses. It is unattached to everything, and yet is the sustainer of all; is without attributes, yet is the enjoyer of the Nature; It exists outside and inside all living beings; is subtle, and hence incomprehensible. It is very far but is also very near. (XIII.14–15)

अविभक्तं च भूतेषु विभक्तमिव च स्थितम्, भूतभर्तृ च तज्ज्ञेयं ग्रसिष्णु प्रभविष्णु च |
ज्योतिषामपि तत् ज्योतिस्तमसः परमुच्यते, ज्ञानं ज्ञेयं ज्ञानगम्यं हृदि सर्वस्य विष्ठितम् |

It is indivisible, yet appears to be divided in the living beings. Know the Supreme One to be the sustainer, annihilator and creator of all beings. It is the source of light in all luminaries, and is entirely beyond the darkness of ignorance. It is knowledge, the object of knowledge and the goal of knowledge. It dwells within the hearts of all living beings. (XIII.16–17)

Swamiji appeared quite charged up while explaining the verses. He said, The expressions here require long explanation but it will bore you, so I will say it in a few words. Just know that these verses have given birth to many wrangling philosophies in India.

Consciousness is that which knows; as in, that which knows the entire existence. Imagine a state when there is no transformation of existence, like waves in the ocean. Naturally the only thing to exist then would be existence Itself. Thus, pure existence Itself is consciousness since It alone knows and exists. There being no two, these have to be one. And you can love only that which exists or seems to exist to you, so this pure existence has to be Love. Thus existence-consciousness-love are the same and undivided in their true form. Quite simple, isn't it?

Was it? I was not sure.

And yet, due to our identification with senses and objects, we feel existence-consciousness-love to be divided, differentiated, attainable, etc. It is due to this differentiation that we, the masters of the universe, imagine a God for us, create one, and then love or fear Him! It is like loving a statue that you have created, as described in the Greek story of Pygmalion! In the case of consciousness, however, if we pray to what we have created, we ultimately become immortal, since that is what we are. This is the gist of the verses.

Not only this, but when we love someone, it is our own love that extends to that person and then we run after them! It is the same with our love for knowledge, wealth, fame, etc. We run after others without ever realizing that we are running after something to get what is already ours and with us!

Bhai, if not anything, the knowledge of this will make your extra effort to run after something decrease.

By now I had become used to learning unsettling facts from Gita. Even then, I asked, But what about, 'knowledge, the object of knowledge and the goal of knowledge' being one? That is not clear.

Normally we see the world through the triad of subject-object-action, as in seeing or experiencing. But to realize that existence-knowledge-love are one and same, the triad has to vanish, and will vanish since there are no two! That is why you, your beloved and the act of love become one at the highest state of love. This is true of knowledge, meditation, acts – everything.

Incidentally, this is the highest ideal of Vedanta, which has also been taken up by Sufi saints.

Hmm, said I. What was there to argue when I was unable to grasp it all? The immensity of the ideas floating around me was overwhelming.

Why spirituality?

य एवं वेत्ति पुरुषं प्रकृतिं च गुणैः सह, सर्वथा वर्तमानोऽपि न स भूयोऽभिजायते |

Those who understand the truth about the Supreme Soul, the individual soul, Nature with its qualities, does not get born again. (XIII.23)

The goal of spirituality is to take you out of the cycle of birth and death – anything less than that is not spirituality. So, what is being marketed as spirituality in the present times is not what it claims to be. But spirituality sells, and hence all these peddlers of neo-spirituality continue to cheat the gullible.

Know the complete canvas. It is only then that you will have a desire to achieve the highest. A little bit of nibbling here and a bit of biting there can take you nowhere.

How to be spiritual?

Swamiji, Gita talks about too many paths to freedom. How will a common man choose the right one?

Choose any path prescribed by the sacred books of your religion and then stay steady on it. That is the way to supreme knowledge. There is no inferior or superior path in it; there are only paths. As Gita says here:

ध्यानेनात्मनि पश्यन्ति केचित् आत्मानम् आत्मना, अन्ये साङ्ख्येन योगेन कर्मयोगेन चापरे
अन्ये तु एवम् अजानन्तः श्रुत्वान्येभ्य उपासते, तेऽपि चातितरन्ति एव मृत्युं श्रुतिपरायणाः |

Some strive to perceive the Supreme Soul within their hearts through meditation; some do so through discrimination between the real and the unreal; while many others struggle to attain it by the path of action. Many others who are unaware of these spiritual paths, hear about God from others and then they cross the ocean of death through devotion. (XIII.24–25)

You can thus see how one can go beyond the cosmic body (universe) through a proper spiritual effort made by one's head, heart or hands, or the combined effort of all these. Take up one path and go beyond your limits set by Nature. That is spirituality.

Beyond illusions

Swamiji was silent for a while and then said, This one time, an interviewer asked me who is an enlightened person in the present times. I jokingly said that I was one. Sorry to say that this got published in a major newspaper! What I was trying to tell them was that anyone can claim to be a spiritual person, as is happening all the time in India. The knowledge of self being subjective, there is no way to prove or disprove someone's claims, which makes the gullible fall for the chimera.

Even then there are some ways by which you can get a glimpse of the greatness of a spiritual person, as expressed in these two verses.

समं सर्वेषु भूतेषु तिष्ठन्तं परमेश्वरम्, विनश्यत्सु अविनश्यन्तं य: पश्यति स पश्यति |
समं पश्यन्हि सर्वत्र समवस्थितम् ईश्वरम्, न हिनस्ति आत्मना आत्मानं ततो याति परां गतिम् |

A realized person sees the presence of God everywhere, so he does not injure the self by self, that is, they do not degrade themselves by the acts of their mind, and thus they reach the highest goal. How? Since, they know that all actions are done by Prakriti and that the Self is beyond action. (XIII.27–28)

A realized person never ever indulges in undignified acts. To uplift the spiritual consciousness of the society they may take some unusual steps, but they never degrade their social conscience. When we act in a foul or filthy way, it is because we identify ourselves with the body, senses, mind, ego, etc. This identification is the false self. It is due to this falsity that we create bondage and rebirth for us.

Once this identification is cut asunder by realizing one's true self, mukti (liberation) is spontaneous. When one sees that all actions are done by Prakriti and that they are the Self, meaning pure consciousness, which is beyond any action, then they can neither crave nor avoid anything. In addition, whatever they do to continue living in the world cannot leave an impression on them, since impressions belong to the mind, but their conjunction with the mind has then been cut asunder!

To see and treat everybody with an equal and compassionate eye is the most important quality of the enlightened. Be enlightened, bhai! Nothing less than that should be your goal!

Is God responsible for our mess?

You might wonder that if the Supreme Lord is the Self of all embodied beings, how can He be unaffected by their acts, since the sin and virtue affect the real doer. Gita explains the point with an emphatic denial of our conclusion that God is responsible for our mess.

यथा सर्वगतं सौक्ष्म्यात् आकाशं नोपलिप्यते, सर्वत्र अवस्थितो देहे तथात्मा नोपलिप्यते |
यथा प्रकाशयति एकः कृत्स्नं लोकमिमं रविः, क्षेत्रं क्षेत्री तथा कृत्स्नं प्रकाशयति भारत |

As the akasa *(space) that pervades all things is not stained by objects, even so the Self dwelling in the body does not get stained; and, as the one sun illumines the whole world, so does the kshetrajna illumine the kshetra without getting affected by the defects of the body. (XIII.32–33)*

Space contains everything – good and bad – but it is never treated as good or bad because of what it contains. God is just like that; all are contained in Him, but He is never affected by the ills or virtues of the beings. God is the illuminator of the body and the universe, without getting affected by what He illuminates.

In Hinduism, God is thus seen as the power behind everything, whilst staying unaffected. This privilege cannot be with God who meddles in our affairs! Nice, na?

Is this the most difficult chapter? I asked.

Swamiji smiled.

Easier said than done, I thought when I completed my notes. But then I remembered how Swamiji had once told me that nothing can be achieved till the time is right. However, one should listen to such thoughts so that we can inculcate them when the right time comes knocking.

My one wish is that I can keep all this in my memory till that time comes.

XIV

THE DYNAMICS OF LIFE

We were walking toward our point of start for the day when Swamiji asked, Have you ever felt like crying out 'Et tu Brutus?'

Yes Swamiji, I have been stabbed in the back quite a few times in my life, both personally and professionally; probably more than what one usually gets. But I moved on.

Choosing the right company

One big reason why we get stabbed in the back, he said, is that we are not careful when choosing who we surround ourselves with. There are two situations in which we choose our close ones – the personal and professional, as you pointed out. If you consider society to be a large pond, then people here are like varieties of fish through which you have to sift. Crucially, your choice will remain confined to the pond that is at your disposal and the fish that it has to offer, which often are not tailored to your preferences.

Regarding choosing your mates on the professional front, let me narrate a story from the great Mahabharata. After the Pandavas had won the war, enjoyed their new-found power for some years and grown old, they finally felt extremely sick of the killings that they had committed during the war, and so they travelled to the Himalayas to give up their bodies. As they walked, each of the five started falling dead, including Draupadi – their common wife – who fell first. When asked, Yudhisthira, the eldest, told Bhima the defects of each of them that had led to their deaths. Draupadi fell down because of her partiality to Arjuna, Sahadeva was overproud of his wisdom, Nakul of his beauty, Arjuna of his pride and Bhima himself fell due to his gluttony. However, Yudhisthira had never told them of their defects earlier and instead had led them as a team.

What we can learn from this story is that when you lead a team, you must do so without pointing fingers at them, or else they will turn against you. Why? Because people are born with a certain blueprint, and hence, even if they want to, they cannot change their nature and flaws in this life. If one makes effort over several births, then these may finally change. So, the best thing is to focus on one's strength and not on one's shortcomings, since you cannot overcome them. This is true for your team, too – focus on the strengths of your members. Popular teachings like 'work on your weakness' are silly when seen in this light.

But, while choosing your personal companions, you have to be careful. Remember, 'trust not those who are not content'.

This was unacceptable for me, so I objected vehemently. I do not agree with you, Swamiji. How can we progress unless there is discontent within? Even you said that religion begins when there is dissatisfaction. Aren't you contradicting yourself?

Bhai, diluted inconsistency is the crown of the wise, while stubbornness is the suicidal vest of the fool. As you can guess, I do not want to cause an explosion! However, what I said was 'discontentment from the world leads to spirituality'. The desire to know yourself is neither an ordinary kind of desire nor the ordinary kind of knowledge that we are familiar with. So, my words are consistent, although they may be interpreted as being inconsistent.

It is like the Maya that you have been talking about – a mass of confusion, I joked.

He laughed innocently. The power to appreciate a joke about himself showed his inner strength. I appreciated that.

As for growth, he said, it comes through one's commitment and not through the acts born of nervous energy. It has become fashionable these days to equate unbridled passion with expressions like drive or work ethic. But remember that, humans made progress through commitment and not through passion.

As mentioned by you, we have been talking about Maya and Prakriti quite a bit. These, and their equivalent terms, play an important role in Hindu religion and culture, so it is good to know how they influence and affect us in our daily life, as also in spirituality.

Prakriti (nature) comprises the three gunas (qualities) – sattva, rajas and tamas – in perfect balance. When creation begins, prakriti gets active, with the three gunas remaining together while also trying to overpower each other. The entire creation, along with all universes and their inhabitants, is a mere play of these gunas.

It was stated in the seventh chapter that the Lord creates, sustains and destroys the universe through His two aspects – matter and spirit. Although the soul residing in the body is one with God, it wrongly identifies itself with the three gunas of Prakriti due to ignorance, and is then born in various bodies, suffering the good and the bad produced by the actions of the body. This chapter discusses the three gunas.

If you understand the character of the three gunas, you will be able to judge people and make the right choice. And if you want to be spiritual, you have to first get rid of your sloth by being active, and then become noble by attaining stability from within. It is then that you reach the launching pad to spirituality!

The three qualities within us

The three qualities – sattva, rajas and tamas – pervade everything in the universe. They stay together, try to overpower each other and bind the soul by deluding it. Everything in the universe, including human beings, is a mixture of these. The people around us are all different because they contain varying proportions of these three qualities.

सत्त्वं रजस्तम इति गुणाः प्रकृतिसम्भवाः, निबध्नन्ति महाबाहो देहे देहिनम् अव्ययम् |

Sattva, rajas and tamas – these three gunas, born of Prakriti, bind the soul in the body. (XIV.5)

The gunas are the finest particle in creation. How fine? Finer than the mind, since it is the gross product of the gunas.

Of the three gunas, sattva is stability, rajas is kinesis and tamas is inertia. Whatever is in the universe is the interplay of these three.

The biggest credit of prakriti is not the creation of the universe but its power to ensnare the soul through the three gunas. However, this binding is not real, for if it were real then the soul would get into bondage again and again, and mukti would never be possible. The embodied soul, known as jiva, is the reflected consciousness of Brahman, the Absolute. When creation takes place, Brahman appears as God, Isvara, who always remains beyond the gunas but the jiva thinks itself to be one with the sights created by the three qualities. Thus, the fundamental difference between God and us is that we, as soul, get deluded by the gunas and think ourselves to be bound, while God is ever free from any such entanglement.

How we get ensnared

How the gunas bind is shown next.

तत्र सत्त्वं निर्मलत्वात् प्रकाशकम् अनामयम्, सुखसङ्गेन बध्नाति ज्ञानसङ्गेन चानघ |
रजो रागात्मकं विद्धि तृष्णासङ्ग-समुद्भवम्, तन्निबध्नाति कौन्तेय कर्मसङ्गेन देहिनम् |
तमः तु अज्ञानजं विद्धि मोहनं सर्वदेहिनाम्, प्रमाद आलस्यनिद्राभिः तन्निबध्नाति भारत |
सत्त्वं सुखे सञ्जयति रजः कर्मणि भारत, ज्ञानमावृत्य तु तमः प्रमादे सञ्जयति उत |

Of these, sattva, being purer than the other two, is illuminating and full of well-being, so it binds the soul by creating attachment for happiness and knowledge.

Rajas is of the nature of passion arising from worldly desires and affections, and so it creates attachment to actions.

Tamas, born of ignorance, stupefies all embodied beings, and thus deludes all through negligence, laziness, and sleep.

Sattva attaches to happiness, rajas to action, and tamas to ignorance. (XIV.6–9)

There is nothing much to explain in these verses. It must be remembered that even noble qualities like knowledge and happiness are attributes of the mind, and hence belong to the realm of Prakriti. Those who want mukti must outgrow these, too. This is the fundamental difference between Vedanta and other religions that preach a person to be good. Although, virtues like goodness and nobility must be cultivated, since these are stepping stones to the Highest, they are not the ultimate state.

Sri Ramakrishna's story of the three robbers beautifully highlights this fact. In the story, a merchant is waylaid by three robber brothers, sattva, rajas and tamas. Despite being a thief, the sattva robber nobly does not want to hurt the victim, and even shows him the path to the town. Thus, though sattva cannot go anywhere near freedom or take someone there, it can guide the way. The other two – rajas and tamas – plot to plunder, hit, harm and damage the merchant in every possible way. There is no question of their going anywhere near the town, that is, they cannot lead a person to freedom.

Those who want to be achievers or to die with their boots on, have a predominance of rajas. They are deep in the world of matter and often use others as stepping stones to further their interests.

People with predominance of tamas are those who have a tendency to cause hurt. They are by nature vicious, cruel, demanding and toxic. If they get angry, they can go to any length to harm even their close ones.

Bhai, be wary of those having much of rajas, and keep a safe distance from the tamasik types.

However, these three qualities are present in all of us. If we did not have tamas, then we would not be able to sleep; and if we did not have rajas, we wouldn't be able to wake up! It is only the predominance of a particular guna that determines the nature of a person.

I was impressed. The reason for many of my follies in making friends and associations had suddenly become clear. I softly muttered my thanks, to which Swamiji turned back and asked if I had said something.

Nothing, I said.

I then changed the topic by asking if he had ever suffered because of bad company. Yes, many times, he answered gleefully, as if it was a matter of big achievement for him.

But how could that be, when you know these scriptures so well?

Tell me, he countered, who is a greater fool – those who make mistakes knowingly, or those who do so unknowingly?

What a question to ask! No fool like an old fool, as they say. The serial offenders are the worst ones.

Fine! Then tell me, who is more likely to burn their hand? The one who knows an object to be hot, or the one who holds it without knowing that? Well, the answer is obvious. Once you know what is right and what is wrong, you become very careful while indulging in wrong acts or engaging with the wrong types. As for me, I know who the bad ones are and that they may harm me, but even then I let them come near me due to various compulsions. You, however, are driven by your passions and necessity, and hence need to know how to stay safe.

No doubt in that!

Are you evolving?

As I have been telling you, these three qualities, which are the finest particles of creation, live together and try to overpower each other all the time. For example, we sleep and also wake up; get angry and forgive. Our love may change into hatred in a moment, day turns into night every day, fruit ripens and then rots ... the list goes on. These are all instances of one guna being overpowered by the other.

रजस्तमश्च अभिभूय सत्त्वं भवति भारत, रजः सत्त्वं तमश्चैव तमः सत्त्वं रजस्तथा |

It is in the nature of the gunas that sometimes sattva prevails over rajas and tamas, sometimes rajas dominates sattva and tamas, and at other times tamas overcomes sattva and rajas. (XIV.10)

You can understand which of the three gunas is currently predominant in you by examining how you feel and behave. The pattern of life, too, can be understood through this.

सर्वद्वारेषु देहेऽस्मिन्प्रकाश उपजायते, ज्ञानं यदा तदा विद्यात् विवृद्धं सत्त्वमित्युत |
लोभः प्रवृत्तिरारम्भः कर्मणामशमः स्पृहा, रजस्येतानि जायन्ते विवृद्धे भरतर्षभ |
अप्रकाशो अप्रवृत्तिश्च प्रमादो मोह एव च, तमस्येतानि जायन्ते विवृद्धे कुरुनन्दन |

When, the light of intelligence shines through every sense in this body, then it should be known that sattva is predominant. Greed, activity, the undertaking of actions, unrest, longing – these arise when rajas is predominant. Darkness, inertness, miscomprehension, and delusion – these arise when tamas is predominant. (XIV.11–13)

When sattva increases, you become intelligent, and your sense organs become extra powerful. Know that to be a fact. Wherever you see an intelligent person, they will have more of sattva.

However, do not confuse intelligent people with clever and smooth talkers. They are cunning types and so have more of rajas. Whenever they cannot get the right prey, they sink into tamas.

You might wonder if the predominance of these qualities matter in life. The answer is yes. The quality of life in this birth and the type of birth in the next is determined by the kind of qualities you have. The next two verses say:

Those who die with the predominance of sattva are born among the learned; those who die with a preponderance of rajas are born among people driven by work; while those dying with tamas take birth among the dull and the uncultured.

The idea is that you get what you want. If you do not choose to be noble, then you will be born among shirkers or shriekers!

I furtively checked Google for the word 'shrieker', but it failed to provide an answer. I concluded that Swamiji meant the active types.

Swamiji continued, The chapter then goes on to stress on the importance of going beyond the three gunas, which essentially means to meditate deep and transcend the empire of the mind to be what a person truly is – Atman.

Once true knowledge dawns, you go beyond getting attached to the play of the gunas or getting into a blame game towards them – you become neutral towards the play of Nature. The three gunas continue to play through your body until you are alive, but you do not care whether good or bad plays through you!

The way to freedom

Swamiji concluded by saying that for spiritual seekers, the way out is to love God.

मां च यो अव्यभिचारेण भक्तियोगेन सेवते,
स गुणान् समतीत्यैतान् ब्रह्म भूयाय कल्पते |
ब्रह्मणो हि प्रतिष्ठाहम् अमृतस्य अव्ययस्य च,
शाश्वतस्य च धर्मस्य सुखस्यैकान्तिकस्य च |

Those who serve Me with an unswerving devotion, they go beyond the gunas and become fit to be one with Brahman, for, I am the abode of Brahman, the Immortal and Immutable, of everlasting dharma and of Absolute Bliss. (XIV.26–27)

Sri Krishna is God. When personified he appears with form, and in his impersonal form, He is Brahman. That is where the idea that Sri Krishna is the abode of Brahman comes from.

For a devotee, the best way to attain mukti or be one with Brahman is to worship God in whatever form they love. A very interesting discussion on this comes in the next chapter.

I finish off this note with the feeling that the chapter was relatively easy to understand, if not fully accept. And it was definitely quite practical. A great help in personality management.

XV

THE WAY TO GOD

Some years ago, I chanced upon a poster promising '*Gita Saar*' – the Essence of Gita – in Hindi. It had some nice quotes from the sacred text, of which I remember only one: *Jo ho raha hai, theek ho raha hai* – whatever is happening is fine, or something like that. But till now, I had not come across any statement even remotely connected with that idea. So, I asked Swamiji about it. Was I missing something?

He laughed loudly, and said, I, too, have come across that poster somewhere. What is interesting about that poster is that not a single statement on it is from Gita!

He then added, You know, Gita must hold the world record for the maximum number of interpretations and commentaries, as also an uncountable number of misrepresentations! You yourself had made strong allegations against it, which you must have realized by now are far-fetched.

You can say that.

Gita is a *moksha shastra*, meaning that it teaches you how to be one with God. Everything else in it or about it is incidental, like props to take the philosophy forward. In an effort to make this work practical, some overzealous people misinterpret it or talk selectively from it to suit their needs.

Hmm.

Your perseverance in listening to the explanation of Gita shows that you must have developed a liking for it, and so you won't get bored if I explain the fifteenth chapter in full, since it is revered as a complete scripture. Imagine! In a mere twenty verses, this chapter presents the entire spectrum of spirituality, religion and the world! What great minds our sages had! And to think that today we take pride in dealing with trinkets in comparison to the gems that the sages left for us!

I did not agree with him, but stayed silent, since I was preoccupied with some ideas from the previous chapter, which were buzzing around my head.

Samsara, the world

Swamiji began with a description of samsara, which roughly translates to 'the world', but actually means our existence and interactions with the universe, including our rebirths.

He said, 'God and mammon cannot be served at the same time as two swords cannot be put in the same scabbard' – these words of Jesus Christ are true for every seeker of spirituality. Those who want to attain liberation, or love God with unswerving devotion have to be detached from samsara – that which slides all the time. This chapter begins with a description of samsara through the analogy of an *asvattha* tree, so that an aspirant may understand its nature, develop dispassion towards it, and then acquire love and knowledge of God.

ऊर्ध्वमूलम् अधःशाखम् अश्वत्थं प्राहुरव्ययम्,
छन्दांसि यस्य पर्णानि यस्तं वेद स वेदवित् |
अधश्चोर्ध्वं प्रसृतास्तस्य शाखा गुणप्रवृद्धा विषयप्रवालाः,
अधश्च मूलानि अनुसन्ततानि कर्मानुबन्धीनि मनुष्यलोके |
न रूपमस्येह तथोपलभ्यते नान्तो न चादिर्न च सम्प्रतिष्ठा,
अश्वत्थमेनं सुविरूढमूलं असङ्गशस्त्रेण दृढेन छित्त्वा |
ततः पदं तत्परिमार्गितव्यं यस्मिन्गता न निवर्तन्ति भूयः,
तमेव चाद्यं पुरुषं प्रपद्ये यतः प्रवृत्तिः प्रसृता पुराणी |

Samsara is spoken of as an eternal ashvattha tree rooted above and branching below, whose leaves are the Vedas. He who knows it, is a real knower.

The branches of the tree extend upward and downward, nourished by the three guṇas, whose buds are the objects of the senses. The roots of the tree hang downward, causing the flow of Karma in the human form. Below, its roots branch out causing (karmic) actions in the world of humans.

The real form of this tree is not perceived in this world, neither its beginning nor end, nor its continued existence. But this deep-rooted ashvattha must be cut down with the strong axe of detachment.

After that, one must go in search of the foundation of the tree, which is the Supreme Lord, from whom streamed forth the activity of the universe a long time ago. By taking refuge in Him, one will not have to return to this world again. (XV.1–4)

The world, with all its beauty and charm, is ultimately a big trap for the soul. So, before the soul tries to get freedom, it has to cut the snares and traps completely, meaning that one has to get rid of all attachments, physically and mentally, from the world and its people.

The interesting point to note in these four verses is the stress on the word 'detachment', which happens to be the keyword of Gita. This is true in spiritual life, as also in one's professional and personal life. To be successful and to be at peace in the world, one must maintain at least a little detachment in all that one does, loves, aspires and craves for.

No one can achieve big in life without detachment. Why do we fail to get good grades in exams? Why are we not adored? Why do marriages fail? Why do we get depressed? The answer to all this is just one – lack of detachment from what should not be done. People talk about yoga all the time, without ever realizing that yoga is actually *'viyoga'* – detachment from what is not to be done. To lead a healthy life, one has to stay detached from what is not needed, as well as a little detached from what one wants or already has.

Gita being a scripture, Sri Krishna talks about how to get out of the cycle of birth and death. The first step towards it is to develop detachment from the world. Know that detachment is the key to success; it is also the key to liberation of every kind. People stay in toxic relationships or in a toxic workplace simply because they do not have enough detachment! And even you cannot get rid of your problems for the same reason.

I was startled by the words of Swamiji, which sounded quite prophetic. But more than that, I was surprised to see how the basics of spiritual life are applicable in daily life. I must admit that I had never imagined that religion permeates our life principles so deeply.

The way out of samsara

निर्मानमोहा जितसङ्गदोषा अध्यात्मनित्या विनिवृत्तकामाः,
द्वन्द्वैर्विमुक्ताः सुखदुःखसंज्ञैः गच्छन्त्यमूढाः पदमव्ययं तत् |
न तद्भासयते सूर्यो न शशाङ्को न पावकः, यद्गत्वा न निवर्तन्ते तद्धाम परमं मम |

Those who are free from pride and delusion, who have overcome the evil of attachment, who dwell constantly on the self and on God, who are free from the desire to enjoy the senses, and are beyond the dualities of pleasure and pain – only such persons attain My eternal Abode, which neither the sun nor the moon, nor fire can illumine, (since it is self-luminous). Having attained that, one does not return to any of the worlds ever again. (XV.5–6)

To be spiritual means to give up the world fully and be one with God. There is no other way. The result is permanent joy in which there is no trace of this world or any other. Those who love anything – parents, spouse, kids, friends, wealth, food, etc. – can never be one with that state.

Param dham is the common term used for the highest state of spiritual realization. In that state, the soul realizes its identity with God.

Creation and rebirth

Creation – its origin, sustenance and dissolution – finds an important place in every scripture. In the Veda, too, there is a fair share of this discussion, though *Nasadiya Sukta* of the Rigveda clearly says that these things cannot be explained, since there was no one at the time of creation. It means that you can take any theory that suits your philosophy of life and move ahead. Gita touches on these topics more than once for the same reason – take up what suits your mentality and move ahead. There is no single fixed route to God!

ममैवांशो जीवलोके जीवभूतः सनातनः, मनःषष्ठानि इन्द्रियाणि प्रकृतिस्थानि कर्षति |
शरीरं यदवाप्नोति यच्चापि उत्क्रामतीश्वरः, गृहीत्वैतानि संयाति वायुर्गन्धानिवाशयात् |
श्रोतं चक्षुः स्पर्शनं च रसनं घ्राणमेव च, अधिष्ठाय मनश्चायं विषयानुपसेवते |
उत्क्रामन्तं स्थितं वापि भुञ्जानं वा गुणान्वितम्,
विमूढा नानुपश्यन्ति पश्यन्ति ज्ञानचक्षुषः |
यतन्तो योगिनश्चैनं पश्यन्ति आत्मनि अवस्थितम्,
यतन्तो अपि अकृतात्मानो नैनं पश्यन्ति अचेतसः |

An eternal portion of Mine becomes a living soul and then it draws (to itself) the (five) senses, and mind as the sixth. It is thus that the soul rests in Prakriti. When the soul wants to take birth or leave a body, It takes these six and moves on, the way wind carries fragrance from flowers. The soul experiences the world of objects by presiding over the five senses and the mind.

The spiritually challenged people cannot perceive the soul while it resides in the body and enjoys the sense objects; nor do they perceive it when it departs. But those who possess spiritual wisdom see it clearly. Striving yogis, too, are able to perceive the soul enshrined in the body. However, those whose minds are not purified cannot see it. (XV.7–11)

Considering the sacred nature of the chapter, I had decided not to object to anything that Swamiji said from it. Also, I was not in a position to agree or disagree with the esoteric.

Creation in Vedanta is explained using an analogy of the sun in the sky and its reflection in a bowl of water. The actual sun and the reflected sun appear to be two, but when the water dries up in the bowl, the reflected sun can be said to go back to the sun. In this analogy, the sun is the Supreme Lord, the bowl is Prakriti, and the water in the bowl is the mind. When the water (that is, mind) is emptied, the bowl (Prakriti) continues to be there and can be filled up by some other water (rebirth). But when the bowl itself is destroyed (that is, Prakriti itself is dissolved through right knowledge), that reflected sun can never again come into existence.

In these verses, this very concept of creation and rebirth is explained. At the time of creation, an eternal portion of the Lord (a portion of the Infinite is also infinite) becomes a living soul (jiva) in the world and draws to itself the five senses and the mind from the Prakriti. At the time of death, and later at the time of acquiring a new body (that is, rebirth), the Lord of the body and senses (jiva) is accompanied by the subtle body (which includes senses and the mind). This carrying of the senses, etc. by the jiva is like the wind carrying scent particles away as it passes. Thus, even when the physical body is destroyed after death, the jiva continues its journey with the essential components of the previous body and the mind to work out its Karma through a new body.

This explains why ghosts behave the way do, and how our past life affects our present. Bhai, be careful! What you do now will leave an impression on your senses (in the brain centre) and the mind, and will be carried forward to the next life. It is like an error in a computer program! These errors will pop up whenever the opportune moment (and the worst moment for you!) comes, he teased.

What is the proof of all this? These are the words of the spiritually enlightened. The verses say that the soul cannot be perceived by a common man when it leaves the body at the time of death, or when it dwells in the body, or when it is united with the gunas, or while it experiences the objects. Only the eyes of the spiritually illumined can perceive all this, and luckily for us, even a sincere yoga aspirant can experience these.

Have you experienced any of this, or a ghost?

What to say! If I say yes, you will think me to be proud, and if I say no, then you will think me to be humble. My answering this will not alter your perception. That is why we say that you have to have your own experiences and realizations to believe the sacred words. As Lord Buddha said, '*Atmadeepo bhava*'.

You are avoiding the question.

Casual questions must be answered casually, he said, and then proceeded to the next inscriptions on the slabs.

God and His glory

The next verses narrate some of the glories of God, in continuation with what Sri Krishna had said in Chapter X.

यदा आदित्यगतं तेजो जगद्भासयते अखिलम्,
यत् चन्द्रमसि यच्चाग्नौ तत्तेजो विद्धि मामकम् |
गामाविश्य च भूतानि धारयामि अहमोजसा,
पुष्णामि चौषधीः सर्वाः सोमो भूत्वा रसात्मकः |
अहं वैश्वानरो भूत्वा प्राणिनां देहमाश्रितः, प्राणापान-समायुक्तः पचामि अन्नं चतुर्विधम्
सर्वस्य चाहं हृदि सन्निविष्टो मत्तः स्मृतिर्ज्ञानम् अपोहनं च,
वेदैश्च सर्वैः अहमेव वेद्यो वेदान्तकृत् वेदविदेव चाहम् |

Know that the light of the Sun, the moon and the fire is from me.

I nourish all living beings with My energy by permeating the earth. And, by becoming the moon, I nourish all plants with the juice of life.

I am the fire of digestion in the stomachs of all living beings, and the energy that assimilates the digested food.

I am seated in the hearts of all living beings, and from Me come memory, knowledge, as well as forgetfulness. I am the subject of discussion of the Vedas; I am the author of the Vedanta, and I alone am the knower of the meaning of the Vedas. (XV.12–15)

All power, glory, wisdom – as also their opposites – comes from God. Nay, these are God Himself! That is why the narration says that God is the light of everything.

It has been the belief in India that the moon (lit. soma) is the repository of all sap. When the sap enters a plant, it gets nourished and enriched. The verse says that Lord Himself is that soma, the repository of all sap.

The same Lord also enters the bodies of all living creatures in the form of the *Vaishvanara* fire (the fire that lives in the stomach). Mingling with the prana (upward vital air) and *apana* (downward vital air), He alone digests the four kinds of food (masticated, sucked, swallowed and licked) taken by living beings.

Above all, He is seated in the hearts of all as the witness of all that is good and bad; from Him comes memory and knowledge and their loss. He alone is the author of the Vedanta (that explains the essence of the Veda), the Knower of the Veda and He alone is to be known through the four Vedas.

The interesting thing in these verses is the mention of forgetting as coming from God! Memory, ah! How it propels us forward and also drags us back! Lucky is the person who can forget his past, for God's grace is with them.

I pondered – was I lucky?

Lord – beyond all

द्वाविमौ पुरुषौ लोके क्षरश्चाक्षर एव च, क्षरः सर्वाणि भूतानि कूटस्थोऽक्षर उच्यते |
उत्तमः पुरुषस्त्वन्यः परमात्मेति उधाहृतः, यो लोकत्रयमाविश्य बिभर्ति अव्यय ईश्वरः |
यस्मात् क्षरम् अतीतोऽहम् अक्षरादपि चोत्तमः, अतोऽस्मि लोके वेदे च प्रथितः पुरुषोत्तमः
यो मामेवम् असम्मूढो जानाति पुरुषोत्तमम्, स सर्वविद्भजति मां सर्वभावेन भारत |
इति गुह्यतमं शास्त्रम् इदमुक्तं मयानघ,
एतद्बुद्ध्वा बुद्धिमान्स्यात् कृतकृत्यश्च भारत |

There are two purushas in the world – the kshara (perishable) and akshara (imperishable). All beings are the perishable; while the kutastha (Prakriti, that is, nature) is called the imperishable. But (there is) another, the Supreme Purusha, God, who by pervading the three worlds, sustains them.

As I (God as Sri Krishna) transcend the perishable and am above even the imperishable, therefore I am referred to as Purushottama in the world and in the Vedas. Those who know Me as the Supreme God, they truly have knowledge, and they worship Me with their whole being.

This is the most profound teaching imparted by Me to you, O Arjuna. Knowing this one attains the highest. (XV.16–20)

You may find this portion difficult and abstruse but that is how spiritual philosophy goes. In fact, our commentators have tried to explain this part of Gita variously. But, if you take a comprehensive view of all the Hindu scriptures, or even just Gita, then the meaning becomes plain and simple.

Sri Krishna here talks about the three realities, which are one but appear as three – Soul, Nature and Consciousness. In the example of the sun and the reflected sun, cited earlier, when there is no creation, what remains? You will naturally say 'one sun'. However, we are not talking here about any ordinary sun, but of Reality. To describe that Reality as 0, 1, 2 or whatever, you need an observer, which is not there. So, what remains, remains! It cannot be expressed.

But when we are talking from the standpoint of our existence, there are three realities, of which God is the supreme. The soul or Nature cannot call itself one with God till they are in this state of independent existence.

Shankaracharya, the great teacher of Hindu scriptures, made an amazing contribution to the world of philosophy by introducing the concept of Absolute and Relative (*paramarth* and *vyavaharika*). Once you understand that reality indeed has two distinct states, you will never have any difficulty harmonizing the outlooks of various sects and religions.

Swami Vivekananda had explained these two realities with a simple example. If a person were to travel towards the sun and take photographs at various stages, the pictures will look different, but they will all be of the same sun. Something like this is the case with God in His absolute reality, and God in the relative world.

While concluding, the Lord terms this chapter as *shastra*, scripture, since it contains the essence of the Veda.

I have a small request, bhai. Please try to memorize this chapter and recite it daily after your bath. Consider this to be your *guru dakshina* to me.

After I finished writing my notes on this chapter, I felt moved by Swamiji's request and decided to memorize and recite it daily.

XVI

THE DIVINE AND THE UNHOLY QUALITIES

I was feeling pretty mellow in the morning after my exposure to Chapter XV. If indeed God was the reality, as the chapter describes beautifully, then there was something wrong in our perception of the universe and the way we acted here.

The source of ethics

Lost in the maze of my thoughts, I was listening selectively to Swamiji when one statement from him caught my attention: Do you believe in values?

This made me alert. I replied, What do you mean, Swamiji? Everyone believes in certain values. As they say, *choron ka bhi iman hota hai* – even crooks have their ethics.

Indeed, crooks are more ethical than us, he said, for there would be a summary execution by their tribe or disciplinary action from a kangaroo court in case of a violation! Please do not mind my saying this, but most of the Western world runs on the principle of 'ethics of the crooks'!

What!

Do not get excited without understanding the subject, he said sternly. Values flow from three broad sources. First, from spiritual principles, based on the realizations of sages and prophets; second, when a religiously empowered person dictates right and wrong to their followers; and finally, when some self-proclaimed people of wisdom sit together to impose values on a society.

Of these, the first is the best because of its rationality, the second is good enough but not as rational, while the third is the projection of those wielding power in a particular society. In this third kind, values and laws keep changing unbridled under the garb of the democratic process, although it is only mob justice carried out by the few on the majority.

You don't believe in democracy, do you?

Fully. But let us not get political. The Hindu value system is based on eternal spiritual principles, with an emphasis on unselfishness, meaning one has to be inclusive even in one's daily life. Here, in Gita, Sri Krishna is narrating universal principles of inclusiveness that should be adopted by every society as their way of life.

This chapter elaborates on noble qualities alongside unholy ones. If you remember the description of the three gunas, you will realize that to be noble means to have sattva within you, and to be not-so-noble means to have traits born of rajas and tamas. Why have sattva? That is because it is the launching pad to spirituality. Of course, if a society has some other goals, they will focus on a different value system.

The divine qualities

Sri Krishna first enumerates the *daivi* – divine – qualities, which have been the basis of the Hindu value system, as reflected in books like *Manusmriti*. If you can fully imbibe any of these qualities, you will become an icon, as Gandhiji became because of his practice of non-violence.

अभयं सत्त्वसंशुद्धिः ज्ञानयोग-व्यवस्थितिः,
दानं दमश्च यज्ञश्च स्वाध्यायः तप आर्जवम् |
अहिंसा सत्यम् अक्रोधस्त्यागः शान्तिः अपैशुनम्,
दया भूतेषु अलोलुप्त्वं मार्दवं ह्रीरचापलम् |
तेजः क्षमा धृतिः शौचम् अद्रोहो नातिमानिता,
भवन्ति सम्पदं दैवीम् अभिजातस्य भारत |

Fearlessness, purity of mind, steadfastness in spiritual knowledge, charity, control of the senses, performing yajna, regular reading of the scriptures, austerity, uprightness; non-violence, truthfulness, absence of anger, renunciation, tranquillity, absence of fault-finding, compassion towards all, non-covetousness, gentleness, modesty, absence of fickleness, boldness, forgiveness, fortitude, purity, absence of hatred, absence of pride – these are the divine virtues. (XVI.1–3)

These, as anyone can see, are universal values and virtues that everyone in the world should have. Our Acharyas, who have written commentaries on various scriptures, have explained these terms with minor variations in meaning, but the general idea remains the same. These are the qualities of a gentleman, as also of religious persons and those aspiring for spirituality.

Honesty, integrity, values, virtues

I have a question, Swamiji. The list of virtues that Gita gives us seems to be conflicting. For example, my truthfulness may cause violence, harm or even the death of someone. How would we then decide what to do?

What you say is absolutely correct – this is known as an ethical dilemma. You may be trying to practise some value but end up derailing another. That is the reason why such dilemmas are a wonderful recipe for engrossing stories. Some religious systems have tried to come up with a hierarchy of values, with non-violence or truthfulness on the top, but you cannot really name an alpha-value.

Ordinarily, people are self-centred, with their ideas of 'me and mine' extending up to, say, their family. But this is how animals live, too. To be human means to be inclusive, which comes through the practice of social norms, laws and values.

If a person practices values like truthfulness or not stealing, they are known as honest. However, in most cases, honesty is a lack of opportunity, and at times courage, which shows that it is an external show that depends hugely on who is looking at the practitioner.

Greater than the honest are those who are established in some virtue, irrespective of who is looking at them or applauding them. These are the people who are said to have integrity. They may, if need be, cross the boundaries of values, norms and laws to be true to their self. After all, they don't care what others feel about them. In one word, they go by their conscience, considering what is right at that moment.

I have known honest people and also a few who have integrity. My experience is that you cannot depend on the honest ones when you are in a crisis, for they will try to look good to others and save their own skin. As compared to them, you can always count upon the unconditional support of those having integrity. Honesty makes you a goody-goody, while integrity takes you to personal greatness, and consequently to spirituality. Mere honesty is a struggle to be established in sattva, while integrity implies spiritual aspiration to go beyond the three gunas.

Are you honest or virtuous, Swamiji?

I am not sure about my nature, but I like to help people and make them happy. Laws, morality, honesty are secondary to me.

Isn't that reproachful coming from a monk's mouth?

Not at all, bhai! Ethical dilemmas can be sorted only by those who treat integrity, as in virtues, above values. Stick to your guns of virtue and let the world take care of itself. The entire Mahabharata is about ethical dilemmas, without offering solutions. The idea in the great scripture is: 'Do what you consider to be right, for you will be criticized for what you choose to do when facing an ethical dilemma regardless. Only that your conscience needs to be clear, which again has to be based on your virtue.' There are many instances in the story of Mahabharata when Yudhisthira went against the norm, saying that his mind was established in virtue and hence wrong words could never be a part of his speech. Today, Yudhisthira is a synonym for dharma.

Even if you do not learn anything from our discussion, I would request you to have one simple goal in life – do such acts that your name may go from a mere noun to an adjective! This is possible only if you have integrity based on some virtue or value.

I felt humbled – the sign of inner weakness! To overcome my discomfiture, I suggested that we move ahead.

Are you unholy?

In contrast to values and virtues, there are traits within us that are unholy to varying degrees. We will have a look at these but before that, let me make it clear once again that good and evil do not come from two different sources, but are the natural products of the three gunas working within us. The evil traits are the harvest of rajas and tamas.

दम्भो दर्पोऽभिमानश्च क्रोधः पारुष्यमेव च, अज्ञानं चाभिजातस्य पार्थ सम्पदमासुरीम् |
दैवी सम्पद्विमोक्षाय निबन्धायासुरी मता, मा शुचः सम्पदं दैवीमभिजातोऽसि पाण्डव |
द्वौ भूतसर्गौ लोके-अस्मिन् दैव आसुर एव च,
दैवो विस्तरशः प्रोक्त आसुरं पार्थ मे शृणु |

Pretentiousness, arrogance, conceit, anger, harshness and ignorance belong to asuri *– evil nature. The divine qualities lead a person to liberation, while the asuri leads to bondage.*

Worry not, O Arjuna, you have divine qualities which have been elaborated; and now know about the demoniac traits. (XVI.4–6)

This is another of my favourite chapters. I knew a monk who used to humorously say that most people find themselves mentioned in scriptures. When asked to explain, he would say, read chapter XVI and you will know!

प्रवृत्तिं च निवृत्तिं च जना न विदुरासुराः, न शौचं नापि चाचारो न सत्यं तेषु विद्यते |
असत्यम् अप्रतिष्ठं ते जगदाहुः अनीश्वरम्, अपरस्परसम्भूतं किमन्यत् कामहैतुकम् |
एतां दृष्टिम् अवष्टभ्य नष्टात्मानो-अल्पबुद्धयः,
प्रभवन्ति उग्रकर्माणः क्षयाय जगतोऽहिताः |

They know not proper acts from improper, and hence they neither have purity in life nor good conduct, nor even truthfulness.

They say, The world has no purpose, has no moral order, and is without God. It is brought about by sexual union due to lust, what else? Holding fast to such views, these misdirected ones, with petty intellect and cruel deeds, grow to be the enemies of the world threatening its destruction. (XVI.7–9)

In today's world, most people hold these ideas as their philosophy and truth of life! This is the YOLO theory that you were mentioning. Isn't it amusing that thousands of years ago, too, there were people with such an outlook? Viewed philosophically, this outlook has been demolished completely, but it keeps rearing its head through the thinking of the dimwits, rooted in selfishness.

THE DIVINE AND THE UNHOLY QUALITIES

People with such an outlook are not only devilish but also engaged constantly in the destruction of the world. Look around and you will find that the history of the world is mostly about these devil-incarnates who have time and again turned lush green fields crimson with the power of their sword.

Shockingly, if a person has any of these traits, know that they will have all of them sooner or later.

I was shaken from within, hoping that these were just loose ideas floating on meaningless sound waves. Unfortunately, the barrage of pointers continued to scorch me.

काममम् आश्रित्य दुष्पूरं दम्भमानमदान्विताः,
मोहात् गृहीत्वा असद्ग्राहान् प्रवर्तन्ते अशुचिव्रताः |
चिन्ताम् अपरिमेयां च प्रलयान्ताम् उपाश्रिताः, कामोपभोगपरमा एतावत् इति निश्चिताः
आशापाशशतैर्बद्धाः कामक्रोधपरायणाः, ईहन्ते कामभोगार्थम् अन्यायेनार्थसञ्चयान् |

Filled with insatiable desires, full of hypocrisy, pride and arrogance, holding unholy ideas through delusion, they work with impure resolve.

Obsessed with endless desires that end only with their death, they regard gratification of lust as the highest, and feeling sure that to be the only goal in life.

Bound by hundreds of wishes, given over to lust and wrath, they strive to hoard wealth through unfair means for their gratification. (XVI.10–12)

इदमद्य मया लब्धम् इमं प्राप्स्ये मनोरथम्,
इदम् अस्ति इदमपि मे भविष्यति पुनर्धनम् |
असौ मया हतः शत्रुर्हनिष्ये चापरानपि, ईश्वरोऽहम् अहं भोगी सिद्धोऽहं बलवान्सुखी |

आढ्योऽभिजनवानस्मि कोऽन्योऽस्ति सदृशो मया,
यक्ष्ये दास्यामि मोदिष्य इति अज्ञानविमोहिताः |
अनेकचित्तविभ्रान्ता मोहजालसमावृताः, प्रसक्ताः कामभोगेषु पतन्ति नरकेऽशुचौ |

Their thoughts are like I have gained this much today, and shall fulfil this desire of mine in near future. This much is mine for the present, and by tomorrow I shall have more. That enemy has been destroyed by me, and others too I shall destroy. I am the lord, I enjoy, I am successful, powerful and happy. I am rich and cultured. Who else is equal to me? I will perform yajnas (to have fame), I will make charities (to be famous), I will rejoice.

Thus, deluded by ignorance, bewildered by many a fancy, covered by the meshes of delusion, addicted to the gratification of lust, they fall into foul hell. (XVI.13–16)

There is nothing to explain in these verses; you can see how the world is hurtling towards self-destruction with these and other similar thoughts.

What is indeed surprising is that Gita is nearly 3,500 years old, if not more – even in those times, people had such cravings! It simply means that the essential nature of people does not change with the passing of months, seasons and years. Only those who want to go beyond this madness bring about an inner change for their own sublimity. What more is there to say?

This chapter holds a mirror before you with the words, Mirror, mirror on the wall, who is deadliest of us all?

I wanted to appreciate the rhyme but was too shaken.

What leads you to hell?

त्रिविधं नरकस्येदं द्वारं नाशनम् आत्मनः,
कामः क्रोधस्तथा लोभः तस्मात् एतत् त्त्रयं त्यजेत् |
एतैर्विमुक्तः कौन्तेय तमोद्वारैः त्रिभिर्नरः,
आचरति आत्मनः श्रेयस्ततो याति परां गतिम् |

There are three gates to the hell of self-destruction – lust, anger and greed. Therefore, one should abandon all three. Those who have gone beyond these three gates of darkness, alone strive to become blessed. (XVI.21–22)

Gita is not a self-help book or a motivational one, but a spiritual book whose only aim is to take a person to self-realization. So, at times it has to put a finger in our eyes to show how we err and why.

The crux of this chapter is to stress the importance of getting rid of rajas and tamas tendencies. When you have big aspirations, or want to be victorious and lord over others, you have a lot of rajas within you. And if you have too much of violence within you that makes you feel like ruining others or destroying them, know that there is a lot of tamas within you. These two gunas will slowly bring about a devastating transformation within you and make you the devil incarnate soon enough. So be careful!

To get rid of devilish qualities, practise overcoming your insatiable desires, anger and greed. If every other method fails, then pray to God to remove these shortcomings in you.

Otherwise, you will have to wait for a long time to get out of the hell that you create for yourself. Period.

Period! No, there could be no period to this. The discussion had shaken my sensibilities and I decidedly wanted to grow up. I had to do it, if not for anything else then simply for my own well-being.

XVII

THREE ATTITUDES

I am not sure what my feelings were as we approached the completion of this humongous discussion on the sacred Gita. Indeed, it is to my credit that I had held on for so long, listening to ideas and words which were often out of depth for me.

By now, my conclusion was that Gita is indeed an impressive book of spirituality, but it is difficult for first timers to remember all that it contains. So, I asked Swamiji if this was a problem others faced, too.

The problem you mention, said Swamiji, is universal. For that matter, no spiritual work can be comprehended by going through it just once. Our minds are quite gross and so we can grasp only crude ideas, whereas spiritual truths are extremely subtle, so it takes ages to comprehend and consequently remember them. You can memorize a spiritual work but comprehending it is a completely different matter. The devout recite these works regularly to stay connected with the Divine, but the meaning dawns upon them only when they are ready for it.

How will I know if I am ready?

You understand something or learn a subject only when you work it out for yourself. No amount of teaching or studying can make you 'know' a subject unless you are nearly ready for it. A teacher can at best make you take one step beyond the boundary of what you already know or can confirm what you have already figured out.

For example, India today has the highest number of universities in the world, but how many great scientists are we producing? Close to none. Why? It is because in most cases, the teaching is meant to shove information inside heads that are not yet ready for it. This is even truer for spiritual knowledge – we collect only information, without ever letting it mature into knowledge. Information comes from outside while knowledge comes from within. The words of Gita or Bible or Veda are mere pointers to Truth, which you have to first know, then think deeply over, and finally understand. By God's grace someday that understanding may ripen into experiencing it.

To summarize, you are ready for knowledge when you have worked it out by yourself. When people criticize religious people for not living up to their ideals, the same allegations can be made against them for not being a scientist simply because they have studied science!

Coming back to your question, there is a popular story from the Mahabharata, according to which, long after the Kurukshetra war was over, Arjuna once requested Sri

Krishna to teach him Gita again, since he had forgotten it. Sri Krishna was quite annoyed and said that it was extremely irresponsible of him to have forgotten it, and that he himself was in a state of highest yoga when he had delivered it, so it was not possible for him to do so again! This story sums up the subtlety of spiritual teachings – the teacher has to be in a high state of yoga and the disciple has to be fully receptive.

I was relieved that modern gadgets had helped me record all that Swamiji was saying!

When we reached the first stone carving of the seventeenth chapter, he said that it was about three kinds of shraddha, a word which is difficult to translate into English.

It roughly means the orientation and attitude of a person that regulates their acts, he explained. Once shraddha for something is lost, the bond between the person and that 'other' breaks down irrevocably. Take, for example, marriage. If a person loses shraddha for the institution of marriage, you can guess the consequences, and if shraddha for the spouse is lost, then the fate of their marriage is a forgone conclusion.

You are what your shraddha is

In spirituality, which is our topic of discussion, shraddha means the disposition of a person born of an affirmative faith, conviction and reverential attitude towards spiritual reality. A person is made of their shraddha, they are that shraddha, and that shraddha is them.

Shraddha is of three types, as everything else in life – sattvika, rajasika and tamasika. A person with sattvic shraddha moves towards knowledge and happiness; with rajasik shraddha one pursues the path of action that leads them to pain and suffering; and tamasik shraddha takes its adherents to ignorance and delusion. This chapter describes the three kinds of shraddha or attitudes.

सत्त्वानुरूपा सर्वस्य श्रद्धा भवति भारत, श्रद्धामयोऽयं पुरुषो यो यत् श्रद्धः स एव सः |

The shraddha of each is according to his natural disposition. A person consists of their shraddha, and they are verily what their shraddha is. (XVII.3)

You are what your disposition or attitude is. Your acts, thoughts, behaviour and worship will be shaped accordingly. The next verses (4–6) talk about how sattvika people worship celestial gods (like Indra), rajasika people worship demigods, and tamasika people worship ghosts and spirits. When worshipped with shraddha, these deities respond to their prayers, but that cannot lead a person to the highest spiritual realization.

Know a person by their food habits

आयुःसत्त्वबलारोग्य-सुखप्रीतिविवर्धनाः, रस्याः स्निग्धाः स्थिरा हृद्या आहाराः सात्त्विकप्रियाः
कटु अम्ललवण अत्युष्ण तीक्ष्णरूक्ष-विदाहिनः, आहारा राजसस्येष्टा दुःखशोकामयप्रदाः |
यातयामं गतरसं पूति पर्युषितं च यत्, उच्छिष्टमपि चामेध्यं भोजनं तामसप्रियम् |

The foods which augment vitality, energy, strength, health, cheerfulness and appetite, which are savoury and succulent, nourishing and tasteful, are liked by the sattvika.

Excessively bitter, sour, saline, hot, pungent, dry and burning food, are liked by the rajasika. This kind of food produces pain, grief and disease.

The food that is stale, tasteless, stinking, cooked overnight and uchchhistha (already tasted by someone or leftover food), is liked by the tamasika. (XVII.8–10)

Hindus have traditionally been quite fussy about food. These three verses of Gita show how the nature of a person can be known by the kind of food that they take. Also, we lay a lot of stress on food not tasted or offered to someone else, since it becomes uchchhistha, known popularly in Hindi as *jootha*. The purpose behind this categorization is to let people know what will encourage mental purity in them.

What about non-vegetarian food, wine, fast food, etc.?

You will be surprised to know that neither Gita nor any of the Hindu scriptures – and by scriptures I mean the main ones and not the popular books written by some saint – prohibit non-vegetarian food. In fact, onion and garlic are a bigger taboo than meat in the *Manusmriti*, the greatest law book of the Hindus. If you apply the criteria mentioned here, you will know what to eat and what to avoid.

As for wine, it is not encouraged. There are mentions of its prohibition in various books, partly because it is fermented, meaning stale, and mostly because it takes away the alertness of the mind.

However, in spite of all the fuss regarding food intake, Hindus have been quite liberal in such matters and allow people to eat what they want, cautioning them of the consequences of becoming tamasika, which takes you downward in life, as mentioned earlier.

Three types of worshippers

अफलाकाङ्क्षिभिः यज्ञो विधिदृष्टो य इज्यते, यष्टव्यम् एवेति मनः समाधाय स सात्त्विकः |
अभिसन्धाय तु फलं दम्भार्थम् अपि चैव यत्, इज्यते भरतश्रेष्ठ तं यज्ञं विद्धि राजसम् |
विधिहीनम् असृष्टान्नं मन्त्रहीनम् अदक्षिणम्, श्रद्धाविरहितं यज्ञं तामसं परिचक्षते |

That yajna (or worship) is sattvika which is performed unselfishly, with the idea that it has to be performed as their way of life or as a responsibility.

Rajasika yajna is when a person has strong desires to fulfil through them, or when they want to make a show of it.

Tamasika yajna is performed without proper rituals, and is devoid of the mantras, gifts and shraddha. (XVII.11–13)

This section is very interesting, since it shows how most Hindus today have degraded themselves in matters of worship. Go to any temple – for that matter, you can go to the Shiva temple here at Omkareswar – and watch the worshippers. See how only few offer their worship properly with mantras, rituals and *daana* (making gifts to the worthy).

If you go to the temples of a metro city, the situation appears worse. People purchase some sweets as offerings, and present a long list of demands to God, with no proper procedure for the puja, etc. Tell me bhai, is God such a fool that He will fulfil your demands simply because you have offered Him some laddoos?

Anyway, at least they are doing something, even if that be tamasika puja. Maybe someday some sense may grow in them and then they may evolve to be sattvika.

Types of self-control

Be it the food that you like or the type of worship you perform, everything stems from self-control, which, as you can guess, is of three types.

देवद्विज-गुरुप्राज्ञपूजनं शौचम् आर्जवम्, ब्रह्मचर्यम् अहिंसा च शारीरं तप उच्यते |
अनुद्वेगकरं वाक्यं सत्यं प्रियहितं च यत्, स्वाध्याय अभ्यसनं चैव वाङ्मयं तप उच्यते |
मनः प्रसादः सौम्यत्वं मौनम् आत्मविनिग्रहः, भावसंशुद्धिः इत्येतत् तपो मानसमुच्यते |

Worship of God, respecting the Brahmins, as also Guru and the elderly, purity, straightforwardness, continence and non-injury are control of the body.

Words that do not cause distress, are true, inoffensive and beneficial, as well as regular recitation of the scriptures, are control of speech.

Serenity of thought, gentleness, silence, self-control and purity of purpose are control of the mind. (XVII.14–16)

One funny thing that I have observed in this life is that we want to control others, but rarely do we try or even think to apply control over ourselves. Look wherever you may, it is all self-implosion leading to suicide, murder, depression, divorce and other negative acts that stink of lack of self-control. Things have gone so bad that I'm left to wonder if I am an alien in my own land and times!

Swamiji, the word used in Gita is *tapah*, which you translated as control. Is that correct?

Yes. Tapah, from which *tapasya* has come, is any act in which a person commits themselves completely; stretching over years and decades, thinking of nothing else. This generates heat within and can make a person achieve the impossible. So, every tapah is a kind of self-control, withdrawing from the pleasure hunt and undignified acts.

Right ho! But, what about the worship of the Brahmins mentioned here? Isn't that a parochial attitude?

No, not at all. A society must learn to respect its elders and the learned if it wishes to remain alive and cultured. Compromise these two, and soon the society will be in the hands of ruffians. In earlier times Brahmins had knowledge, and hence the term. The implied meaning is to respect the learned.

Now that you mention it, Swamiji, I also feel that people hardly respect others.

Well, if you go to villages you may see the last glimmers of these values, but in general we have lost the battle with the Western I-me-mine-ism. This has to change or else we will perish as a culture. Strong words but true, nevertheless.

Dana: Making gifts

Dana, meaning gifting as a religious act, plays a very important role in the Hindu religion. You might have heard of Christian charity, in which the donor feels themselves to be superior to the one to whom the charity is being made. In the Indian traditions, however, as stressed in the *Manusmriti*, the right kind of dana is when a person makes gift as a religious act, and more importantly, both the giver and receiver feel honoured and blessed. If it is not so, then dana degenerates into charity, which bloats one's ego instead of leading them to sattva.

दातव्यम् इति यद्दानं दीयते अनुपकारिणे, देशे काले च पात्रे च तद्दानं सात्त्विकं स्मृतम् |
यत्तु प्रत्युपकारार्थं फलम् उद्दिश्य वा पुनः, दीयते च परिक्लिष्टं तद्दानं राजसं स्मृतम् |
अदेशकाले यद्दानम् अपात्रेभ्यश्च दीयते, असत्कृतम् अवज्ञातं तत्तामसम् उदाहृतम् |

Dana made to a worthy person with the idea that it should be done as a religious duty, without consideration of anything in return, at the proper time and in the proper place, is stated to be sattvika dana.

And what is given with a view to receiving in return, or looking for some result (like going to the heaven), or reluctantly, is rajasika dana.

Gifts made at the wrong place or time, to unworthy persons, without showing respect, or with contempt, is tamasika dana. (XVII.20–22)

Recently I came across the term 'return gift'. Believe me, it was so shocking to me that my *vairagya* from the world increased. Why make a gift if you expect a return gift? What kind of society are we creating? Why are even children's birthday parties becoming about 'partying', instead of instilling values in them? Why can't these higher-ups of society teach their kids the values of dana? But no. They only understand enjoyment through the basic functions of their bodies!

The importance of this discussion does not lie in judging people but in realizing that a conscious practice of sattvika habits will help you become noble. The central note of sadhana in the Hindu religious system is that what the greats do spontaneously, a sadhaka has to make efforts to do. That helps people acquire the kind of personality that one copies.

Of course, if you do not want to be noble, then who can force you into it?

Cultivating noble qualities

The chapter concludes with the suggestion of how to make things pure in case there is some doubt about it.

ॐ तत्सदिति निर्देशो ब्रह्मणः त्रिविधः स्मृतः, ब्राह्मणास्तेन वेदाश्च यज्ञाश्च विहिताः पुरा ।
तस्मात् ओमिति उदाहृत्य यज्ञदानतपःक्रियाः, प्रवर्तन्ते विधानोक्ताः सततं ब्रह्मवादिनाम् ।

'Om Tat Sat' – these three words are the symbolic representations of the Supreme Brahman since the beginning of creation. From them came the priests, scriptures and yajna (held sacred by the Hindus). Therefore, when performing worship, making dana or undertaking penance, it is customary to begin by uttering 'Om'. (XVII.23–24)

Om (made of combined sound of A, U, M) is the verbal representation of God. Whenever this sacred word (which is actually a sound) is uttered, the inherent goodness of a thing or act gets manifested. Om is also used to express consent, and to make things pure and holy.

Personally, whenever I travel, I always utter 'Om' before sitting down to make the place pure. It is like sprinkling Ganga water to purify things.

In the end, the Lord says that even if a person is ignorant of scriptural injunctions, they should lead their life with proper shraddha and make efforts to cultivate habits that are entrenched in sattva.

Whenever a person feels that his gift, worship or austerity may be impure, they should purify it by uttering 'Om Tat Sat'. In this way they will cultivate noble qualities, and ultimately attain the highest.

Since it was my last night at Omkareswar, I hesitantly invited Swamiji for dinner. He firmly declined, saying that monks should never venture out of their dwellings after sunset. I felt sad for the separation that was to take place the next day, but then reminded myself that separation is the only eternal law of life.

It was midnight when I completed the note on this chapter, which is simple and yet profoundly practical. Good for me that I could grasp some of the ideas well and identify where all things nosedived for me.

I tossed and turned in bed, thinking how my perception of life has undergone a change. I stayed awake till the late hours only to wade into sleep barely an hour before I was to meet Swamiji for the last time.

XVIII

FREEDOM

The cacophony of the alarm clock shoved me out of the bed as never before. I quickly got ready, without caring for the number of hours that I had spent fishing for dreams. It was imperative for me not to let go of even a single minute of Swamiji's company on our last day together.

Swamiji welcomed me with his usual smile. By now, I knew that meeting and separation did not matter to him. If he was not expressing his wisdom to the willing, he would live in his own inner world without needing the company of anyone. How I wish I could do that, too! But was I a person of the inner world who could dwell there without a care in the world? I don't think so. Maybe that is one of the more serious problems affecting us in present times – we cannot live by ourselves!

On our way, we talked of this and that, reminding each other that it was the last day of his explaining Gita to me. He, too, was to go back to his place within a day or two.

The last chapter of Gita, he said, is partly an extension of the entire work and also a summary of the ideas that are spread across the previous chapters, in an altogether different way. In the process, it presents the gist of the Vedas, the Upanishads and the Hindu way of life.

In the first twelve verses Sri Krishna discusses the difference between sannyasa and *tyaga*, which are quite technical, but I will explain the idea.

Renunciation of duties without understanding the higher philosophy behind it, as has been the wont in India since ages, is tamasika tyaga; renunciation due to fear of physical suffering or pain is called rajasika tyaga; but performance of these actions as a matter of duty, and without any greed or fear, is called sattvika tyaga. So, the wise ones, endowed with sattva qualities, do not give up their duty even if they are disagreeable, nor do they feel any attachment to jobs that they like. 'Avoid not, seek not' is key.

It reminds me of the Karma yoga that you talked about.

So true! It is unfortunate that many in India have been tamasik tyagis for ages.

Now, since it is impossible for anyone to give up work entirely, it is better that they do their activities without any attachment or aversion. This would make them noble and maybe even saintly. A good example would be brushing your teeth. As kids we never liked to brush, but as we grew up, we realized that it is a must to maintain our oral hygiene. Just like that, to maintain your spiritual hygiene you must do all your work as duty with utmost dispassion. The more dispassion and perfection, the better you will become as a human. This is true evolution, and not what we read in the works of Darwin.

Let me give you a shock, Swamiji. Many young people do not brush their teeth these days unless they have to meet someone.

Is that so, he said. If it is true then know that they will be doomed soon, with a fat bank balance but without anything to do with that. Soon they will be like the mythical king Midas whose touch turned everything to gold, leaving him with nothing to love!

The dynamics of action

A little sadness had begun to seep into his voice, but then he pulled himself up and continued.

We work, he said, but we rarely try to understand its nature or dynamics. And I can assure you that no scripture or self-help book explains these in a better way than Gita. The next three verses explain how all that we do – physically, mentally or verbally – has five factors behind them.

अनिष्टमिष्टं मिश्रं च त्रिविधं कर्मणः फलम्, भवति अत्यागिनां प्रेत्य न तु संन्यासिनां क्वचित् ।
पञ्चैतानि महाबाहो कारणानि निबोध मे, साङ्ख्ये कृतान्ते प्रोक्तानि सिद्धये सर्वकर्मणाम् ।
अधिष्ठानं तथा कर्ता करणं च पृथग्विधम्, विविधाश्च पृथक्चेष्टा दैवं चैवात्र पञ्चमम् ।

The three-fold results of acts – pleasant, unpleasant and mixed – accrue even after death to those who are attached to their acts. But, for those who are detached, there is no such result.

Know the five factors behind all actions, as taught by the great sages.

The body, the soul, the senses, prana (the vital energies of the body) and daiva (the divine) are the five factors behind every action. (XVIII.12–14)

There are four kinds of action that people perform: *nitya* (duties), *naimittika* (acts performed on special occasions), *kamya* (acts with desire) and *nisiddha* (prohibited acts). The first two types purify us, while the last two are not good for spiritual aspirants.

The lord says that whatever the act, it will require five factors – body, senses, prana, soul and daiva to accomplish it. The word daivam, or divine, may mean divine providence or the presiding deities of the senses. There are five prana that work within a living body.

I wished to say 'Objection, Milord!' but refrained.

Swamiji continued, You may wonder wherefrom the gods have entered here, and how they can affect our work, since we are the one who labour for success. But know this to be a fact: everything in the universe, inert or sentient, has the presence of the divine behind it. Likewise, we have the divine as our innermost being, and so does the universe. It is thus that our senses and organs, too, have the presence of the divine as the source of their respective actions. For example, the deity behind the eyes is Sun, and behind the hands is Indra, etc. But because we are focusing on the practical side of Gita, we will let go of the discussion on this topic.

Ask any *firang*, and he will say that their achievement is due to their effort. But they do not know that there are wheels within wheels in everything that we do. When the god of stomach is not happy with you, you develop such indigestion that cannot be cured by any medication!

Let us move ahead, Swamiji.

Oh yes. I only wish to add that whenever you do any work, personal or professional, keep these factors in mind so that you can pay attention to proper compliance for peace and prosperity. Having a mere 'compliance officer' in a company to see the legality is not enough; have a spiritual compliance unit for your company.

A spirituality compliance officer? My friends will be assured that I have gone nuts after my visit to the Lord of all nuts, Shiva!

Your life, your choice, bhai.

He then continued, The greatest of work managers are those who do not let their identification with results overpower their actions.

यस्य नाहंकृतो भावो बुद्धिः यस्य न लिप्यते,
हत्वाऽपि स इमान लोकान् न हन्ति न निबध्यते |

He who is free from the 'I' sense and whose buddhi (intelligence) is not coloured (by good or evil acts), then even if he kills all, he actually neither kills nor gets bound (by that act). (XVIII.17)

We are back at where we had started in the second chapter: 'You grieve over what should not be grieved for!' This is the central idea of Gita as also of Hindu dharma – the Atman is infinite. Anyone who knows themselves as Atman knows no duality, and hence is beyond good or bad, since they alone are everything.

For me, too, this is the *moola mantra* – the ultimate ideal of life. How I wish that I can someday reach this state of non-identification with my acts!

Please do not mind my saying this, Swamiji, but earlier you mentioned some verses as dear to you.

Indeed. It is important for you to know that whatever we discussed in Gita is like a ladder to this verse. Your unselfish work, worship, discrimination, being established in sattva – these are all stepping stones to reach this state. When I had mentioned the verse *anityam asukham* ... there, too, the goal was this verse only.

So, gear up for the battle, young man, and go, conquer the world. Bring glory to yourself, your family, society and the country. Be great by performing your duty so unselfishly that God Himself may reveal His Self to you and say, 'Look, I alone exist. There is no birth or death, no cause and effect, no time and space, no mind or matter – I, and I alone exist.'

Raw energy seemed to be flowing out of Swamiji's body and words, and it seemed to be influencing me, too.

In a raised voice, Swamiji continued, Sri Krishna then narrates some more classifications. You should know these to lead a better life.

Three kinds of understanding

सर्वभूतेषु येनैकं भावम् अव्ययमीक्षते, अविभक्तं विभक्तेषु तत् ज्ञानं विद्धि सात्त्विकम् |
पृथक्त्वेन तु यत् ज्ञानं नानाभावान् पृथग्विधान्, वेत्ति सर्वेषु भूतेषु तत् ज्ञानं विद्धि राजसम्
यत्तु कृत्स्नवदेकस्मिन् कार्ये सक्तम् अहैतुकम्,
अतत्त्व अर्थवत् अल्पं च तत्तामसम् उदाहृतम् |

The knowledge that makes a person see One unified existence in all beings – undivided in the divided things – is said to be of sattvika nature.

When one sees different realities of various types in all beings as separate from one another (that is, one sees different souls in different bodies with different characteristics, such as happiness, misery, etc.), then that knowledge is called rajasika.

And the knowledge that results in seeing the whole in one limited thing (like imagining God in one name, form or idol), then it is of tamasika type. (XVIII.20–22)

Sri Ramakrishna used to say that an inferior devotee thinks that God resides in heaven, a mediocre devotee thinks that God resides in his heart, and a superior devotee sees God as all pervasive.

Thus, a man with tamasika knowledge sees his body as the real self, and also thinks that the Lord is confined to a single image or symbol. The primitive religions held similar views. Even those who believe that their God is the only true God belong to this kind.

Strong words, Swamiji.

I am not saying this; Gita is explaining things for us. Limitedness is tamasika, while the infinite is sattvika.

Three kinds of acts

नियतं सङ्गरहितम् अरागद्वेषतः कृतम्, अफलप्रेप्सुना कर्म यत् तत् सात्त्विकमुच्यते ।
यत्तु कामेप्सुना कर्म साहंकारेण वा पुनः, क्रियते बहुलायासं तत् राजसमुदाहृतम् ।
अनुबन्धं क्षयं हिंसाम् अनपेक्ष्य च पौरुषम्, मोहात् आरभ्यते कर्म यत् तत् तामसमुच्यते ।

Unselfish action performed in accordance with the scriptures and free from desires or dislike is sattvika.

Action prompted by selfish desire, done with pride and full of stress, is rajasika.

The acts initiated out of ignorance or delusion, without thought to one's own ability, and disregarding consequences, loss and injury to others is tamasika. (XVIII.23–25)

India is slowly waking up from deep tamas to rajas, as we discussed earlier. The darkness of ignorance and sloth that had enveloped us for thousands of years is finally giving way to the light of knowledge. So, it is important for every Indian to know what is right and what is not so right. For this, we cannot have any better book than Gita.

Swamiji seemed to be getting emotional. His voice had gone soft. He held my hand and said, Bhai, you are a rich person, so do something for your country and fellow citizens. There are four goals of life – *vidya*, *sampad*, seva, *tyaga*. You have now acquired vidya – the knowledge from Gita in matters of personality, mind and acts. With this newfound wisdom, go back to work, generate wealth, that is, sampad, and with that wealth go out and help people, seva. Help people know the truth; help them financially, academically, in becoming strong, stable and vigorous. Do all this and become great. And finally, when you have become full of inclusiveness through the ideals of service, give up all – tyaga – to be one with your spiritual nature. There is nothing else to be done in life. Do it.

We sat down in silence to let the waves of emotion pass. After a while, Swamiji exhaled deep, got up and started explaining further.

How good a worker are you?

मुक्तसङ्गो – अनहंवादी धृति उत्साह-समन्वितः,
सिद्ध्यसिद्ध्योः निर्विकारः कर्ता सात्त्विक उच्यते |
रागी कर्मफलप्रेप्सुः लुब्धो हिंसात्मकोऽशुचिः, हर्षशोकान्वितः कर्ता राजसः परिकीर्तितः |
अयुक्तः प्राकृतः स्तब्धः शठो नैष्कृतिको-अलसः, विषादी दीर्घसूत्री च कर्ता तामस उच्यते |

A person is a sattvika worker if they are free from egotism and attachment, endowed with enthusiasm, determination and equipoised in success and failure.

The rajasika workers are passionate, result-oriented, greedy, violent, impure and prone to elation and dejection.

Tamasika, the worst kind of workers are undisciplined, vulgar, stubborn, deceitful, slothful, despondent and procrastinators. (XVIII.26–28)

I am sure that this will help you in your workplace to judge people!

Yes, Swamiji. But how do I change their attitudes?

According to Gita, one has to work hard to overcome tamas, and then practice unselfishness to overcome rajas. Unfortunately, you cannot force ideals on people. As discussed earlier, you have to work with them and then bring them up gently.

Three types of buddhi

The discussion is now about the types of buddhi. As with many such technical terms, it cannot be translated into English, except for the loose word, intellect. Buddhi, as compared with intellect, is that faculty of the mind which gets enforced by the words of elders, teachers, scriptures and by one's conscience. It is actionable, meaning that a mere theoretical knowledge of correctness is not enough; one has to act accordingly and thus keep one's thoughts and acts completely under control and in conformity to the norms of dharma.

प्रवृत्तिं च निवृत्तिं च कार्याकार्ये भयाभये, बन्धं मोक्षं च या वेत्ति बुद्धिः सा पार्थ सात्त्विकी ।
यया धर्मम् अधर्मं च कार्यं चाकार्यमेव च, अयथावत् प्रजानाति बुद्धिः सा पार्थ राजसी ।
अधर्मं धर्ममिति या मन्यते तमसावृता, सर्वार्थान् विपरीतांश्च बुद्धिः सा पार्थ तामसी ।

Sattvika intellect knows the difference between proper and not proper action, duty and non-duty, grounds for fear and not to be afraid, and factors causing bondage and liberation.

Rajasika intellect has a distorted apprehension of dharma and its opposite and also of right action and its opposite.

Tamasika intellect does not know the difference between dharma and adharma, and sees untruth as truth. (XVIII.30–32)

The idea is clear about what the right kind of dharma should be. To be honest, I am not very happy with the state of understanding that people have in matters of religion these days. I sincerely hope that people get back to studying scriptures to know what a great treasure our ancestors have left for us.

The holding power

Have you heard of the expression 'second wind' coined by William James? According to him, when you continue to work even after you are dead tired, you get a huge surge in your energy levels that makes you achieve the impossible, but leaves you completely drained for a long time. Most creative people depend on this.

I told him that I knew of the term but not about its coinage.

These Americans! They are always looking for a new propellant for themselves, like a dog looking for new kind of petrol to put on its tail to make it run faster! William James was no exception.

We, the Hindus, believe in dhriti – the holding power that retains us on course even when we feel tired. This is quite an unusual word and the idea that it represents is wonderful. Most of us do not feel like doing our chores simply because we lack dhriti, and thus fail to be successful. Interestingly, most mothers have a lot of dhriti. Even if they are dead tired, they get up to take care of their child.

धृत्या यया धारयते मनःप्राणेन्द्रिय-क्रियाः, योगेन-अव्यभिचारिण्या धृतिः सा पार्थ सात्त्विकी |
यया तु धर्मकामार्थान् धृत्या धारयते-अर्जुन, प्रसङ्गेन फलाकाङ्क्षी धृतिः सा पार्थ राजसी |
यया स्वप्नं भयं शोकं विषादं मदमेव च, न विमुञ्चति दुर्मेधा धृतिः सा पार्थ तामसी |

Dhriti, the fortitude, by which the functions of the mind and body are upheld through spiritual understanding is sattvika.

Rajasika dhriti is that by which one holds on to duty, pleasures and wealth, out of their desire for results.

Tamasika dhriti is that by which an ordinary mind does not give up sleep, fear, grief, despondency and conceit. (XVIII.33–35)

In case of sattvika dhriti, your power to do work remains uninterrupted because it draws energy from your higher faculties, established in spiritual reality. It is said that gods like Indra have sattvika dhriti, the Asuras have rajasika, and the demons have tamasika dhriti.

Wherever you see people shirking their duty out of laziness, fear, grief, etc., know them to have tamasika dhriti.

If you look around, you will see how most people do not practice religious rituals simply because their dhriti is tamasika. Those who claim to be 'spiritual and not religious' may actually belong to this category.

Is your happiness of the right kind?

यत् तदग्रे विषमिव परिणामे-अमृतोपमम्, तत्सुखं सात्त्विकं प्रोक्तम् आत्मबुद्धिप्रसादजम् |
विषयेन्द्रियसंयोगात् यत्तदग्रे-अमृतोपमम्, परिणामे विषमिव तत्सुखं राजसं स्मृतम् |
यदग्रे चानुबन्धे च सुखं मोहनम् आत्मनः, निद्रा-आलस्य-प्रमादोत्थं तत्तामसम् उदाहृतम् |

Sattvika happiness is born of clear intellect rooted in spiritual reality. In the beginning it is like poison, but at the end it is like nectar.

Rajasika happiness arises from the contact of object with sense. It is like nectar in the beginning but ends like poison.

Tamasika happiness begins and ends in self-delusion arising from sleep, indolence and miscomprehension. (XVIII.37–39)

To make the distinction clear, whenever a person works hard to achieve noble things, the effort is painful, but the result is full of joy, like in studying. When one works out of passion and emotion, which often drain a lot of energy, even the ultimate outcome is usually painful. Most young people will vouch for this.

The worst kind of happiness, tamasika, is born of wrong understanding, which results in more and more self-delusion. Laziness breeds more laziness!

I pondered whether my happiness over the years had been of the sattvika type. Probably not, for most of my inner kicks ended in external kicks.

How work becomes worship

To remind you for the nth time, the Gita is a spiritual book whose purpose is to lead a person to self-realization, irrespective of their gender, occupation or nationality. This, Sri Krishna explains in two verses.

स्वे स्वे कर्मणि अभिरतः संसिद्धिं लभते नरः, स्वकर्मनिरतः सिद्धिं यथा विन्दति तत् शृणु |
यतः प्रवृत्तिः भूतानां येन सर्वमिदं ततम्, स्वकर्मणा तम् अभ्यर्च्य सिद्धिं विन्दति मानवः |

Devoted to one's duty, one can attain the highest perfection. How? By performing duties, a person worships God from whom all have come into existence, and who pervades all. (XVIII.45–46)

The best way to worship God is to perform one's duty sincerely and unselfishly. What is duty? It is the responsibility one chooses and that society expects them to perform. Imagine a ticket checker on a train. His dharma is to help people even if they do not have a ticket, and not merely to throw the law book in their faces. But what is the ground reality? Let us not even discuss that. Believe me, no amount of going to the temples or reading the sacred books can save them from the fall.

But who cares?

Anyway, this idea is further elaborated in the next verse.

श्रेयान् स्वधर्मो विगुण: परधर्मात् स्व अनुष्ठितात्,
स्वभावनियतं कर्म कुर्वन् आप्नोति किल्बिषम् |

Better is one's own dharma even if that be unattractive, than the dharma of another that may look appealing. He who does the duty ordained by his own nature incurs no evil. (XVIII.47)

Gita stresses a lot on svadharma – one's duty as fixed by the varnashrama, which was explained in earlier chapters. However, now that such system is no longer in practice, the duty of a person is simply defined as 'what one has taken up and what others expect from them in that endeavour.' It is a simple principle.

For example, if you are into business, your svadharma will demand that you look after the welfare of your staff, and generate wealth for the society. If you are motivated by self-interest, then you can never aspire to grow internally, although you may have some quick worldly success.

In the case of the ticket checker discussed above, if they give up their dharma of service and take up the dharma of others – the cheats – then you can guess what the consequences will be!

So, the message of Gita regarding work is: stay true to your svadharma. Period.

The result of leading an ideal life

People often ask what they will gain by being religious. What to say to these know-it-alls! Anyway, Lord Sri Krishna answers this.

सर्वकर्माणि अपि सदा कुर्वाणो मद्व्यपाश्रयः, मत्प्रसादात् अवाप्नोति शाश्वतं पदमव्ययम्

By performing duties and taking refuge in Me, people attain the highest spiritual state by My grace. (XVIII.56)

God's grace descends in the form of spiritual understanding in a mind that has been made pure by performing one's duty without any selfish motive.

What if you do not follow the words of God? You must have heard of the famous dictates of Abrahamic religions, according to which if you obey the command, you will go to heaven; and if you don't obey, then the inferno of the purgatory awaits you.

But the Hindu religion does not function that way. It simply says: 'Perform your duty unselfishly, place your mind in God, and you will be free from all kinds of bondage.' And what if one becomes a shirker? Well, your very nature will force you to work. So, it is better that you give your mind the right orientation to convert your work into sacred duty, and thus become blessed.

However, even if you do not listen, no hell-fire will be stoked for you. Enjoy laziness, corruption and dereliction of duty; let people down, sample all the worldly pleasures you want – just know that it will only prolong your suffering by that much.

Your life, your choice.

यदहंकारम् आश्रित्य न योत्स्य इति मन्यसे,
मिथ्यैष व्यवसायस्ते प्रकृतिस्त्वां नियोक्ष्यति |
स्वभावजेन कौन्तेय निबद्धः स्वेन कर्मणा,
कर्तुं नेच्छसि यन्मोहात् करिष्यसि अवशोपि तत्|

If, driven by arrogance and pride, you decide not to fight, know that your decision will be in vain, since your very nature will compel you to fight, O Arjuna.

Compelled by your inner nature, you will be driven to do what you refuse to do – that which is your duty. (XVIII.59–60)

If you remember, the original 'moral dilemma' posed by Arjuna was whether or not he should take part in the war. To this, the Lord says that Arjuna's very nature as a born warrior will make him take part in the war even if he does not want to engage in it. So, his sulking is only delaying the inevitable.

In an interesting story by Sri Ramakrishna, there was a monk who tried to persuade a king to give up everything and come with him to the forest to lead the life of a hermit. The king laughed and said that his inner nature was such that even if he went to the forest, he would create an empire there!

Interestingly, people often talk about the nature of others, and at times use expressions like 'pro', without actually realizing how important nature is in everyone's life. A duck will take to water and a swan to the sky – there can never be an exception.

Personally, I have seen many monks who continue to be driven by their inner nature and keep working according to their nature. But what indeed changes is their outlook towards life, and their unselfishness. That is how they grow.

In the present times, the education system, social set-up and work environment rarely care for all this, as a consequence of which there is a constant conflict within us. So, you should try to implement this test of personality in your workplace if you want to outpace your competitors. You will soon see the wonderful result it produces.

God rules all from within

ईश्वरः सर्वभूतानां हृद्देशेऽर्जुन तिष्ठति, भ्रामयन् सर्वभूतानि यन्त्रारूढानि मायया |
तमेव शरणं गच्छ सर्वभावेन भारत, तत्प्रसादात् परां शान्तिं स्थानं प्राप्यसि शाश्वतम् |
इति ते ज्ञानम् आख्यातं गुह्यात् गुह्यतरं मया,
विमृश्यैतत् अशेषेण यथेच्छसि तथा कुरु |

God dwells in the hearts of all living beings, O Arjuna, and by His divine power He makes them move like a marionette on a machine.

Take refuge in Him with all your heart, and then by His grace you will attain supreme peace (and) the eternal abode.

Thus, I have explained to you this knowledge that is more profound than all. Think over it deeply, and then do as you wish.
(XVIII.61–63)

Just look at the apparent contradiction in this verse. In the beginning, Sri Krishna says that it is He who makes everything move, but He later tells Arjuna to apply his mind and do what he considers fit.

This apparent contradiction explains the famous conflict among the theologians about 'God's will' and 'self-effort', for instance. There are innumerable theories and philosophies affirming and attempting to explain, one of the two stands.

However, these three verses show how God's will and your will are one and the same. Sri Ramakrishna used to tell a story in which a mad elephant was running down a road, while its mahout was shouting to everyone to run away from it. A novice in religion, instead of listening to the words of the mahout, sat down on the road to pray to the elephant, since he had been taught that: 'God is present in all beings'. Inevitably, the young man was thrown by the elephant. When his Guru later asked why he had behaved that way, the disciple sheepishly repeated the philosophy that he had learnt. The Guru rebuked him by saying, Indeed God alone is all, but by the same argument the mahout also is God. Why didn't you listen to him?

God's will expresses itself in the words of scripture and one's Guru. It is only selfishness that colours the words of the Lord and makes us behave erroneously in the world. Though religious preachers may try their best, people will not give up their selfishness easily. Or perhaps that selfishness will not let go of the mind easily, and so people will continue to be controlled by their petty ego. Therefore, the real goal in life is to make ourselves pure by giving up selfishness; what then arises in the mind will be the voice of God.

Indeed, all that we do is from God. The false sense of ego comes from God, and the effort to be unselfish, too, comes from God. So, why not listen to the words of the masters and struggle to be unselfish? Selfishness is the world, unselfishness is God!

Be unselfish. This is the whole of religion, and the whole of sadhana.

The essence of Gita

सर्वधर्मान् परित्यज्य मामेकं शरणं व्रज, अहं त्वा सर्वपापेभ्यो मोक्षयिष्यामि मा शुचः |

Directing all your thoughts towards me, take refuge in Me alone. I will then liberate you from all sins; fear not. (XVIII.66)

This verse sums up Gita, and it is also highly technical. Sri Krishna here asks Arjuna – and through him, all of us – to give up all dharma, which means every 'sense of duty', as also bad acts. The idea is to perform all actions, good or bad, with a complete sense of surrender to God. In return, God will take such a devotee out of the cycle of birth and death. It is this cycle which is sinful, and not merely the acts as commonly understood.

This is also in consonance with verse seventeen, where the Lord said that, He who is free from the idea of 'me' is not affected (by good or evil), nor is bound (by the action).

Whatever your approach may be in spirituality – worshipping God with form or without form – the selfish 'me' has to go. Once it is gone, your sense of good and bad, virtue and vice, too, will melt away. You will realize that to attain one undivided consciousness, which is our real nature, is our birthright and only duty in life. Do this, whether through your work or worship.

Drawing the net

With these words of Sri Krishna, Gita concludes its teachings. As a mark of gratitude, Arjuna says:

नष्टो मोहः स्मृतिः लब्धा त्वत्प्रसादात् मयाच्युत,
स्थितोऽस्मि गतसन्देहः करिष्ये वचनं तव

My delusion is destroyed, and I have gained my smriti through your grace, O Lord! I am firm; my doubts are gone. I shall act according to your words. (XVIII.73)

The crucial comment from Arjuna is on 'smriti' – the state of mind that knows what is right and wrong. This is attained through consciously shaping the mind with the words of the scriptures, teachers and elders, as explained earlier.

In most cases, we behave badly because our selfish desires overpower our smriti. So, my dear brother, go back to your life and keep your smriti ever effulgent.

Gita then concludes with the words of Sanjaya, who had been narrating the happenings in the battlefield to the blind king Dhritarashtra.

यत्र योगेश्वरः कृष्णो यत्र पार्थो धनुर्धरः, तत्र श्रीर्विजयो भूतिः ध्रुवा नीतिः मतिर्मम |

Wherever is Krishna, the Lord of Yoga, wherever is Partha, the wielder of the bow, there is prosperity, victory, expansion and right policy: such is my conviction. (XVIII.78)

And the words of Sanjay proved prophetic! Arjuna won the war despite all odds.

May we feel the presence of Lord in our heart. May He guide us forever towards freedom, Swamiji concluded and went silent.

Our parikrama was complete. As on other days, we reached the main Omkareswarnath Shiva temple after crossing the Bhima gate. But, unlike previous days, Swamiji took me inside the temple and bowed before the Lord, thanking him for letting us complete such a wonderful endeavour without any setback.

We then parted ways – he continued his journey to the world beyond, and I, my journey in the world.

GITA ROLLS ON

My stay at Omkareswar was over. I walked towards the bridge that would take me to the mainland, where my driver was waiting for me. When I reached the middle of the bridge, I turned around to look at Swamiji.

He was gone.

That was when I also realized that I had forgotten to ask for Swamiji's name and contact details. How stupid of me, I thought! Maybe our journey together was meant to end there. Or perhaps we would bump into each other again, like a comet visiting Earth a second time, only to fade into the vast expanse, never to be seen again.

I let out a sigh and walked towards my hotel, and then to my car.

On my way, I kept pondering on Gita and its relevance. I will sum up my thoughts in a few sentences:

1. What is the dharma of a brave man when his innocent wife is put to the ultimate public shame of being disrobed in front of the world? Should he avenge that?
2. If war becomes inevitable due to rightful reasons, is it fair to turn away from it? I think that it is our own escapism

or a newfound fad to criticize everything that belongs to the Hindu religion that makes us think differently. No one had heard of such criticism even fifty years ago!
3. Gita is more about the philosophy of life than about the art of war. It shows how to make one's personality a complete whole, instead of letting it remain disintegrated.
4. A unified personality can make a person attain anything in life – success, wealth, freedom and mukti.

My musings were interrupted when a call came from the office, informing me of some crisis in the company.

Unlike previous occasions, I smiled and said, No problem, I am coming.

SELECT BIBLIOGRAPHY

This work is entirely from memory. However, the books which I studied related to this work over the years are mentioned here.

- *Srimad Bhagavad Gita* (Various editions) by Gita Press
- Swami Swarupananda, *Srimad Bhagavad Gita,* Kolkata: Advaita Ashrama.
- Swami Nikhilananda, *The Bhagavad Gita,* Kolkata: Advaita Ashrama.
- Swami Mukundananda, *Bhagavad Gita: The Song of God*
- *Complete Works of Swami Vivekananda,* Kolkata: Advaita Ashrama.
- Swami Nikhilananda (tr), *The Gospel of Sri Ramakrishna*
- Samarpan, *The Hindu Way,* New Delhi: Pan Macmillan India.
- His Eastern and Western Disciples, *Life of Swami Vivekananda* by
- Samarpa, *Living Hinduism,* New Delhi: Niyogi Books.
- Edwin Arnold, *The Song Celestial: A Poetic Version of the Bhagavad Gita*
- Samarpan, *The World of Religions*, New Delhi: Niyogi Books.

THANK YOU!

So, finally my work on Gita is complete! Looking back, I can proudly admit that this work could never have come into existence without the will of Bhagavan, call Him by whatever name and remember Him in whatever form. Without the Lord's blessings, Gita could not have come out in this unique form.

My humble regards to the elder monks of my organization who patiently taught me the subtle nature of scriptures over the decades. Also, the kindness of my brother monks has been phenomenal, and has given me the strength to carry on with the noble work. My sincere namaskar to all of them.

The journey of life brought before me many friends and loved ones who were there when I needed them. Though most of them have now moved towards a different destiny, I fondly remember them all and acknowledge their contribution in my growth. Thank you, dear ones!

My heartfelt thanks to my great friends whose love and care for me can never be repaid! They are the strength of my staying power in the service of my mother religion. Some of them prefer not to be named. My thanks to them.

My deepest and most sincere gratefulness to Sri K. Gopalakrishnan, Bangalore and Ms Moumita Kundu, London, who have been with me on this work from day one of the project. Both of them went through every chapter and every line multiple times, correcting, editing and making suggestions. I also had countless discussions with Sri Gopal ji on this work. No words of thanks can be enough for what they have done.

My thanks to their family members, too, who allowed me to encroach on their time and space. In addition, Ms Mary Gopalakrishnan and Mr Arnab Kundu are my good friends and admirers of my work. Thank you, dear ones.

My grateful thanks to Sri Ajay Nayak, IAS (retd.), who has been with me during turbulent times, encouraging me all the way in doing this kind of work. His words of appreciation and admiration have been a great power source for me even during my darkest days. This work owes hugely to him, for discussing with me many times how to go about it. Thank you, dear brother.

Whenever I complete writing a book, I fondly remember Sri Abhayanada ji, IPS (retd.), his wife Dr Nutan Anand and Sri D.N. Gautam, IPS (retd.) who have been great well-wishers of mine from the day that we first met some decades ago, and who never had any doubts about my capabilities even when I was immersed in deep tamas.

My fond gratitude and love to Sri Rebanta Bandyopadhyay, USA, who has been a great friend and support for many decades. Now his adorable wife Ms Susen Bandyopadhyay, and their three wonderful kids Tushti, Turni and Shara too have extended warmth, love and appreciation towards me. Thank you, dear family!

Thanks also to Sri C. Sridhar (IAS) and Sri Ajey Ranade (IPS) who have been great admirers of my work and have often gone through the manuscripts of my work before these went to the press.

Ms Shiwangi has been with me like a doting mother and indulgent friend through my good and bad days for three decades now. Thank you, Shiwangi for being there when no one seemed around. Her husband Sri Devmurty ji, a great friend of mine, has always been around me to lend a supportive hand. Now their son, Kartikeya, too, has started lending his words of admiration. Thanks to this wonderful family for being there for me at all times.

Dr Hema has been a great source of support to me in various ways for more than a decade. My life has been steadied due to her great contribution. I and my books owe so much to her. The name of this book was suggested by her. Thank you, my dear friend!

My excellent friends Sri Dibyajyoti and Sri Rajshekhar have been pillars of support in my life. In spite of their busy schedules, they have been with me whenever I needed them. They listened to my ideas, went through the manuscripts and suggested a thing or two. Grateful thanks my beloved ones!

Ms Payal Garg has been a great friend and admirer of my books and has been untiring in her efforts to make my works popular. Thank you, my good friend.

Mr Shyam Anand Jha, Muzaffarpur, who works in management education, has taken a lot of responsibility that I was supposed to carry. Without his active support, even my monastic life would not have been possible. Thank you, sir.

A special thanks to Ms Indrani Ghosh who has been looking after our efforts selflessly. She, too, went through the manuscript of this work and suggested some important insertions.

I would like to thank my good friends Sri Avinash Singh and Ms Adrija Sen who have been bedrock of support for me for decades. Thanks also to Ms Piyali Dutta and Sri Arpan Chakraborty for being so supportive in my life.

Dr Aparna Jindal and her husband Sri Varun Jindal have a huge contribution in this work. Some of the expressions in this book have been directly copied from Dr Aparna's conversations with me. Being a fast reader, she completed every chapter that I wrote in a day and sent her feedback to quickly make them reader-friendly. Sri Varun ji has been a great help in our other projects, too. Thank you, bhai! I owe the expression 'bhai' in this book entirely to him.

My heartfelt thanks to Ms Aditri Kundu, London; Ms Divya Gaur, Uttarkashi; Ms Srijana Banerjee and Ms Kritansha Pandey, Kathmandu, who are young admirers of my work. It is due to them that I know how young minds work. Of them, Ms Divya deserves special thanks for being of great help, unknown to her, decades ago.

My good friends Sri Rajdeep Mukherjee of Pan Macmillan India, Sri Vijay Sharma ji and Ms Teesta Guha Sarkar, publisher of the book, have been very kind to bear with me patiently during the formative stage of the book, as also during its production. Thank you so much! These three impressed upon me the importance of this of work and asked me to complete it urgently.